# Assessing Educational Achievement

EDUCATIONAL ANALYSIS
General Editors: Philip Taylor and Colin Richards

CONTEMPORARY ANALYSIS IN EDUCATION SERIES
General Editor: Philip Taylor

Contemporary Analysis in Education Series

# Assessing Educational Achievement

*Edited by*
**Desmond L. Nuttall**

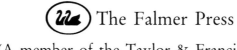 The Falmer Press

(A member of the Taylor & Francis Group)
London and Philadelphia

UK      The Falmer Press, Falmer House, Barcombe, Lewes, East Sussex, BN8 5DL

USA    The Falmer Press, Taylor & Francis Inc., 242 Cherry Street, Philadelphia, PA 19106-1906

---

© Selection and editorial material copyright D. L. Nuttall 1986

First published 1986

**Library of Congress Cataloging in Publication Data**

Main entry under title:

Assessing educational achievement.

    (Contemporary analysis in education series)
    Bibliography: p.
    Contents: Assessing for learning / Harry Black — The prospects for public examinations in England and Wales / Henry G. Macintosh — Australian examination systems / Graeme Withers — [etc.]
    1. Educational tests and measurements — Addresses, essays, lectures.  I. Nuttall, Desmond L.  II. Series.
LB3051.A766  1986  371.2′6  85-20679
ISBN 1-85000-056-5 (pbk.)

Typeset in 11/13 Garamond by
Imago Publishing Ltd, Thame, Oxon

Jacket design by Leonard Williams

*Printed in Great Britain by Taylor & Francis (Printers) Ltd, Basingstoke*

# Contents

# General Editor's Preface

The assessment of educational achievement is at times more than a reasonable public concern: it verges on public hysteria. Part, though not all, of the reason for this is a failure to grasp the nature and limitations of educational assessment. Even among educators there is only a limited grasp of the complexities of assessing educational achievement, and about some forms of assessment there is simply prejudice.

This highly professional and very readable collection of essays, skilfully edited by Desmond Nuttall, should go a long way to setting matters right and placing them in perspective. Moreover, the collection shows that there is an international dimension to problems of assessing educational achievement, at least in the English speaking world.

What the collection also amply illustrates is that there are many inventive and educationally committed minds at work in the field of educational assessment. If this could be fully appreciated by those who demand the assessment of educational achievement, then the best effects of assessing achievement could be realized and the worst mitigated.

*Philip Taylor*
*Birmingham*
*December 1985*

# Editorial Introduction

About three years ago, an issue of *Educational Analysis* (Volume 4 Number 3) edited by me was published under the title 'Assessing Educational Achievement'. I was very pleased when the publishers invited me to edit a second collection, since there have been many important developments in the intervening period. I was equally pleased when all the original contributors (save one) agreed to update their contributions in the light of subsequent developments in their fields. Many have radically revised their chapters to reflect the rapid pace of change in national policies, and all have brought them up to date by incorporating new information, new data and new references. The only original contributor who did not feel able to update his article was Roy Forbes, then of the Education Commission of the States, the body responsible for the National Assessment of Educational Progress (NAEP). In 1983, the Education Commission of the States was unsuccessful in its tender to take on the next phase of NAEP, and Educational Testing Service won the contract. Appropriately, the new Executive Director of NAEP, Archie E. Lapointe, kindly agreed to write about American developments.

The assessment of educational achievement serves many functions in education. In one guise, it is an integral part of teaching and learning, though most assessment is carried out informally — through questions and answers in class, through observation of students at work — rather than through the formal and artificial means of tests and examinations. Yet it is these more formal types of assessment that inevitably catch the public eye and generate debate and research (the latter occasionally informing the former). The research has usually been of the technical kind, investigating the efficiency of the tests as measuring instruments and as predictors of future success; until recently, relatively little research had been carried out on their social, psychological and educational effects, but such as has been done aligns with the mood of the times to question many of the forms and functions of assessment in education.

The chapters in this volume contribute to this process of questioning. They fall into three main sections: the first section comprises four chapters that look at the assessment of the individual and the second, four chapters that review the use of the assessment of individuals as a way of assessing the performance of educational institutions or the educational system as a whole. The final section consists of three chapters that are more theoretical, grappling with problematic conceptual issues in the field of educational assessment.

In the first chapter, Harry Black, drawing on his experience of diagnostic and school-based assessment, indicates how assessment might be developed to be of direct value to teacher and student (formative assessment) with particular emphasis upon criterion-referenced procedures. To achieve this, though, we need to break away from the dominant model of summative assessment, as epitomized in the British examination systems. These systems show signs of moving towards a greater degree of criterion-referencing; Harry Black sees danger in this move if it re-establishes an ascendancy for summative assessment. In the next chapter, Henry Macintosh examines the developments in the examination systems of England and Wales, a difficult task since there have been so many proposals for change in recent years and final decisions on many of them are imminent. On one, the common system of examining at 16+, a decision was announced in June 1984, confounding the predictions of Henry Macintosh and many others; a new examination, the General Certificate of Secondary Education, *is* to be introduced from 1988, but on terms dictated by central government that drastically reduce the autonomy of teachers. At 17+, there is still a ferment of activity but, at 18+, the dominant position of the universities seems likely to continue to stifle long-overdue reform. In Australia, too, as Graeme Withers reveals in his chapter, the universities exert a dominating influence on the curriculum and assessment at the point of transition from school, though alternatives to examinations are gaining ground, not without controversy. In contrast to Britain, though, Australian states have almost completely abolished examinations below the level of university entrance, and allow schools to develop their own courses and assessments.

In the final chapter in this section on assessment of the individual, Tricia Broadfoot points to the bugbear of assessment selection. While selection (for different forms of further and higher education as well as for employment) is still required of the educational system (and while examinations have other important societal functions to perform, for example in controlling the curriculum), any alternative to public examinations has to fulfil these same functions. Many of the alternatives, like pupil profiles in Britain and *orientation* in France, may therefore prove to be retrograde rather than progressive. Only through alternatives that challenge the functions themselves might we find a way forward.

Assessments of individuals are frequently aggregated to provide assessments of classes (and teachers), institutions and the educational system. The current emphasis on the accountability of public institutions, not least schools, is the theme underlying the next group of four chapters. Stewart Ranson, John Gray, David Jesson and Ben Jones analyse the concept of accountability in their chapter and show how dangerously simplistic the use of public examination results to judge the effectiveness of schools can be. Moreover, the publication of examination results required under the law serves to signal and reinforce the predominant academic emphasis of British schooling, an emphasis that other initiatives in assessment documented in earlier chapters are seeking to undermine.

A little of the pressure on examination results as measures of the efficiency of the educational system was removed by the establishment, in 1974, of the Assessment of Performance Unit (for England, Wales and, later, Northern Ireland). In her chapter, Caroline Gipps offers a critique of the work of the APU showing how, often through lack of forward planning and proper analysis of the problems, it has so far failed to meet a number of its objectives, while succeeding in others. Somewhat surprisingly, perhaps its greatest success is in the production of new and imaginative methods of assessment that might be of great value to the teacher in the classroom.

Without systems of public examinations, the USA and the individual states were early in the business of testing for assessing the efficiency of the system and the institutions. The chapter by Archie Lapointe shows how concern about educational performance is as great as ever, and how demands for testing show no signs of abating. Indeed, the experience and familiarity with the use of test results over the past twenty years has created a new level of sophistication in the expectations of professional and lay publics. NAEP, under its new management led by Archie Lapointe, is responding by making a series of changes designed to enhance its effectiveness (though in my own chapter I am critical of some of these changes). In Canada, too, assessment of the performance of educational systems flourishes and grows more complex, as the review by Les McLean demonstrates. But we do not always know what to do with the results of these testing programmes, nor do we pay enough attention, McLean feels, to the issue of validity, a topic that he examines closely and critically. My own chapter, the first in the final section, examines another thorny issue in national and local assessment, the measurement of change in performance over time. Change has to be related to a constant (a measuring instrument or a measurement scale) but the constant appears elusive.

The final two chapters are, in my view, the most important and most enduring in the collection. Harvey Goldstein's provides a clarification of models underlying the concepts of equating and comparability, the latter one of the most researched aspects of public examinations in Britain. His main conclusion (that the difficulty of an examination and its relevance to a syllabus are inherently confounded) implies that only in very special circumstances is it possible to investigate the comparability of standards empirically. Otherwise, comparability is a myth as I have argued elsewhere.[1]

The last chapter, by Bob Wood, draws together many of the issues raised in earlier chapters, such as the dominance of the tradition of individual differences and the search for technical, rather than educational, improvement. He offers a programme for educational measurement that would surely appeal to all the contributors to this volume, and indicates some of the promising lines of development that can already be detected. In common with the other chapters, but more explicitly, his chapter conducts and orchestrates the reconstruction of educational measurement that is long overdue.

Desmond L. Nuttall
The Open University

## Note

1 NUTTALL, D. (1979) 'The myth of comparability', *Journal of the National Association of Inspectors and Eductional Advisers*, autumn, pp. 16–17.

*Section 1*

# Assessment for Learning

*Harry Black*
*Scottish Council for Research in Education*

In 1980, a survey in Scotland (SCRE, 1980) showed that while 87 per cent of secondary schools claimed to have an assessment policy for reporting purposes, only 29 per cent had a policy for other non-reporting assessment. Furthermore, of the former, 40 per cent of these schools had a *written* policy, but only 36 per cent of those with non-reporting policies had it in written form. That only one in ten schools has a policy in this vital area formally committed to paper is not evidence that assessment for reasons other than reporting does not take place. But it is symptomatic of the low priority given to assessment for reasons other than reporting at an organizational level.

Other simple comparisons substantiate the point. Consider the amount of time, energy and money spent by both individual teachers, and schools in general, on setting and marking continuous assessment tests, end of session examinations and mock 'O' levels. Reflect on the money spent by examination boards and the number of assessment specialists employed by them. Read, if you can find a sabbatical term, the literature on the technology of assessment for reporting and certification. Compare these in turn with the complete lack of support normally given to teachers in devising and applying procedures to pinpoint their students' learning problems, with the virtual absence of outside agencies to develop formative assessment instruments and procedures, and the limited literature on the topic.

There can be little doubt that summative assessment, which can be defined simply as assessment of the outcomes of education for purposes of reporting or certification, dominates the educational psyche of assessment. Formative assessment, which can be thought of as comprising forms of student evaluation carried out to monitor progress with a view, where appropriate, to altering the final outcomes, holds a position somewhere behind the closed and private door of the classroom.

Yet it would be wrong to argue that formative assessment is an innovation. Teachers have always taken account of learning difficulties in their classrooms and reacted to them. Questions are asked at a class and individual level, mistakes are noticed as the teacher wanders about the classroom. Spelling, punctuation and substantive errors are corrected in written work, and common errors are noticed when tests are marked. Teaching and learning, except in the extreme case of programmed learning, are interactive, and informal formative assessment is a vital element in the whole process.

The obvious question then is that if formative assessment has long been part of the tradition of teaching, why should one draw comparisons with summative assessment? By implication one appears to be dissatisfied with the status quo. Are there not enough bandwagons to jump on without pushing one which might interfere with sound existing teaching practice? This paper *challenges* this common stance by making four assertions.

1 There is evidence that the nature of formative assessment has long been an issue;
2 Formative assessment as practised is not all that it might be;
3 There is evidence that carefully thought out formative models can make a substantial difference to learning;
4 Sound formative assessment needs is own technology and this is *not* the developed technology presently made available to teachers.

## Formative Assessment as a Longstanding Issue

There are not many names from the educational world of the mid-nineteenth century which have retained their position amongst present day scholars. Amongst the few, Charlotte Mason, a teacher in the middle-class schools of Victorian England, and Helen Pankhurst of Dalton, Massachusetts, are known for their development of child-centred education. Their challenge was essentially to the way in which students learn. But a resultant change was to the nature of assessment. The extent of the change was such as to make Taylor (1965) note that when the Dalton plan was introduced to some schools in this country 'The convention that written work was always to be corrected resulted in masters disappearing in a blizzard of paper.'

Awareness of the issues was not confined to teaching methodology. An interesting early example of formative assessment technology can be found in a letter written by the Reverend George Fisher, Principal of Greenwich Hospital School, and quoted by E. Chadwick (1864). In it he describes a scale book which provides examples of works of differing levels of attainment and which can be used as a fixed standard against which to compare the work of individual pupils. In addition to his scale for writing he states that:

> By a similar process values are assigned for proficiency in mathematics, navigation, scripture knowledge, grammar and composition, French, general history, drawing and practical science respectively. Questions in each of these subjects are contained in the 'scale book' to serve as types not only of the difficulty but of the nature of the questions for the sake of future reference.

That there existed an awareness of the importance of formative assessment from the early stages of formal education cannot be in dispute. But two things happened which turned the focus elsewhere. First, the introduction of public examinations directed the attention of teachers to goals beyond their own classrooms. Second, the development of intelligence tests, especially in the United States, turned the attention of assessment specialists to the development of instruments which would sort pupils into a normal distribution of attainment. Formative assessment, of course, continued to take place but its development was dwarfed by the burgeoning summative tradition.

The most significant development which took place in the first sixty years of this century was the construction of standardized diagnostic tests. These were largely confined to basic skills in number and language. Thus, for example, Buswell and John (1926) produced a diagnostic test in arithmetic and provided a chart and manual for the teacher. In other cases diagnostic tests were built into textbooks. But today such tests are seldom used in schools, not least perhaps because modern conceptually oriented mathematics is less easily tested in this way than the basic number skills of traditional arithmetic.

In the 1960s, however, several significant developments took place in the United States where standardized testing had become a substantial industry. Programmed learning, which was seen at the time as a bright new solution for the child-centred tradition, became the focus of considerable attention. But the essence of programmed learning was that students should successfully complete a unit of work or 'frame' before they moved on to the next. The function of formative tests in such a system is to ascertain whether a student has, or has not, attained the intended outcome of the frame. But the test-conscious educationists who tried to apply their norm-referenced technology to the situation found that it did not work. They did not want to know who had performed best on the frame, nor to have the students spread on a normal distribution. And so the term 'criterion-referenced test' was coined by Glaser (1963) to describe instruments which would best allot students to mastery or non-mastery states.

Coincident with these developments, formative assessment was being applied by Bloom and his colleagues (1971 and 1976) in a mastery learning context. In both these cases the technology and the role of formative assessment were clearly distinguished from that of summative assessment.

## Formative Assessment in British Schools

The British assessment tradition has had different priorities over the last twenty years. The influence of summative assessment and, in particular, external certificates, has had a dominant role in teacher thinking. The advent of the CSE and Mode III syllabi may have been a watershed in curriculum thinking, but its impact on formative assessment must be in doubt. In particular, teachers have developed skills which are appropriate to the construction of summative internal examinations. We have also moved en masse towards the 'progressive' notion of continuous assessment. As a result, school assessment is dominated by staccato forms of the old end-of-session examinations. Continuous assessment in action means continual examination for reporting, and to make matters worse, many teachers are doing it rather well because of the skills they have picked up from the exam boards.

The problem is that the price we have had to pay for a better summative assessment model in schools has actually reduced the likelihood of formative assessment taking a more prominent role. Black and Dockrell (1980), for example, noted that in most cases where they saw continuous assessment taking place, feedback was in the form of a general attainment grade giving no real information about specific strengths and weaknesses. Furthermore, assessment typically took place at the end of each unit of work by which time it was too late to take remedial action. In a later study (Black and Dockrell, 1984), they show that some teachers think that continuous assessment as practised is a real obstacle to the introduction of diagnostic assessment procedures. The reason is that the pressures of carrying out systematic continuous *and* diagnostic assessment are seen as placing intolerable demands on preparation, marking and testing time.

Of course, there are many examples of interesting practice in formative assessment to be found in British schools today. Black and Broadfoot (1982), for example, give a number of case studies of formative procedures in both primary and secondary schools. But the disturbing aspect of their description is that what is described in the case studies has to be seen as innovation not just by the writers but by the teachers themselves.

In fact, it is difficult to gain a clear impression of the extent and nature of formative assessment as practised by individual teachers either in the past or today. Not only does one have to breach the defensiveness of teachers in describing what their approach may be, but observational studies are necessary to evaluate the use which is made of the data collected. There is no doubt that some teachers carry out formative assessment both effectively and conscientiously. Many others are conscientious but ineffective. Others are neither. It is also the case that teachers from different subject backgrounds have differing traditions to live up to. Equally, in some schools, a deliberate policy of requiring teachers to perform certain assessment tasks means that formative assessment is expected to be carried out. But the facts about what actually takes place are not readily available, and even when they have been gathered, are sensitive in the extreme. Three points can, however, be made.

1   There is evidence that both parents (SCRE, in progress) and pupils (Black and Dockrell, 1984) rank formative information highly in terms of the feedback they would like from assessment.

2   Where teachers are put in the situation of developing alternative formative assessment models, they typically admit that their existing procedures were not designed with individual feedback of learning problems as a high priority (Black and Dockrell, 1984).

3   There is evidence that carefully planned programmes of formative assessment can have a wide range of positive impacts on learning and teaching.

## The Impact of Alternative Formative Models

The essential difference between most existing formative procedures and the alternative models described here is the extent to which they are systematic. Their focus and intention is the same as that of the formative assessment ideal of most teachers. But rather than happening haphazardly or by chance, they are carefully planned integral parts of a teaching and assessment strategy designed to systematically support student learning.

Probably the best documented model is the 'mastery learning' approach developed by Bloom and his associates in the United States. In Bloom's (1976) account of mastery learning he states that the approach begins

> With the notion that most students can attain a higher level of learning capability if instruction is approached sensitively and systematically, if students are helped when and where they have learning difficulties, if students are given sufficient time to achieve mastery, and if there is some clear criterion of what constitutes mastery.

Proponents of the model claim that the use of mastery learning techniques can result in 80 per cent of students in a class attaining the same standard as the top 20 per cent of students taught by the same teacher using conventional techniques. They further claim that students will develop more positive attitudes to learning, because as they are given frequent evidence of their success, they will spend more of their classroom time on active learning and they will develop the skill of seeking help when they have diagnosed that it is needed.

Underlying the approach is a recognition of the important relationship between three elements of the learning process: what a student has already attained (cognitive entry characteristics), his attitude to the learning opportunity (affective entry characteristics), and the nature of the teaching available (quality of instruction). In the conventional teaching situation the extent to which a student's cognitive entry characteristics are appropriate to a new element of learning is largely uncontrolled. In consequence, many students enter a new learning situation with less than optimum attitudes which are in turn cumulatively demotivating.

Where mastery learning is used the teacher is required to allow the students to master each sequential unit of work. In consequence, each element of learning in the hierarchy takes place when students have mastered the previous element. They therefore support their enhanced cognitive characteristics with more positive attitudes and hence reduce not only the variance in student attainment, but also the variance amongst *rates* of attainment.

The claims made from existing mastery learning studies are impressive, although it has to be stressed that their relevance to the typical British classroom is as yet not established (for relevant research, note McIntyre *et al.*, in progress). In particular, even coping with the diminished learning rate variance reported in the more optimistic of existing studies has considerable implications for the way learning would have to be managed. Furthermore, it has to be recognized that most applied experience of the approach in the American context is confined to fairly straightforward reading or number development. Other studies relate mastery to the content of chapters in textbooks. In neither of these cases does one recognize the freedom and diversity of expected outcomes of learning from the British classroom. In consequence, the case for the model is diminished neither by its logic nor its reported successes, but by it being unproven as a reflection of our existing priorities.

An associated approach, but one which is less demanding in its expectations and implications for learning management is the diagnostic assessment model which arose from the deliberations of the Dunning Committee on Assessment in Scotland (HMSO, 1977). The Committee stated that:

> Diagnostic tests enable teachers to gain detailed information on the particular points of difficulty for each pupil, information which is necessary if there is to be improvement of performance. In such tests the responses selected by pupils from a number of options can indicate that a certain concept or process has or has not been grasped. The subsequent action is to select and offer alternative learning experiences to remedy the difficulties diagnosed. The tests are not easy to design, and at present are relatively under-developed across the curriculum and for different age ranges. Nor are they necessarily easy to apply and teachers may well require assistance in devising, acquiring, and using them.

It went on to recommend that research and development work should be instigated in the area. Amongst resulting studies has been the Diagnostic Assessment Project of the Scottish Council for Research in Education.

The Diagnostic Assessment Project (Black and Dockrell, 1980, 1984) was essentially teacher-based. The starting point was action research to develop diagnostic approaches to the problems that collaborating teachers wanted to tackle in their own classrooms. From this a model was derived which provided guidelines for other teachers wanting to apply the approach themselves.

Several points distinguished this Scottish Diagnostic Assessment model from the American mastery learning approach. First, considerable emphasis is placed on teacher freedom in deciding the outcomes which are to be assessed. Teachers applying the model are exhorted to reflect the true variety of their intended outcomes by choosing to diagnose attainment of the most crucial rather than those which are easy to assess. Considerable stress is placed on the variety of diagnostic instruments which can be constructed to assess not only conventional low-order cognitive outcomes but also expressive, affective and high-order intentions. Furthermore, the focus of the instruments is intended to be the assessment of discrete small-scale domains each covered by a number of items rather than the large-scale 'chapters' typical of much of the American literature.

Second, the limitations placed on teaching style and learning management are less strict. It is expected that at frequent points time will be made available for individual or group remedial work on diagnosed problems. But the rate at which students are able to learn is not necessarily dictated by the mastery of the whole class. Instead it is accepted that in many cases the intended outcomes can be developed longitudinally but some modular outcomes may not be mastered by all students, and that those who have already mastered the core will be encouraged to master extension outcomes. In short, provided that the teacher is able to accommodate some individual remedial work in his programme, the diagnostic approach is considered suitable for a wide variety of teaching styles and management plans.

Third, considerable emphasis is placed on the use of appropriate criterion-referenced assessment technology. The Project has tried to develop the approach in such a way that it can be used by teachers. In turn, this has led the researchers to question some of the trends in the current American literature and this is a point to which I will turn below.

Encouraging results have been obtained from the research. Teachers have reported that they consider it to be both professionally acceptable and a valuable teaching aid. It has helped them to focus more clearly on their reasons for teaching and helped them to pinpoint individual learning difficulties. Students have seen the diagnostic instruments as a valuable aid to learning and data has suggested a significant increase in attainment, although longitudinal studies such as those reported in the mastery learning literature have not yet been carried out. Observation and interview suggest that although the approach is more time consuming in its design than traditional continuous assessment, experience progressively reduces the time teachers take to use it. In brief, therefore, there is considerable evidence that systematic formative models of this kind can have substantial benefits for both teaching and learning.

## The Technology of Formative Assessment

Just to touch on this issue requires a substantial paper on its own and so only a few brief points will be made here.

First, it is clear from research experience that teachers are not well versed in the technology of instrument construction for formative purposes. This is not surprising, of course, because the criterion-referenced approach which is appropriate to such assessment is relatively new and is not the assessment model currently used for external certification.

Second, it would be dangerous to assume that systematic formative models require the teacher to become a specialist in most of the current criterion referenced technology. In fact most recent trends in this area have been appropriate to the needs of minimum competency testing in the United States. The context of formative assessment places different priorities on the technology.

In essence, there are two fundamental differences between criterion-reference for diagnostic purposes and its application for summative purposes. First, the consequences of mis-classifying students in diagnostic assessment are far less dire. If you make an error in deciding a young person's competence at the end of his or her education, you are substantially influencing their life chances. If you mis-classify someone as not understanding an element of learning in a diagnostic test, the worst you will do is to give them extra remedial help which they may not need. Clearly, therefore, there can be a greater tolerance of unreliability in the diagnostic context.

It would not, however, be appropriate to use this as the sole argument for questioning many of the procedures proposed in the criterion-referenced literature. Indeed, such a course could be dangerous. It could lead to tolerance for poor and essentially useless diagnostic tests which might do more harm than good. Furthermore, while many of the solutions proposed are unnecessarily complex for most situations in which disgnostic tests will be constructed, the basic issues will not and should not go away.

However, there is another crucial difference distinguishing between diagnostic and summative criterion-referenced assessment. In the latter, the pressure is very substantially to report attainment in general terms. This creates substantial problems for criterion-referenced assessment designs. It is very difficult to conceptualize criteria for the attainment of, shall we say, 'Organic Chemistry' or 'Following Instructions', both of which are possible domains for summative profiles. It is even more difficult to establish a homogeneity for tests and instruments assessing such large-scale domains without resorting to complex and often contentious psychometric techniques.

The foci appropriate to diagnostic assessment are, however, much smaller in scale. They are single well-defined concepts or skills which are crucial to the learning process. It is information on attainment of these which teachers and pupils find most useful in determining the next educational step. By fortunate coincidence, it is also these which posed the fewest problems in criterion-referenced instrument construction.

Clearly, therefore, these points raise a number of fundamental issues with regard to the current national interest in 'grade-related criteria' and other second cousins of criterion-referenced assessment. It could well be that we will witness, over the next few years, a psychometric bandwagon in the technology of criterion-referenced assessment design. The focus will almost certainly be on the large-scale domains which have greatest appeal to examination board interests. It is highly likely, therefore, that workers in this field will place considerable emphasis on issues such as the statistical procedures appropriate to manipulate 'observed' scores into 'true' scores, the complex issue of optimum test length and on the use of procedures such as item response theory to choose option test items.

Inevitably we have to recognize that the educational system is obliged by the needs of society to provide information on the summative attainments of young people. Furthermore, a move towards criterion-referenced assessment design for these assessments could well be an improvement if it was done sensitively and with sufficient resources. Not only would it provide young people with a clear understanding of what is expected of them to achieve academic success but by establishing national criteria, it could pave the way for the abolition of a substantial number of the examination boards which absorb a disproportionate slice of the declining educational cake.

However, should this move towards criterion-referenced summative assessment take place, it has to be recognized that a summative orientation might again come to dominate thinking in the area. If this should lead to the emphasis on teacher assessment skills in criterion referencing being for summative purposes in the same way that CSE internal assessment turned many subject teachers into continual examiners, we will not have capitalized on the substantial potential that criterion-referenced testing has in supporting teaching and learning.

## Conclusions

There is already evidence that teachers can construct and apply sound formative criterion-referenced tests for diagnostic purposes if they are given appropriate support (Black and Goring, 1983). There is ample evidence that, at least in Scotland, there is a substantial interest in this approach amongst teachers and educationists beyond the classroom (for example, McCall *et al.*, 1983; Mortimer, 1983; Perfect and Robinson, 1983; Simpson and Arnold, 1983). This chapter has tried to show that systematic formative assessment can have substantial and beneficial effects on teaching and learning and has argued for the explicit recognition of the need to develop *appropriate* skills amongst teachers.

As in much of education the problem is one of priorities and tradition. Assessment has long been seen as competitive and comparative. While it can fulfil this role it is, in fact, much nearer to the needs of students and teachers in its formative application. Schools virtually close down for two weeks while the external examinations are held. Many hours of teacher effort are devoted to setting and marking the instruments. If the same could be found in one session to allow teachers to gain sound formative skills and then develop appropriate assessment policies, the benefit for future years would be substantial.

## References

BLACK, H.D. and BROADFOOT, P.M. (1982) *Keeping Track of Teaching*, London, Routledge and Kegan Paul.

BLACK, H.D. and DOCKRELL, W.B. (1980) *Diagnostic Assessment in Secondary Schools*, Edinburgh, SCRE.

BLACK, H.D. and DOCKRELL, W.B. (1984) *Criterion-Referenced Assessment in the Classroom*, Edinburgh, SCRE.

BLACK, H.D. and GORING R. (1983) *A Diagnostic Resource in Geography*, Edinburgh, SCRE.

BLOOM, B.J. (1976) *Human Characteristics and School Learning*, New York, McGraw-Hill.

BLOOM, B.J., HASTINGS, R. and MADAUS, G. (1971) *Handbook on Formative and Summative Evaluation of Students' Learning*, New York, McGraw-Hill.

BUSWELL, G.T. and JOHN, L. (1926) *Diagnostic Chart for Individual Difficulties, Fundamental Processes in Arithmetic*, Indianapolis, Bobbs-Merrill.

CHADWICK, E. (1864) 'Statistics of educational results', *The Museum*, 3, pp. 479–84.

GLASER, R. (1963), 'Instructional technology and the measurement of learning outcomes: Some questions', *American Psychologist*, 18, pp. 519–21.

HMSO (1977) *Assessment for All*, Edinburgh, HMSO.

McCALL, J., BRYCE, T.G.J. and ROBERTSON, I. (1983) 'Assessing foundation science practical skills in the classroom', *Programmed Learning and Educational Technology (PLET)*, 20, pp. 11–17.

McINTYRE, D. *et al.* Research in Progress, Assessment and teaching in the first two years of secondary schools, project funded by the Scottish Education Department, University of Stirling.

MORTIMER, G.J. (1983) 'The application of diagnostic assessment to the teaching of historical skills', *PLET*, 20, pp. 18–26.

PERFECT, H. and ROBINSON, J. (1983) 'An approach of diagnostic testing in the Scottish "O-grade" biology course', *PLET*, 20, pp. 27–35.

SCOTTISH COUNCIL FOR RESEARCH IN EDUCATION (1980) National survey on school-based assessment as part of the Perceptions of School-Based Assessment Project, SSRC-funded, unpublished.

SCOTTISH COUNCIL FOR RESEARCH IN EDUCATION (in progress) Perceptions of School-Based Assessment Project.

SIMPSON, M. and ARNOLD, B. (1983) 'Diagnostic tests and criterion-referenced assessments: Their contribution to the resolution of pupil learning difficulties', *PLET*, 20, pp. 36–42.

TAYLOR, L.C. (1965) *Resources for Learning*, Harmondsworth, Penguin.

# The Prospects for Public Examinations in England and Wales

*Henry G. Macintosh*
*Southern Regional Examinations Board*

Given the almost weekly appearance of incompatible statements by major bodies about the single system of examining at 16+ and given the multiplicity of equally incompatible documents and speeches upon public examinations past, present and future which flow endlessly from politicians, the Department of Education and Science (DES), Her Majesty's Inspectorate (HMI), the Secondary Examinations Council (SEC) and the examining boards, not to mention the Further Education Units (FEU) and the Joint Board for Pre-Vocational Education (JBPVE), anyone attempting an article such as this one on the prospects for public examinations in England and Wales is on a hiding to nothing and can only get it wrong either in whole or in part. If only, says the author, I could just wait a week or a month or a year, then all would be crystal clear or at least a degree or two less muddy. It is instructive in this regard to compare the original article I wrote for the first edition.[1]

Ironically there was, I believe, a better case at Easter 1984 when this article was written for asking for a delay of a month than at any other time over the past year or eighteen months. Within the next month the Consultative Document on the Certificate of Pre-Vocational Education (CPVE)[2] will appear and will receive a very wide circulation; the Secretary of State is expected to make his long awaited pronouncement upon a single system of examining at 16+ and a statement will be made on the introduction of the Intermediate or 'I' level (apparently now to be called 'AS' or Advanced Supplementary). The DES is also at the present time digesting the comments it has received upon its draft policy statement on Records of Personal Achievement for School Leavers[3] and will shortly announce the criteria which bids for financial support for pilot studies in this area will have to meet. The first fruits of the work undertaken jointly by all the GCE boards on developing a common core within major subjects at GCE 'A' level will show itself in the June 1984 examinations. Action in respect of all these matters will go a very long way to determining the prospects for public examinations in England and Wales and a very uncertain prospect it is. That the examining boards themselves recognize this uncertainty — and here one is not only referring to the GCE and CSE boards but also to bodies like the Royal Society of Arts (RSA), the City and Guilds of London Institute (CGLI), and the Business and Technician Education Council (BTEC) — is shown by the multiplicity of potentially competitive activities in which they are currently engaged. These range from the licensing of driving instructors to the construction of basic skill tests and from developing local certificates to assisting local education authorities (LEAs) in the construction of graded tests and profiles.

What conclusions might realistically be drawn from all this flurry beyond the general observation that public examinations in England and Wales, far from becoming rationalized as many had hoped, are becoming a bigger and even more unhelpful jungle? I would suggest four. Firstly that GCE 'A' level will remain unchanged and that 'AS' when it is introduced will take the form of a half 'A' level. Secondly, that regardless of what Sir Keith Joseph may say or do about a single system of examining at 16+, the GCE and CSE boards will continue to produce joint syllabuses and examinations which will attract progressively fewer and fewer candidates. Thirdly, that the CPVE will prove extremely attractive to many students at 17+ and will relatively rapidly turn out to be the culminating point of a new 14–18 curriculum. In both curriculum terms and as an alternative model for public examining the CPVE has great potential, but it could also turn extremely sour and lead to a deeply divisive curriculum. Fourthly, there will be a marked increase in LEA-initiated records of personal achievement or profiles underwritten, in many cases, by existing examining boards acting as accrediting and validating agencies. These rather dogmatic, even extreme, suggestions require justification and the remainder of this chapter will be devoted to trying to provide this.

### Examinations at 18+

First GCE 'A' level. When talking about examination reform in the United Kingdom there is a tendency whenever 'A' level is reached to pause respectfully and announce that normal transmission will resume shortly. The history of attempts to reform 'A' level, apart from using up almost every available letter in the alphabet, has shown all too clearly that there is no collective will to broaden it on the lines of, say, the Scottish Higher. With the current cutbacks in places in higher education and a refusal even to consider lengthening the three-year honours degree courses, the costs of making any such change would probably now prevent it, even if the will was there. There has also been very little inclination to alter existing assessment methods or to expand significantly the range of subjects included. Real change therefore seems extremely unlikely, and 'A' level will in consequence continue to exercise a quite disproportionate influence upon curriculum thinking and assessment practice within a comprehensive school system.

'AS', of course, represents yet one more attempt at 'A' level reform. In the current circumstances it seems inevitable that breadth will not be introduced at the expense of standards and that 'AS' will, therefore, become in effect a contrasting or complementary half 'A' level for those with realistic aspirations for higher education and the professions, i.e. the two or three 'A' level student with expectations of a grade C or better. The resulting *de facto* grouping requirement can only make the whole examination more difficult. There are, of course, possibilities for introducing new subjects at 'AS' and a number of interesting current Alternative Ordinary (AO) syllabuses come to mind here. There are also possibilities for widening the range of assessment techniques used, to include for example greater emphasis upon orals and upon coursework, but as is so often the case logistic and administrative considerations will determine what actually happens in a situation where entries and hence fee income will in any case be small.

It will be interesting to see whether in the event the universities replace 'O' level with 'AS' as part of their general admission requirements but, even if they do not, there ought to be a sharp reduction in future in the number of students taking 'A' level in conjunction with 'O' level and/or 16+. In view of the well-known British preference for entering examinations because of their status rather than their suitability, this reduction may well take time and will depend in the last resort upon the availability of acceptable alternatives.

## Examinations at 16+

Given that it has now had an eighteen-year run which almost rivals that of *The Mousetrap*, the steps on the road towards a single system of examining at 16+ have been well documented, notably by Nuttall[4]. The introduction to the Consultative Document for the CPVE draws attention to three basic questions which it suggests have been emphasized in the public debate over the pre-vocational education of young people. These are as follows:

(i) What kind of curriculum ought to be provided by our institutions?
(ii) How ought that curriculum to be delivered?
(iii) How should the performance of young people be properly assessed?

These questions apply with equal force to courses leading to a single system of examining at 16+, and indeed to any courses which lead to some terminal qualification, but public debate upon them in relation to 16+ has been conspicuous by its absence. Instead, central government itself through the DES has increasingly taken the initiative in examination reform as the basis for establishing greater central control over the secondary curriculum — a control which it does not possess in law. At 16+ the present government's main vehicle for this purpose has been the development of national criteria, both subject-specific and general. Recently there has been a major thrust towards developing grade-related criteria within subjects as the first step in a shift towards criterion-referencing — a shift which has the personal support of the current Secretary of State, Sir Keith Joseph. The work undertaken upon national criteria which require government approval has further delayed the date for introduction of a single system and has led to growing disillusionment amongst many in education about the likely outcome.

One of the main causes of this disillusionment has been the insistence throughout by central government (and by the present government in particular) on the need to preserve within the new system the standards of one of the two examinations to be included in it, namely GCE 'O' level. Unless the Secretary of State can convince his Cabinet colleagues that 'O' level standards will be maintained in a single system, there will be no formal approval given for it. The price being paid for this — and it is a heavy one — is differentiated assessment in almost every subject, and hence a perpetuation of selection at age 13 or 14 and little or no incentive to experiment with either new subjects or new approaches to assessment — opportunities which ironically some of the subject-specific criteria actually encourage.

The snail-like progress — in marked contrast to the speed with which the CPVE has been introduced (it will be certificated for the first time in 1986 on courses commencing in September 1985) — has encouraged the 16+ groups of GCE and CSE boards, operating in the main not as integrated units but as loose federal structures, to develop and make available in increasing numbers their own joint syllabuses. These, however, lack the benefits of common certification and freedom of choice. The real problems of developing 'meaningful' grade-related criteria within single subjects (nothing less than the identification on a subject basis of the elements and structure of the curriculum), quite apart from the need to convince party colleagues, make it likely that the Secretary of State will not set a date for the introduction of a single system in his forthcoming statement. He is far more likely to propose further work on grade-related criteria leading to a gradual 'harmonization' of the two existing systems — a word which he has invented and is now trying to get the examining boards to define. If this happens then the examining boards themselves may well decide that they have had enough and work out arrangements between themselves for the operation of joint 16+ syllabuses — arrangements which will effectively mark the end of CSE, and the CSE boards. In such circumstances the result could be even more divisive, bureaucratic, retrogressive and obsolescent (to quote Nuttall[5]) than would be the case if a single system was introduced on the present government's terms.

Small wonder then that the opposition grows louder every day not only to the age-related irrelevance of the proposed single system but to public examinations as a whole and looks increasingly to the development of alternatives. Amongst these although very different in nature are the CPVE and Records of Personal Achievement.

## The Certificate of Pre-Vocational Education

The CPVE is run by a Board set up in 1983 jointly by the CGLI and BTEC, which bodies supply ten of the thirteen Board members, the other three coming from the RSA, the GCE boards and the CSE boards. The Joint Board has an independent Chairman — an industrialist appointed by the Secretary of State. It thus comes very definitely from the further education stable — the Certificate of Extended Education (CEE) was the school horse for the 17+ stakes. Given the economic and political climate of the late 1970s from which it emerged this is hardly surprising but its FE connections have had significant consequences both for its design and for the way in which it had been perceived by many in education.

Let us first look at its design as outlined in the Consultative Document. This document poses a number of key questions to which the Joint Board clearly wants answers in order to help it make up its mind, but the basic design does not fall into this category and will not therefore be materially altered. Unlike the majority of public examinations taken by students in schools, the CPVE is not based upon published course statements or syllabuses — usually single subject in nature — from amongst which choices can be made and which can be taken in batches or one at a time. Instead it consists of a curriculum framework made up of three elements: a common core, vocational studies and additional studies. The first two (the core and vocational studies) are mandatory and taken together must occupy not less than three-quarters of the time available in a full-time one-year course. The additional studies, whilst encouraged and recorded on the certificate, are not mandatory. In the determination of this model the Joint Board has been markedly influenced by the work of the FEU and in particular its 1979 publication *A Basis for Choice* (ABC): *Report of a Study Group on Post-16 Pre-Employment Courses* — a sub-title not without significance.[6] In addition to advocating a curriculum framework very similar to that proposed by the Joint Board, ABC also strongly pressed for the use of profile reporting — a process hitherto associated in the UK with experimental work in schools notably in Swindon, Totnes, Evesham and on a national scale in Scotland. A parallel or complementary curriculum input from the schools side of comparable quality was unfortunately not forthcoming at this time due in part to the growing problems faced by the Schools Council.

The core comprises the following ten areas which are intended *jointly* to provide a set of aims, objectives and typical learning experiences for a CPVE programme. These are as follows:

Personal and career development
Communication

Numeracy
Science and technology
Industrial, social and environmental studies
Information technology
Skills for learning, decision making and adaptability
Practical skills
Social skills
Creative development

The vocational studies, which it is intended should be closely integrated with the core in terms of promoting learning opportunities and skills development, are to be based upon clusters of activities which have a common purpose and related learning objectives. The determination of specific vocational areas has yet to be made but it has been suggested that the eleven occupational training families identified by the Institute of Manpower Studies and the Manpower Services Commission could provide a rational and workable basis although their long-term value has yet to be determined. It may well be, however, that in the operational version of the CPVE a smaller number of more broadly-based categories such as 'Working with others' or 'Processing information' will be used, or an opportunity provided for students to take general vocational studies. The chosen areas will, however, provide the basis for three types of course, namely

(i) orientation, in which the students will sample a number of areas with a view to channelling existing interests and assisting future choice;

(ii) exploration, mainly within an area which is already attractive or interesting to particular students;

(iii) preparation for entry to a chosen vocational field involving one or more areas.

The third element, the additional studies, are intended to serve one or more of the following purposes:

(a) to provide a natural extension to the core and vocational elements of the framework;

(b) to provide a natural extension to the vocational elements in some areas to the level of industrial competence;

(c) to provide studies associated with the creative arts, physical, community and other group activities;

(d) to allow for special educational needs.

They can thus bridge the divide between training and general education or enable one or the other to be pursued in greater depth. The nature and range of the additional studies are one of the questions upon which the Joint Board does require advice, and the decisions eventually taken here are likely to have a significant effect upon the attractiveness of the CPVE for a wide range of students.

Throughout the proposals relating to the three elements there is constant reference to the coherence of the whole programme and to integration both within and between elements. These features, which are combined with marked flexibility in the choice of course content, are both built deliberately into the overall programme and do not result from the choice of particular examination courses by individuals and institutions as is the case with GCE and CSE. The instrument for ensuring this happens is the criteria for programme approval or validation laid down in a section entitled 'Maintenance of Quality'. As well as a description of the content through which it is intended to meet the overall requirements for the CPVE, these criteria require details of how the programme will be organized, resourced, taught and evaluated. Amongst the criteria listed, for example, are not only such things as an appropriate balance of core, vocational and additional studies and the inclusion of all the elements of the core, but also opportunities for review of progress by the students, for programme negotiation, for staff development and the provision of resources. The levels of programme scrutiny which such criteria require and the mechanisms for ensuring that what is alleged should happen does indeed happen are of a very different order from those used by most existing examining boards and would require them to adopt a very different role vis-à-vis both student and institution. It is a role which involves on the one hand a direct and specific impact upon the workings of institutions and on the other the provision of support and advice. Such a role is not without difficulties and tensions, and will certainly require those involved to establish rather different organizational structures and employ rather different staff from those in current examining agencies.

An approach such as that envisaged for the CPVE also makes possible a much closer and more positive interaction between assessment and learning than is currently the case with other public examinations. If this is to become a reality, however, the assessment and certification procedures proposed are crucial. Whilst the rather sparse information provided on these two topics in the Consultative Document makes many of the right noises, there are other less satisfactory suggestions and there is clearly much more work to be done in both these areas. For example, the CPVE with its emphasis upon specific objectives, cross-curricular skills and profile reporting lends itself far more to criterion-referencing than a subject-based examination such as the GCE or CSE. In order to take advantage of this, however, it is not pertinent to talk about absolute consistency of measurement from place to place and from year to year. Comparability and 'can do' assessment are uneasy bedfellows even when there is relatively little emphasis upon subjects. Furthermore, if it is really intended that assessment within the CPVE will take place for both formative and summative purposes then it makes little sense to provide external centrally set assessments. The concentration should instead be upon externally moderated local assessments. Finally, the relationship between experience and achievement expressed in terms of skills is not nearly as simple or as clear-cut as the Consultative Document tends to suggest, nor is it easy to devise appropriate means of testing the skills once they have been identified. Much work needs to be undertaken, in particular, on the development of integrated assignments set within the context of specific institutions — exercises which again do not lend themselves to centrally set assessment.

Enough should by now have been said to suggest that the proposals for the CPVE have the capacity to match the curriculum and assessment needs of many more students than the single system at 16+. Unfortunately its origin and its present FE base do not help rational consideration of its merits and potential. Ever since Callaghan's Ruskin speech in 1976, central government has consistently argued that the school system has not adequately catered for the economic needs of the nation and that the future output of the system must be geared more closely to the requirements of employment. Given the present government's predilection for an examination-led curriculum there is no doubt that the CPVE (or the 17+ examination as it then was) was conceived originally as an instrument for shifting the curriculum along 'more appropriate lines'. The struggles that led to the emergence of the Joint Board, although shorter, were no less messy and byzantine than those which have affected 16+, but in this case they were polarized into FE versus schools and hence once again into training versus general education. The school examining boards, particularly the CSE boards, resented the cavalier treatment given to a decade's experience with CEE and this insensitivity has turned many potential friends of the CPVE into enemies. The disconnection of examination reforms at 17+, which are the direct responsibility of the Joint Board, from those at 16+ and 18+ over which Schools Branch at the DES and the SEC exercise responsibility has further reinforced the views of those who see the government as deliberately creating a divisive curriculum through examination change. In this scenario, the elite growing ever smaller will ultimately take 'A' level and the hewers of wood and drawers of water growing ever larger will ultimately take the CPVE. The latter, while currently only certificating one-year full-time post-16 courses, also has the capacity to provide terminal assessment for a 14–18 pre-vocational curriculum which CGLI and BTEC appear to think they have been ordained by God to provide for a waiting and grateful people.

For all these reasons and a fair amount of prejudice besides, the CPVE has been seen in many quarters as the examination flag carrier of the new vocationalism. The distinction between pre-vocationalism (education for employability?) and vocationalism (education for employment?), if it was ever realistic, has been largely lost in this argument. Maurice Holt, in a recent article entitled 'Vocationalism — the new threat to universal education'[7], produces a good (albeit somewhat extreme) example of this point of view. He opens with the following:

> A fundamental decision we have to make about education is whether it should transform the mind so as to equip us for independent judgment and rational action or whether it should be directed towards practical skills for particular ends. This is the distinction between liberal education — education for freedom for tackling problems as yet unknown — and schooling as training for instrumental tasks as they are currently perceived.

Given views such as these, it is not surprising that the CPVE has had a bad press even before its final form is known. However, even those who hold Maurice Holt's views are not happy with the present public examining system. It is, they will say, too subject-based, too dominated by the needs of higher education, and too uninformative. Current interest in and experimentation with graded tests and profile reporting, the development of the Oxford Certificate of Educational Achievement (OCEA)[8] and the Hargreaves Committee proposals for improving secondary schools in ILEA[9] all underline this unhappiness and all emphasize the need for an assessment system which reflects instead of directs the curriculum and which is more open, more flexible, more positive and less age-related. No other country would surely ever refer to its public examinations as 16+, 17+ and 18+.

The views of critics such as Holt are not justified in my opinion. The Consultative Document for the CPVE suggests that the Board has begun to generate a life of its own and has freed its thinking from that of the two bodies which set it up in a number of important respects. For example, it has recognized that a majority of its clientele will be educated in schools and not colleges of further education and that, in consequence, the core should be capable of realization to a greater degree than was once envisaged through single subjects, something that is possible without sacrificing cohesion. It has also recognized that the need to develop social and creative skills is as important for the constructive use of leisure time as it is for improving employability. There is still much that needs to be done — for example, a willingness to allow agencies other than the Joint Board itself to submit proposals for CPVE accreditation as off-the-shelf packages, a less instrumental view of communication, a wider definition of what is or is not vocational. Another matter for concern is the slightly peripheral position still given to additional studies. While no longer the pariahs they once were when it was feared that they might be used to distort the basic purpose of the CPVE, additional studies are still not accorded mandatory status. Given the extended target group envisaged by the Joint Board this is essential. These problems are all, however, perfectly capable of resolution given the will to try. What is needed first, therefore, is not a philosophical attack upon the CPVE but a practical look to see whether the kind of curriculum needs which people believe to be necessary for secondary schools can be encompassed and evaluated within the framework proposed by the CPVE, considered not as the basis for a one-year course but as the basis for a 14–18 curriculum. If the answer to such an analysis is 'yes', then the CPVE could indeed replace 'O' level and CSE, and do more than any other single act to rationalize the present examination jungle.

There would appear to be two major obstacles to such a development. First, the continuance of an unaltered 'A' level and, second, teacher attitudes, on the one hand to assessing their own students and on the other to teaching a less subject-bound curriculum. Despite the widening of the target group for the CPVE to include virtually all post-16 full-time students except for those for whom 'A' level is a realistic target at *present*, the nature of 'A' level and its prestige will inevitably cause a substantial number of students to be entered for 'O' level or 16+ as a stepping stone to 'A' level whether or not this makes educational sense at the time. Progression both into and out of the CPVE is vital because, if something which purports to be pre-vocational turns out to lead nowhere, the disenchantment will be that much greater. Progression in terms of exemption through credit transfer ought to be relatively easy to negotiate with bodies like BTEC, CGLI and the RSA although empire-building may well hinder progress. If the CPVE remains geared to one-year courses, there is an equal need to look at ways in which achievement on the YTS core can be credited for the CPVE. There are indeed a whole host of ways in which the notions of progression and credit transfer need exploration in the interests of young people who take examinations and courses set by different bodies at different times. Progression through exemption is not, however, practicable in the case of 'A' level and the question for the potential 'A' level student therefore becomes 'Can I realistically proceed from the CPVE to "A" level in the light of their respective demands?' Given that the time scale over which young people will undertake their education will inevitably lengthen and become less continuous in the future, the answer to the student's question could be 'yes' provided that the status of additional studies within the CPVE is reappraised. These could then be used as the first stage in a three-year course culminating in 'A' level. There is no obstacle incidentally under the proposed arrangements to 'AS' courses being taken as additional studies. Genuine 'A' level students with realistic aspirations for grade C or better in two or three subjects would have no need to take 'O' level or 16+, the relevant preparatory examinations being provided by the institutions at which they were studying. TVEI too would fit very well into an examination system which involved only the CPVE and 'A' level. The CPVE profile could record the achievement of those who left at 16 or 17 or indeed at any point between, and 'A' level the achievement of those who left at 18, 19 or beyond.

The second obstacle, namely teacher attitudes, is much more serious, I believe. No real reform of public examinations in England and Wales can be achieved unless teachers are willing to accept full responsibility for the assessment of their own students. Acceptance of full responsibility does not mean the absence of systems of moderation to underpin teacher judgments in the interests of public relations, if for no other reason. Secondary school teachers remain curiously ambivalent in their attitude to this issue. It is in part a matter of time and resources, in part a matter of training, and in part a matter of historical dependence upon an external system of public examinations. Unless teachers come off the fence and commit themselves to accepting the challenge, any reforms will be an empty shell. The CPVE, and indeed any major reform of the curriculum intended to gear it to the needs of all children, must inevitably involve a reduction in the influence of single subjects and place much greater emphasis upon the development of skills and concepts taught through content selected for its appropriateness for the purpose in hand. Given the training that most present teachers have undergone, this presents a real challenge to their competence and hence to their confidence and self-esteem as teachers. It is vitally important therefore that a curriculum framework such as that proposed for the CPVE does not rule out absolutely the use of single subjects as a part of the overall programme. An analysis of the proposed core and of, for example, the work undertaken by the Geography 16–19 Project[10] on ABC would suggest that this position can obtain with the CPVE.

All this may seem a pipe-dream and the arguments put forward in this article may appear superficial and oversimplified but, given that the following three propositions command substantial agreement, as I believe they do, then a CPVE/'A' level combination could provide a realistic solution:

1  That GCE 'A' level will not change in the foreseeable future and will indeed be reinforced in its present form through the introduction of 'AS'.
2  That the present examination jungle is both wasteful of resources and unhelpful to the mass of young people.
3  That we still wish to retain some system of national public examinations in England and Wales below 'A' level.

If such a combination is not tried then it is likely that the present examination system will break into a thousand fragments. It may be that this is what the government wishes and it intends to divide and rule in the examination jungle not by accident but as a result of deliberate policy.

### Records of Personal Achievement

In considering the fourth of the suggestions made at the outset of this chapter, namely that there would be a marked increase in LEA-initiated records of personal achievement, one enters into rather calmer waters, not least because it is possible for their development to take place in a whole variety of different circumstances. The crucial question, however, is what these records will turn out to be. It is possible to see them simply as a knee-jerk reaction to the inadequacies of existing public examinations. There is, however, far more to them than the provision of alternative systems of certification. The introduction of a well-designed recording system has wide-ranging and extremely important implications for institutional organization, for motivation, for relationships between students, teachers and courses, for teaching and assessment styles, for curriculum patterns, for guidance programmes, for recording systems and for staff training.

The extent to which a significant investment of resources will be put into their development will depend upon their relative importance within the field of examination reform by comparison with other means of providing information about young people. This will largely emerge from national decisions in relation to 16+ and 17+ and how these are reflected in actual take-up by students and teachers. The government draft policy statement on records of personal achievement has been well received but it seems at present to be a relatively low-key development.[11] It intends to involve all students within the 11–16 age range, thus covering the transfer between primary, middle and secondary. The government has also indicated that funding for pilot schemes will be available and has suggested that these could with advantage involve LEAs and examining boards. The pilot study which the Dorset LEA is undertaking in cooperation with the SREB involving some eighteen to twenty-five schools is likely to be fairly typical of such studies, although not all will use such a record as a means of implementing LEA curriculum statements or produce a wide range of in-service training materials as this proposal intends to do. The success of these pilot studies will determine to a substantial degree the way in which the records are subsequently used and the extent of that usage. It will be particularly important in this context, therefore, to establish their credibility with local employers and the community at large. Once again staff development and the extent to which teachers really wish to be involved in the assessment of their own students will be crucial to their success. For a more detailed critique of profiles and records of achievement, see the chapter by Broadfoot in this volume.

### Conclusions

One ought to conclude an article with a title such as this one with some consideration of the future prospects of those who run the examinations — the boards. Put fairly starkly, the CSE boards are almost certainly doomed unless they can either work closely with their constituent LEAs in providing an assessment advisory service, or can become involved in CPVE accreditation and moderation (an option which the Joint Board may prevent), or can integrate with other boards in order to extend the range of services they offer. There are already clear signs that the first and third of these activities are beginning to happen. It is also clear that such activities will require fewer and rather different staff from those presently employed. The GCE boards will continue to exist because of 'A' level (and 'AS' if and when it comes in) and some will also continue to examine overseas although this work is both more demanding and less profitable than it used to be. For some boards, notably Oxford and Cambridge, 'A' level work will probably be sufficient, for others, notably the Associated Examining Board, it will not. This Board, in particular, will need to diversify its assessment activities as it is already starting to do. Again such work will require fewer and rather different staff. Whatever the ultimate scenario, the examination industry like most of British industry will change: it will need to become more competitive and more market-orientated; it will certainly need to become more cost-effective and by law (if for no other reason) it will have to become more open in its disclosure of information. It will also need to become more technically competent in order to provide advice and training in assessment matters. Validation and accreditation are likely to become increasingly significant activities.

This chapter started by suggesting that the reader might with advantage compare it with the previous one of the same title that appeared in the first edition.[12] It might, however, be more fruitful — and it might even raise a smile or an eyebrow — to read this chapter in about a year's time in order to compare it with reality.

**Notes**

1 MACINTOSH, H.G. (1982) 'The prospects for public examinations in England and Wales', *Educational Analysis*, 4, 3.
2 JOINT BOARD FOR PRE-VOCATIONAL EDUCATION (1984) *The Certificate for Pre-Vocational Education: A Consultative Document*.
3 DEPARTMENT OF EDUCATION AND SCIENCE (1983) *Records of Personal Achievement for Young School Leavers: A Draft Policy Statement*, London, HMSO.
4 NUTTALL, D.L. (1984) 'Doomsday or new dawn? The prospects for a common system of examining at 16+', in BROADFOOT, P.M. (Ed.) *Selection, Certification and Control*, Lewes, Falmer Press.
5 *Ibid.*

6 FURTHER EDUCATION UNIT (1979, reprinted 1983) *A Basis for Choice: Report of a Study Group on Post-16 Pre-Employment Courses,* London, Department of Education and Science.
7 HOLT, M. (1983) 'Vocationalism: the new threat to universal education', *Forum,* 25, 3.
8 OXFORD DELEGACY FOR LOCAL EXAMINATIONS (1983) Oxford Certificate of Educational Achievement Newsletters Nos 1 and 2.
9 INNER LONDON EDUCATION AUTHORITY (1984) *Improving Secondary Schools: Report the Committee on the Curriculum and Organization of Secondary Schools* (The Hargreaves Report), London, HMSO.
10 SCHOOLS COUNCIL (1982) *17+: The Geographical Component of 17+ Pre-Employment Courses,* A Joint Geography 16−19 and Itchen College statement.
11 DEPARTMENT OF EDUCATION AND SCIENCE (1983) *op. cit.*
12 MACINTOSH, H.G. (1982) *op. cit.*

# Australian Examination Systems: Eight States of the Art

Graeme Withers
*Australian Council for Educational Research*


Some three years ago, a general survey of Australian public examination systems was attempted by the present author (Withers, 1982). Since that statement, many of the themes which were noted as emerging trends have come to some sort of resolution, some have disappeared entirely, and a few new developments have appeared which are worthy of comment. However, several fundamental understandings are needed to inform the discussion.

Australia has no one examination system common for all its secondary school children, nor does it have one institution to organize and oversee such examinations as do take place across the continent. This makes the writing of a review such as this a tricky exercise — the fine art of generalization becomes even finer when one is trying to define and interpret 'trends', 'themes', or commonality across eight separate systems. The complexity of the eight systems is well demonstrated by a review such as Aldrich-Langen's (1983). The occasional sweeping statement in this chapter should, therefore, be handled cautiously. Often I have tried to locate a development or pinpoint an evolutionary stage by using names of states: this too has its problems. To say that a particular theme has been taken up in one state is not to attribute it exclusively — other states may be working on it too. State reputations are still jealously guarded in such matters.

A public examination system in Australia is either set up and run directly by a state or territory education department, or it may be administered by an autonomous institution funded by a state government, with links to an education department but not controlled or funded by it. The latter relationship leads to some uneasiness at times, especially when control of an examination is only one part of a wider brief to supervise aspects of secondary education.

One notable feature of the last few years, in this regard, is the tendency to review administrative arrangements and functions. South Australia has recast its public examinations board; Western Australia has instituted a series (to some, a plethora) of formal inquiries into the conduct of secondary education and its attendant examination policies; major (Victoria) or minor (Queensland, Tasmania) reviews of program and policy have either been conducted or are in the process of public scrutiny. An acceptable generalization to apply to at least four of these systems (WA, Queensland, ACT and Victoria) is that public comment, in newspapers as well as professional journals, is now constant and, while not always welcome or particularly well-informed, is keeping the examining and certifying authorities very well aware of their public responsibilities.

## Gradual Abolition of Examinations Below Year 12

This is another acceptable generalization about public examinations across Australia: examination systems as such are now almost solely concerned with the final year of secondary schooling, which we shall for convenience label Year 12 (even such nomenclature is not common across state boundaries). The 1960s and 1970s saw the gradual abandonment of externally administered examinations in more junior years. Victoria, for example, once had a set of five, in Years 8 to 12, each covering all the traditional subjects, each offered annually, with certificates attached, to fulfil the functions of exit qualifications for school leavers and tests to verify academic progress. With the increasing retention rates and the gradual rise in school leaving age, the need to provide the former fell away, and it is now left to schools to conduct the assessments necessary in Years 8 to 11 — a definite (if prolonged) act of mercy towards secondary students. There are occasional 'scares' about the possible reintroduction of more junior examinations: a 1983 ministerial enquiry in Tasmania may yet institute a formal 'school certificate' examination at the equivalent of Year 10. The impetus to such moves tends to be party-political, and none so far has tested the strength of possible opposition from teacher unions.

## School-based Curriculum Development and Assessment

A second major strand in public examining is a gradual shift towards greater control by the teaching profession over such examinations as do exist. The process is by no means completed, and the signs of a backlash against it, fostered by various other parties interested in the products of secondary education, are many and widespread across the country. Nevertheless, a comparison of the early 1960s and the mid-1980s reveals a substantial increase in the amount of power delegated to, and responsibility accepted by, practising teachers. And this is one occasion where a sweeping summary might be accepted, to varying extents, for all eight systems: such a change has been officially fostered. For example, in Queensland, in 1971:

> the Radford Committee recommended the abolition of the junior and senior public examinations ... replacing them with a system of moderated assessments. The further recommendations ..., relating to courses of study, intended that schools should have greater autonomy in curriculum design and assessment, to cater more adequately for individual differences in ability and interests among secondary school students. They also intended that the basis of involvement in decision making with regard to school curricula and assessment techniques should be widened. They further intended that teachers should experience greater professional challenge and stimulation, while secondary school students should experience higher motivation, greater freedom in choice of subjects, and the opportunity to proceed at a pace commensurate with their ability and experience. In the area of assessment ..., in addition to the traditional concern for knowledge and understanding, assessment should also be concerned with the processes of learning and with a wider range of qualities and achievements. (Queensland Board of Secondary School Studies, 1979, p. 1)

While the system implemented in Queensland has for some time been the subject of formal review — the so-called 'ROSBA', or Review of School-Based Assessment, process — and much of it critical, the fundamental principles still stand. The 1979 review and others before it, while seeking to make adjustments and direct attention to new emphases, particularly in regard to enhancing public accountability and the quality of the information yielded about students, reaffirm the spirit of the Radford proposals: 'We believe, as did the authors of the Campbell Report [an earlier (1975) review], that the strengths of school-based assessment outweigh its weaknesses' (*ibid*, p. 64).

Another point to be noted is that while the Queensland system has not been directly imported into any other state, its principles established a local context of change, and gave heart to many elsewhere that such changes were possible, workable, and some, perhaps, even likely. A postscript: in case it seems odd that such a scheme should be described in an article on public examination systems, it should be disclosed that Queensland operates a parallel, certifying, public examination for those not in schools, and that the school-based assessments are scaled, by use of a three-hour examination — the Australian Scholastic Aptitude Test (ASAT) — for which all secondary students sit. Students do not receive personal scores on the latter; data are aggregated for inter-school scaling, and tertiary entrance allocations are made according to the resulting scores.

The Year 12 system of accreditation (a process known elsewhere, particularly in the United Kingdom, as 'validation') as used in the Australian Capital Territory, similarly allows schools to develop, teach, and assess their own courses, at Years 11 and 12, while reserving the right to the ACT Schools Authority to moderate the products (students and their scores) by means of ASAT. Other states share and, idiosyncratically, develop the theme of school-based curriculum development. For example, the Victorian Government set up in 1977 the Victorian Institute of Secondary Education (VISE), after long, hard committee work reviewing developments in Queensland, elsewhere in Australia, and overseas. The VISE policy statement on curriculum and assessment, published in 1979, acknowledges these sources, particularly an OECD review:

> In our view the assessment of a pupil's progress and achievement by schools rather than by a single external examination is a critical factor in the reform of upper secondary curriculum. ... in view of the need to cater for an increasing proportion of young people in upper secondary education who will not proceed to traditional tertiary education we feel that schools will function more effectively when carrying out their own assessment and we therefore welcome the gradual trend to shift from external examinations to school-based assessment. (OECD, 1976, p. 34)

This latter comment reinforces an earlier Victorian position from a Committee on Arrangements for Secondary Curriculum and Assessment in 1974:

> The teacher should have the maximum freedom to work out a curriculum which has regard to the individuality of the pupil and the characteristics of the region concerned. The pupil should have the maximum freedom to choose between fields of study, and that choice should be as little constrained as possible by requirements of training for a future occupation. (Victoria Education Department, 1974, para. 30)

All this was fashioned into an interim (some would say compromise) policy, giving in part the following set of arrangements:

6.3 The scheme proposed by VISE therefore ensures that schools have a significant opportunity both to devise Year 12 curricula appropriate to their students and participate in the assessment of those students.

Under VISE, schools may establish subjects which are totally devised and assessed within a single school or within a group of schools. Some students may choose to make up their entire Year 12 program from such subjects. These subjects ... will not be assessed using numerical marks. The rationale of these subjects would be destroyed by the consequences of attempting numerical comparisons of results between subjects and between schools. The assessments will be expressed descriptively, or perhaps through letter grades.

6.4 While VISE supports school participation in devising curricula and in conducting assessments in all Year 12 subjects, it will retain external syllabus prescription and external examination as part of the constitution of another group of subjects. (VISE, 1978, p. 8)

The second half of 1983 saw a fairly thorough revision to these arrangements by an Institute working party. This group, through the Council of VISE, published in March 1984 a set of proposals which updated the 1978 policy and laid out for discussion a second stage of devolution to schools and curriculum developers of the responsibility for devising and assessing Year 12 courses. The recommendations would reduce the number of subjects with external examinations from fifty-six to fourteen, and would reduce the weighting of any external component to a maximum of 50 per cent. By far the most radical recommendation so far as the public is concerned is that which abandons percentages in favour of a five-point or a two-point scale, depending on the subject developers' requirements. (More about this proposal will be said below, when the changes involving university and post-secondary education are discussed.) Other proposals are for the continuance of strict accreditation procedures and to maintain the study of English as a compulsory part of the Year 12 curriculum. Victoria has thus come a little closer to meeting the requirements of the official policy of the Australian Teachers' Federation towards assessment, first stated in 1979 and quoted here in full:

> The ATF believes that the interaction of teacher and student in school and classroom is the focal point of school education.
>
> The capability of teachers to adapt to this interaction in accordance with their professional judgment of students' educational needs must not be stifled by external constraints on the school.
>
> Since it is inevitable that any external examination exercises a uniform domination of curriculum in the form of prescribed syllabi, and to a substantial degree of teaching method and student evaluation, external examination systems are opposed by the Australian Teachers' Federation.
>
> The Australian Teachers' Federation affirms that schools alone can properly undertake the responsibilities of determining awards or statements of students' school attainments. It should be understood by employers and the community that any such statements are of necessity based on school attainment only, and therefore in general provide only a guide on the selection of employees which is the responsibility of employers.
>
> Where there is an agreed need to maintain a uniform state-wide standard of attainment in each subject in the certification of school leavers, evaluative support services must, where necessary, be provided to schools to enable them to meet this requirement with minimal interference with the school program and teacher-learning processes.

There are signs, however, that the 'let-the-hundred-flowers-bloom' philosophy of choice and diversity, possible under this policy, is increasingly less popular with some teacher unions which contribute to ATF membership.

### Grouping Subjects for Accreditation

One aspect of the new proposals in Victoria overturns a procedure implemented as recently as 1981. This was the division of Year 12 subjects into 'Group 1' and 'Group 2' according to whether the course descriptions permitted external examinations and the subject was felt to be worthy of such a 'distinction'. This tier (or 'group') notion of varying individual course assessment procedures (according to the origin of the course design or the intended use of the assessments) was echoed in the report of the Committee of Enquiry into Education in South Australia (1980), where the distinctions were even more finely tuned. Several other authorities use the notion of different tiers: for example, the Year 11/12 program in operation in New South Wales from 1975 distinguished between 'Board courses', with syllabuses and examinations set by the Board of Senior School Studies, and 'other approved studies', developed and examined by the schools themselves but accredited by the Board. These latter do not qualify a student for university entrance.

A second aspect of the accreditation procedure which might be noted is the administrative arrangements for accreditation of course designs and assessment procedures by independent expert committees, on something of the British Council for National Academic Awards model. These will continue in Victoria, and have been picked up by the Select Committee of the New South Wales Legislative Assembly (1981). In amongst exhortations to schools to develop special courses for special needs, as well as a whole series of foundation courses at each year level 7–12, their report suggested that each course (in one-semester units) be accredited by a central authority. 'Such courses must gain the approval of the central authority for their implementation' (NSW Select Committee, 1981, p. 3). However, external examination is avoided and Recommendation 17 firmly asserted of all courses at all levels: 'The assessment should be carried out by the school' (p. 6).

### Other Inter-systemic Changes in the 1970s

Before we leave matters of general context and overviews, one or two other points might be worth noting. One is the beginning of interstate cooperation and contact in a field — education — which was awarded by the Australian Constitution as a preserve of the states and, as mentioned before, jealously (and proudly) guarded. The last few years have seen meetings of an Australasian Conference of Examining and Certifying Authorities, and its papers and proceedings are now published (Volumes 1–4, 1980–1983). The agendas for such meetings suggest that common problems (for example, the emphasis in the 1984 program on school-based assessment) have given rise to a real sharing of expertise, if not always common solutions. The New Zealand examining authority also joins these meetings, and trans-Tasman cooperation and contact enriches the enterprise. A second contact is the joint funding, by Western Australia, the Australian Capital Territory, and Queensland, of a scaling test (ASAT) to serve the related but different tertiary entrance systems of each authority. An experimental run of one form of the test in Victoria in the mid 1970s was effectively torpedoed by militant action by a state teachers union, which was campaigning — not at all tongue-in-cheek — for a ballot to replace examinations as the selection device for applicants for tertiary places. There are, as noted below, signs that Victoria may again participate in an experimental run of ASAT, as a result of the renewed interest amongst universities in controlling their entrance procedures more directly.

Another brief overview might be taken of the social and demographic changes affecting senior secondary education. Rising rolls in senior classes were nationwide in the 1970s to about 35 per cent in 1978. The degree to which tapering off of this rise, or falls in the numbers of boys in secondary classes in Year 12, have occurred will not be summarized state-by-state (the rates vary). An acceptable generalization might be that retention rates are rising again, for both sexes, to about 40 per cent in 1983, and that individual school retentivity rates within the systems are the focus of some research attention. Recent studies such as Batten (1983) and Ainley, Batten and Miller (1984) have contributed to the debate about the quality of senior school life, its curriculum and assessment components and procedures, and the relation of these to retentivity rates. Another acceptable generalization might be that by comparison with 1974 (let alone 1964) this year's Year 12 cohort is larger, particularly the number of girls, is more diverse given Australia's immigration patterns and history, and faces the same problems of youth unemployment, competition for tertiary education and credentials, and the circumstances of economic recession as its peers in other Western countries. As well, the contribution that Year 12 curriculum and assessment (and the examination systems involved) can make to a solution of the problems of this transition is, as elsewhere, under constant discussion, and the solutions no less varied or complex than in, say, the United Kingdom or the United States.

## The Issue of Curriculum Control by Tertiary Institutions

Two practical, political, pressure points remain. Universities and tertiary institutions have not quite disabused themselves of the idea that they should determine senior secondary curriculum through control of its assessments. To put it mildly, the results of the Radford scheme have not achieved unanimous popularity amongst Queensland university staffs. And the Victorian Inter-University Subcommittee on University Entrance is still adamant in its refusal to acknowledge scores from certain accredited courses as counting for entrance. This stance sometimes rests on perceived 'defects' in the course, sometimes on 'deficiencies' in its assessment (especially where teacher assessment accounts for the whole grade or mark). The second pressure point is related to this: while the majority of aspirants to tertiary education get a place, there are quotas limiting entrance to particular courses and to particular institutions. Although there are signs that reliance on examination results for such decisions is declining, or being moderated by inclusion of other measures such as interviews, workshop trials, and descriptive (rather than numerical) assessments, expertise at collating and interpreting such profiles is slow to develop. And confidence in the decision-making and its products is even slower to appear.

That the pressure is real and not illusory can be testified to by the fine heads of steam built up in recent months of public debate about some new proposals put forward by two of the older universities which sought to review their entrance policies and procedures. One was perhaps minor — the decision announced by the University of Sydney that henceforth English would be compulsory for matriculation purposes. Some of the steam dissipated when it was found that, of the most recent intake which would have been affected by such a change, only seven of 500 were found not to have possessed such a credential already. The other occasion however is major, and perhaps gives a real indication of the way in which new selection procedures might develop. In November 1983, the Academic Board of the University of Melbourne considered, approved, and published a paper called *Towards New Undergraduate Selection Procedures*. In the documentation and discussion which surrounded this document, it became clear that the University envisaged preparing its own battery of generalized achievement tests (later revised to 'reference tests') in certain key curriculum areas (English, mathematics, physics, chemistry, economics, Australian history among them), together with an aptitude test on the ASAT model. Moreover, it proposed that all aspirants to places should sit for two or three of these tests (in addition to following the normal HSC curriculum with its attendant assessment procedures). The subsequent debate made it clear that the University hoped that it would be joined by all other tertiary-level institutions in Victoria in financing, running, and using this new system for selecting students.

Some relevant facts should be noted. Post-secondary institutions do have severe selection problems: quotas operate for many courses, not only the highly prestigious ones like law, medicine and veterinary science. Candidates come with increasingly diverse experiences and with various certifications of secondary education — 'normal' HSC students now account for about half the University of Melbourne's aspirants for places, whereas a few years ago they made up four-fifths of the annual total. The social mix of this cohort is also not as successful as it might be.

However, two dangers are apparent — and no excuse is offered for use of the word 'dangers'. One is that such a system might develop into a college-board system similar to that in the United States and proliferate beyond the Victorian borders to post-secondary institutions in other states, so that some of the better features of local autonomy in curriculum and assessment procedures would be lost. This highlights the second danger: that the current movement towards greater school autonomy of curriculum defini-tion, conduct of assessments (particularly in their use of non-competitive procedures), and reporting of student achievement will be destroyed by the application of a new level of 'assessment' being overlaid on the present systems, directed from above and, in effect, becoming or at least determining the 'new Year 12 curriculum'.

The University of Melbourne has made no secret of one of its reasons for proposing the system — that it is dissatisfied with the proposals made by VISE and likely to be adopted late in 1984. In particular, the possibility that aggregable scores based largely on external examinations will disappear from the Year 12 certificate (and hence are no longer available as a quick and easy solution to half the University's selection decisions) is seen as a strong argument for the new scheme. The latter has not achieved anything like the expected degree of other institutional or public support, and the debate rages on.

Other solutions are possible:

1   Selection for entrance to prestigious courses, where the most severe pressures are, might be done after a year's introductory study of a general course, arts- or science-based.
2   A single scaling test which is not content-based, such as ASAT, might be sat by all aspirants for post-secondary places and group data used to contribute to selection decisions.
3   Individual faculties might institute entrance tests. The only local model is the Australian Law Schools Entrance Test, a program begun in 1978. At present ALSET is administered only to applicants who have no Year 12 academic history or no local qualifications, and to applicants to universities in few states. But administration to all comers is occasionally mooted.

It will be interesting to see which, if any, of these achieves any implementation over the next five years or so. There are, of course, at least two other general lines along which entrance procedures for post-secondary institutions might develop:

1   Universities and other tertiary institutions might more readily accept the recommendations of schools as to the nature and quality of candidates for admission, and make the best (in a positive rather than a negative sense) of the skills and knowledge with which undergraduates enter and the descriptive assessments they will bring with them. Agreements between all interested parties (save perhaps the students themselves) on what is an acceptable tertiary entrance qualification in the three states which use ASAT have been amicably reached, and are based largely, if not solely, on school-based assessment.
2   Students and schools might 'vote with their feet', remove themselves from participation in formal, official examination systems and rely on individual negotiation for acceptance into tertiary institutions. The only state where this marker is actually operating is, so far as the present author is aware, Victoria. Further discussion of the matter forms the conclusion of this chapter.

The emphasis above is not intended to suggest that examination systems in Australia exist only in the context of transition to further education. Subjects such as English were once seen as 'service subjects' to tertiary educators, a pass implying that the students had obtained a base level of language competence (debate about what this base should consist of raged vigorously). But it was also possible to see such subjects as components in a general education: 'a range of subjects which all pupils should study if they are to be competent citizens ... Experience in all these fields is manifestly necessary' (NSW Education Act, 1961). To which quotation, the 1981 Select Committee retorted: 'Experience in each of these fields is not "manifestly necessary" for all students, though it may be desirable' (NSW Select Committee, 1981, p. 32). The most recent Victorian statement of curriculum and assessment principles also comments on the point:

> Accompanying the changes already detailed, there appears to have been a reorientation of thinking by both the educational and the wider community, about what constitutes an appropriate design for the education of senior secondary school students. While it is difficult to generalize about what the community thinks this appropriate design might be, two trends have become apparent.
> • to decrease the emphasis on restrictive subject specialization;
> • to increase the availability to students of experience across a broad range of subjects beyond those they need as part of their vocational training.
> While these trends rely heavily on schools to take the responsibility for curriculum design, a centralized Year 12 policy such as VISE's also must be sufficiently flexible to take account of such change. At the same time execution of the policy must be sufficiently rigorous to maintain public confidence in the certificate it generates. (VISE, 1984, p. 5)

**Flexibility and Complexity of Year 12 Education**

Despite the reservations already noted about teacher-union or post-secondary institution policy, the current position seems to be one where subject matter of Year 12 courses is increasingly a matter for choice: as flexible a choice, with as large a range of student-responsive sub-choices, as possible. There choices may be made on vocational grounds, to ease the transition to work, or on other personal interest grounds. Though a state's examination system might seem quite complex, like Victoria's, or South Australia's proposed one, the complexity is to facilitate flexibility, and not necessarily a matter of bureaucratic inefficiency. That schools in at least one state are increasingly availing themselves of the range of opportunities is depicted in Figure 1.

Another aspect of the diversity is the increasing popularity of systems which, while running in parallel with formal examination procedure-based systems such as those described in this chapter, are generally conducted at colleges of advanced education or special colleges of 'technical and further education' (TAFE). It might be noted that these programs — Tertiary Orientation Programmes (TOP) or TAFE — account for most of the 'new' 50 per cent of applicants for places at the University of Melbourne, which was mentioned in the previous section.

A few other aspects of the complexity of course nature and choice remain to be described. One current generalized rumour which needs to be tested is that in the humanities area, students are increasingly moving, where such choice is permitted, from 'traditional' Year 12 subjects such as foreign languages, history, and English literature towards subjects titled with vocational descriptions

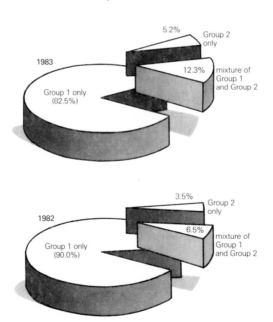

*Figure 1: Relative Balance of Year 12 Enrolments in Victoria, in Group 1 (externally assessed) and Group 2 (totally school assessed) Courses*

such as commercial and legal studies, economics, and secretarial studies. This is not to suggest that they are 'soft options'. Tasmania, for example, approves a course in each at Level III, indicating a syllabus offering what is described as 'additional achievement for the more able pupils'. One assumes that students are selecting them under the (sometimes misguided) impression that they are more vocationally oriented than other humanities courses.

Modular courses (similar to those of the Business and Technican Education Council) exist in most states, and their range extends annually. They fit easily into accreditation systems such as those of the ACT and Victoria, less well in those states where the formal examination structure still exercises a tight hold over student choice. The achievement and maintenance of basic skills in language, while receiving official attention in national assessments below Year 12, are either ignored at that level (most states) or inserted, parallel to the formal examinations, for assessment by school or authority (ACT and Tasmania). Results, in these authorities' jurisdictions, may be inserted on certificates, having been derived from test programs or criterion-referenced assessment routines. The relative simplicity of the issue at a superficial glance is much complicated by the presence of thousands of English-as-a-second-language (ESL) learners in senior forms, particularly in Victoria and NSW. Migrant education programs in schools and special centres attempt a basic skills teaching program to bring students up to the language demands of Year 12 external examinations. The compulsory pass in English for successful completion of the Victorian Higher School Certificate may be achieved for a limited group at a special ESL examination (at least until 1986). But others cope as best they can. The last issue of this type is exemplified in a recent trend towards uniting the counselling, policy, and informational services associated with transition from school, in a single organization together with the curriculum and assessment groups associated with examining in that state. While the assumption that such proximity heightens the flow and interaction of ideas between the two groups remains untested, the attempt to think holistically about the problems of Year 12 is welcome.

## An Alternative System of Curriculum Development and Assessment

On the first occasion when the present author undertook a review of the practices and procedures of Australian examining and certifying authorities (Withers, 1982), the article cited, by way of conclusion, and as a sort of summary of the themes underlying Year 12 curriculum and assessment as they were developing in Australia, the existence in Victoria of the Schools Year Twelve and Tertiary Entrance Certificate Group, commonly known as the STC Group, which offered a genuine and carefully developed alternative to the official structure of examining and certifying Year 12 performance. That paper made the comment:

> In suggesting that this five-year development is a *locus classicus* of the evolution of new structures and relationships within the Australian examining scene, I am not implying unanimous praise and acceptance for such moves across the States, or even within Victoria. Correspondence between the STC group and the registrar of one Melbourne university, if published, would be sufficient to convince even the quickest reader that the pressure points alluded to earlier continue to exist. That the themes and trends embodied in the aims, principles, and operating procedures of the STC group are the ones alive and being discussed across the country, however, I do support. In fact the words 'examining' and 'examinations' seem less and less accurate descriptors of what goes on in curriculum and assessment. (pp. 30–1)

It is pleasant to be able to report that the six schools which formed the original membership of the group have now been joined by thirty-seven more. Also, recent research evidence (Ainley, Batten and Miller, 1984) seems to point to particular success for schools which offer such a program in attracting and retaining students with positive attitudes to Year 12 study.

Briefly, teachers in a group of schools in Victoria were stung into action by the continued existence well into the seventies of a monolithic and seemingly immovable external examination system. They formed themselves and their schools into the STC group. Their Year 12 students did not follow the externally prescribed and assessed courses nor sit final examinations. Instead, an STC group council was formed, with financial assistance from a teacher union and, later, indirectly from the Commonwealth Government's Schools Commission through its Innovations Programme. The Council developed a constitution which *inter alia* contains the following clauses:

3.1 The Group will require the participation of teachers and students and encourage the participation of parents in the development and assessment of the course as a whole and of the individual subjects or units.

3.2 Content of particular subjects or units will not be prescribed centrally.

3.3 The Group will not use or endorse any forms of assessment which grade student against student or school against school for purposes of selection of students to courses of tertiary study or employment or for any other purpose.

3.4 Entry to the course will not be restricted on the basis of academic performance.

3.5 The Group will provide counselling aimed at ensuring that realistic and knowledgeable choices of work or tertiary study can be made by students.

3.6 Syllabuses may vary from school to school and from student to student but will be guided by the underlying values of relevance to the individual student's aspirations, social relevance (which requires recognition of the students' cultural origins and contemporary situations) and interdisciplinary relevance. (STC, 1979, p. 3)

The principles were developed on the basis of the following set of aims:

— to develop courses that meet the diverse needs of students who wish to complete a sixth year of secondary education;
— to share ideas and experiences in curriculum development and assessment;
— to develop appropriate forms of internal assessment;
— to gain access to a broader range of resources and information for curriculum development and resources for use by students;
— to accredit subjects and units developed by member schools;
— to gain acceptance of the courses by tertiary institutions and employers and the community generally. (*Ibid.*, p. 3)

In turn, these aims led to a set of operating procedures for each course, involving:

1 preplanning at school, class, and individual student levels;
2 negotiation between teacher and student or group of students on the form and content of the course;

3  an early start to the evaluation of the course by both teacher and student;
4  conduct of the course;
5  negotiation between teacher and course members of the nature and range of assessments to be made;
6  preparation and editing, by all parties, of the assessments;
7  issue of a certificate to cover all courses.

Initially, membership of the group was given to six schools, all in the Melbourne metropolitan area: by 1979 the number had grown to twelve and has continued to grow ever since. All but one of the participating schools happen to be establishments within the state education system though this is not a limitation within the constitution: private schools could join but in general choose not to. From 1976 to 1980 STC courses of study flourished in the member schools, and the Council negotiated with tertiary institutions, including two universities, to have their alumni selected for courses without the normal Higher School Certificate issued by the 'regular' system. Instead applicants came with an STC certificate indicating units and subjects successfully completed, detailed descriptive assessments of work done in each 'subject', a recommendation for tertiary education, and other material such as references, work experience history and a personal statement by the student. In 1977 one college of advanced education formally recognized the Certificate as equivalent to the official HSC and since then the group has achieved wide acceptance amongst other tertiary institutions and employers.

In 1979, I would guess against the advice of some of their staunchest supporters, the Group Council applied to the then new Victorian examinations body, VISE, for accreditation of its procedures and all its courses, so that the STC Certificate could become a normal VISE-backed HSC. Mutual compromises ensued. The STC Council amended a constitutional article of which it was particularly fond, and permitted the words 'satisfactorily completed Year 12' to appear on its students' certificates (see principle 3.3 above). The Council of VISE delegated to the STC the power to approve courses without further reference to official accreditation committees — and swallowed whole the course design and assessment procedures implied in the constitutional principles. Accreditation was ratified in 1980, and since then students from STC schools have gone on to post-secondary education and employment with a normal HSC.

This system stands as something approaching the antithesis of the proposals for change sponsored by perhaps the most prestigious of the local universities (the University of Melbourne) and detailed in an earlier section. The tension between the state's statutory body for examining and certifying Year 12 (VISE) and the tertiary institutions which use the certificates has been increased by the adoption of many of the principles and procedures of STC by course developers seeking accreditation of other subjects by VISE. It is very much to be hoped that this tension can be resolved in the current round of public discussion on proposed changes, and that the STC system can continue to flourish as it does today. So far it has not been replicated in any of the other seven systems, and any attempt at replication would involve much effort and argument in order to be successful. It would be sad indeed if the impetus and developments which contributed to the current legitimacy and esteem for the course in Victoria were to be lost there as well.

## References

AINLEY, J., BATTEN, M. and MILLER, H. (1984) *Staying at High School in Victoria*, Melbourne, Australian Council for Educational Research.

ALDRICH-LANGEN, C. (1983) *Australia — A Study of the Educational System of Australia and a Guide to the Academic Placement of Students in Educational Institutions of the United States*, Washington, DC, World Education Series, American Association of Collegiate Registrars and Admissions Officers.

AUSTRALIAN CAPITAL TERRITORY SCHOOLS AUTHORITY (1980) *Your Language Matters: A Statement of Year 12 Language Skills*, Canberra (mimeo edition).

BATTEN, M.C. (1983) *Issues of the Eighties: Principals' Perspective and School Practices*, Melbourne, Australian Council for Educational Research.

COMMITTEE OF ENQUIRY INTO EDUCATION IN SOUTH AUSTRALIA (1980) *Report*, Adelaide.

NEW SOUTH WALES SELECT COMMITTEE OF THE LEGISLATIVE ASSEMBLY UPON THE SCHOOL CERTIFICATE (1981) *Report, Part I*, Sydney.

ORGANIZATION FOR ECONOMIC COOPERATION AND DEVELOPMENT (1976) *Review of Educational Policy in Australia: Transition from School to Work*, Paris.

QUEENSLAND BOARD OF SECONDARY SCHOOL STUDIES (1979) *Review of School-Based Assessment*, Brisbane.

QUEENSLAND DEPARTMENT OF EDUCATION (1970) *Public Examinations for Secondary School Students*, by WM C. RADFORD *et al.*, Brisbane.

QUEENSLAND DEPARTMENT OF EDUCATION (1975) *Some Consequences of the Radford Scheme for Schools*, by W.J. CAMPBELL *et al.*, Brisbane.

SCHOOLS YEAR TWELVE AND TERTIARY ENTRANCE CERTIFICATE GROUP

(STC) (1979) *Submission for Accreditation*, Melbourne.

VICTORIA, EDUCATION DEPARTMENT. COMMITTEE OF ARRANGEMENT FOR SECONDARY CURRICULUM AND ASSESSMENT (1974) *Report*, Melbourne.

VICTORIAN INSTITUTE OF SECONDARY EDUCATION (VISE) (1978) *Policy Statement: Year 12 Curriculum and Assessment*, Melbourne.

VICTORIAN INSTITUTE OF SECONDARY EDUCATION (VISE) (1984) *Towards a Revised Policy on Curriculum and Assessment on the Victorian Year 12 Program*, Melbourne.

WITHERS, G.P. (1982) 'Australian examination systems: A review of recent change and development', *Educational Analysis*, 4, 3, pp. 21–33.

# Alternatives to Public Examinations

## Patricia M. Broadfoot
### University of Bristol

What is a public examination? Why do we need alternatives? What might these be like? This chapter is an attempt to answer these three, far from novel but deceptively simple, questions. Indeed, when Hartog and Rhodes published one of the first *technical* studies of the short-comings of examinations in 1935, arguments about their *educational* desirability, in England at least, were already nearly half a century old. Long before there was any very general suspicion that a scientific approach to assessing educational performance typically fell far short of the canons of objective measurement, a considerable number of educationists had come to deplore the constraint examinations exerted on the school curriculum and the emphasis they placed on passive learning by rote and repetition at the expense of a more active, child-centred pedagogy. Among them was Edmund Holmes, who wrote in 1911

> a school that is ridden by the examination incubus is charged with deceit ... all who become acclimatized to the influence of the system — pupils, teachers, examiners, employers of labour, parents, MPs and the rest, fall victims and are content to cheat themselves with outward and visible signs — class lists, orders of merit — as being of quasi-divine authority.

A Report issued by the Board of Education Consultative Committee in the same year showed that similar sentiments were widespread, not least in government circles. And yet in 1917, far from trying to resist the growing domination of the nascent education system by a plethora of examinations, the government gave its blessing to the establishment of a National School Certificate, the first in a dynasty of public examinations which was later to include

'O' and 'A' level GCE (instituted in 1951), CSE (instituted in 1965) and most recently the Certificate of Pre-Vocational Education (CPVE) — a one-year qualification, for the 'new sixth'. Having spent some years flirting with yet other public examinations, it is more than likely that the DES will soon give its blessing to a common system of examining at 16+ and possibly even to the 'Intermediate'-level examination (a shortened 'A' level course, now to be known as the Advanced Supplementary).[1] Coexisting with the GCE and CSE examination boards is a considerable array of more vocationally-oriented accrediting bodies. In England, for example, the Royal Society of Arts (RSA) and the City and Guilds of London Institute (CGLI) examinations have a long and independent history and now comprise a substantial proportion of the examination industry along-side newer arrivals such as the awards given by the Business Education Council (BEC) and the Technician Education Council (TEC), which merged in 1983 to form BTEC.[2]

England has not been unique in her preoccupation with public examining. To enquire into the history of any other mass education system would be to reveal a similar series of '11+', '16+', '18+', vocational and professional public examinations, differing perhaps in style, organization or content, but not in their essential purpose of providing

> a more or less formalized procedure usually separated from the classroom situation which follows after a learning process and in which the candidate has to fulfil appointed tasks or to answer posed questions after which, on the basis of his achievements, he will receive a certificate which gives him some special rights. (Solberg, 1979)

What is it then that gives public examinations their remarkable tenacity in the face of persistent and widespread criticisms of their justice and effects on schooling, including a not inconsiderable body of international research evidence? It has been shown that examinations are biased in favour of particular social and cultural groups and do not provide the equality of opportunity which is their chief *raison d'être* (see, for example, Powell, 1973; Ingenkamp, 1977). They lead to an overemphasis in the curriculum on that which is relatively easily measured — knowledge and intellectual ability — at the expense of that kind of educational progress which is almost impossible to measure, such as attitudes, skills and personal qualities. But even when assessing those kinds of achievement for which public examinations are regarded as most appropriate, they are still prone to considerable inaccuracies of marking.[3] Differences between examiners such as speed of reading, fatigue, competence (see, for example, Dunstan, 1966), ideology (Husbands, 1976), the order and speed of marking, or even the examiner's personal and social situation may affect the marking process (Branthwaite *et al.*, 1981) with the result that there may frequently be considerable variation in the marks awarded for the same piece of work.

There is clearly a strong case for a careful consideration of possible alternatives to public examinations. To the numerous and well-known problems associated with such examinations, of which only a few are set out above, should be added the sheer cost of the industry. In England, for example, in 1977–78 the local education authorities paid £13.5m in entrance fees alone for candidates in GCE 'O' level and CSE. But, if it has been relatively simple to answer, albeit briefly, the first two questions with which I began this chapter — 'What is a public examination?' and 'Why do we need alternatives?' — the third is a great deal more exercising. It is not sufficient to address the problem as simply a question of finding a superficially more appealing instrument to do exactly the same job. Merely to swop 'one-off' examinations for continuous assessment, 'Mode I' for 'Mode III', begs the essential question of what *should* be the role of assessment within the schooling process. Unfortunately, debate at this level has been rare.

## The Social Context of Examination Reform

The search for an alternative to public examinations must begin with an attempt to understand why they play such a central role in contemporary school systems, and hence, what social implications an alternative procedure would have. A second, more practical stage would be an attempt to understand the way in which innovation might best be introduced into any particular education system and the power bases and pressure groups whose support is vital to the successful institution of such an alternative. Thus to answer the third and most important of my initial questions, 'What might these be like?' requires both a value judgment and an analysis: a value judgment about what emphases are to be encouraged in the educational process — given that a backwash effect on the curriculum of public certification-oriented assessment is unavoidable and an analysis of the kind of procedures — if any — which will provide for the best combination of public support and educational desirability in order to achieve this end.

To understand why examinations play such a central role in contemporary school systems it is necessary to go back to their sudden burgeoning in the late nineteenth and early twentieth centuries as an integral feature of the then developing provision for mass schooling. I have suggested elsewhere (Broadfoot, 1979) that this development may be understood in terms of four themes: 'competence', 'content', 'competition' and 'control' — competence attested to, content organized for, competition regulated by and control provided through public examinations. At the heart of this development lay two developing ideologies. The first was that of 'meritocracy' — the selection of people for occupational roles not, as hitherto, on the traditional bases of birth and connections but on a new, more rational basis of individual ability and effort. As people had accepted the old legitimation of privilege, so they came to accept the new legitimation of merit. Similarly they came to accept the second developing ideology — that it was appropriate for schooling, rather than some other social agency, to provide for this selection, by teaching particular competencies (later to become increasingly abstract and unrelated bodies of knowledge) and then 'measuring' who had and who had not reached a given standard. Central to the notion of 'merit' was that failure must be the individual's, not the school's, fault and thus must necessarily be accepted by the individual. It is because public examinations have traditionally been so well able to meet these dual criteria of apparently providing for rational, equitable and acceptable selection by means of relatively simple educational procedures, that they have held sway for so long.

Although the lobby of criticism is increasingly strident in the West, the educational explosion in Third World countries and the consequent pressure on very restricted opportunities clearly demonstrate the vital 'gatekeeper' role public examinations can play. Rejection, whilst it may be unpalatable, must nevertheless be accepted in an apparently fair competition. So successful have public examinations been in this respect that almost the whole weight of contemporary occupational stratification rests upon them. As Eggleston (1984) puts it:

> It is certainly the case that success in competitive examinations is, for most people, an essential prelude to the legitimate exercise of power, responsibility and status throughout mod-

ern societies. Lack of accreditation constitutes a severe limitation and there is abundant evidence that the examination system, despite its technical and ideological critics, enjoys widespread public acceptance.

For this reason alone it is difficult to see how public examinations might be replaced and indeed they are not threatened where they still regulate key points of selection. Where alternatives of one sort or another — usually some form of continuous assessment — are increasingly gaining ground is at those points in the education system which because of 'qualification inflation'[4] are now no longer crucial for selection — typically 11+ and 16+. Britain is atypical of developed countries in this respect in clinging to a 16+ public examination. One of the main reasons for this is that in England the majority of youngsters still leave formal schooling at 16 — in contrast to other developed countries; whilst few now go into jobs, the pressure of unemployment and the large number of applicants for every post encourages employers to continue to resort to the filter of public examination achievements, however ill-suited these may be to their needs. But there is also another reason why public examinations are so hard to reform in England. This is because this country is atypical in its measures for curriculum control in which a highly decentralized system allows almost complete autonomy — at least in theory — to individual teachers and schools. The public examination system provides a not unwelcome check on this freedom both for those who fear too much curricular idiosyncrasy and for the teachers themselves who perceive public examinations as an important protection against possible alternative bases for accountability which might then have to be negotiated.[5]

Thus any attempt to abolish or replace public examinations is likely to be constrained by the degree to which any alternative procedure has as much credibility in attesting competence, in providing some degree of control over what is to be taught and, most important, in regulating and legitimating the process of occupational selection and rejection. In addition to these general functions, an alternative assessment procedure will have to be able to fulfil the specific needs currently met by public examinations in any particular education system. Thus, for instance, in England, public examinations are the major instrument of curriculum control and a school's public accountability. In France, to take another example, they have a very different but equally vital role to play in making a reality of the idea of national unity both in the way they are organized and in the way they are used to regulate entry into a considerable number of professions on a national basis.

There is thus a shifting and delicate balance among educational considerations, social needs and public acceptability, all three of which are a complex, often irrational, mixture of ideology, knowledge and habit. Although it is clearly difficult to assess the precise nature of this balance at any one time, it is important to do so, for it is the context for innovation. Thus, for example, multiple-choice objective testing meets many of the objections about the inaccuracies of examinations and may command a considerable degree of public acceptability, especially since its apparently objective, systematic techniques fit well with the prevailing technocratic ideology. Increasingly, though, such techniques are under fire from educationists who complain that such testing places too much emphasis on shallow regurgitation and too little on reasoned, disciplined thought (David, 1981). Again, to meet the needs of industry for low-paid unskilled workers, it is arguable that there must be school 'failures'. This is unacceptable to most educationists and reflects a fundamental contradiction between formative, diagnostic assessment which must be a central part of the teaching and learning relationship and the 'summative' assessment whose purpose is to provide for selection (Black and Broadfoot, 1982; Hargreaves, 1984).

### Patterns of Change

Nevertheless, recent years have seen the gradual recession of public examinations in many parts of the world, if not in England. In many cases this has been because an alternative assessment procedure has been found which, whilst being acceptable to either educationists or the public, also continues to fulfil the social need, if it still exists, for the regulation and legitimation of selection. A resumé of current practice and aims with regard to School Leaving Examinations, such as that provided by Ottobre (1979), reveals a remarkable similarity in countries as disparate as India and Australia, Iran and Sweden. Crudely, the principal concern is to 'humanize' the assessment procedure; to abolish pass/fail and the fear of failure in favour of grades; to replace one-off examinations by continuous teacher assessment, to extend the scope of the assessment to include not only formal written work but oral and practical work too, and in some cases, personal qualities; to provide for assessment that will be diagnostic and detailed, increasingly cumulative and integrated with the learning process and only culminating in, not solely oriented to, a terminal evaluation. India provides a good example:

> The emphasis will be not on teaching, but on learning. Students will move from passivity to activity; from conformity to creativity and originality; from authoritative acceptance of ideas to enquiry and discovery ... cooperative rather than competitive learning... The whole system of education will be characterized by flexibility and dynamism rather than rigidity and inertia. (Wanchoo and Raina, 1979)

It is too early to evaluate the new certification procedures under the Indian 'ten plus three' scheme,[6] but a very similar example is provided by France, where, except at the level of the 18+ *Baccalauréat* matriculation examination, public examinations have officially been replaced almost entirely by *orientation* procedures.[7] It is worth describing this procedure in some detail since it incorporates principles currently inspiring the reform of formal public examinations in many countries. In addition, the extremely centralized organization of French education has enabled the reform to be incorporated swiftly and comprehensively into the system since first proposed in the well-known 'Haby' reforms of 1975.[8]

## 'Orientation' as an Alternative to Public Examinations

The pressure for public examination reform in France, as elsewhere, was both ideological and pragmatic. There was concern that traditional French schooling was a process of selection based on failure, with class tests, promotion tests, various kinds of certificate examination and, ultimately, the *Baccalauréat* matriculation examination providing for a progressive 'sieving' out of pupils at every stage of the school system — not least of which was *la redoublement* — failure to win promotion to the next class at the end of the school year. Thus immediately prior to the institution of the *orientation* policy, the situation was, as described by Fraser (1971),

> a system that depends upon impersonal assessment of achievement, that has only recently introduced more personal and continuous evaluation, that needs to 'mark' precisely and that must therefore set a syllabus and questions that can be reduced to measurable data. The curriculum is taught abstractly, verbally, precisely. The machinery of examina-

tions needs constant maintenance and minor adjustment, but seems not to be able to cope with the pressure of large numbers of aspiring, articulate students, conscious of their power.

Thus the traditional system placed unacceptable constraints on a curriculum in which the importance of vocational and practical education for the economy were increasingly being recognized. It also created a dangerously large number of disaffected students. Public support for reform was reflected in the results of a recent poll (Jessell, 1980) which showed that 75 per cent of adults would prefer continuous assessment even to the prestigious *Baccalauréat*. Thus the last few years have seen a complete reversal of traditional assessment policy in France. The following words of the then Minister of National Education, M. Beullac, represent a view widely held among parents, if not among teachers, for whom their increasing responsibility for assessment means an equivalent increase in their vulnerability to parental pressure.

What must be avoided above all is *orientation* by failure. There is no career which corresponds with failure, but there are careers which correspond with different dispositions ... *Orientation* cannot moreover be the doing of the school alone. It must be the result of a collaboration between first and foremost the children concerned, the parents who are responsible for them, and the school.[9]

Briefly, the *orientation* procedure works as follows:

Throughout a pupil's school life vocational guidance is based on continuous observation by his teachers, recorded in a cumulative *dossier*, and regular meetings are held between the teachers, a guidance counsellor (*conseiller d'orientation*), a school doctor and psychologist, and representatives of parents. Such meetings are held every year, but the two major ones take place at the end of the second and last years at *collège*, when decisions must be made on the basis of the *dossier* as to the type of studies the pupils will subsequently undertake.

During the spring term before these meetings, the parents are invited to express their wishes concerning the guidance of the child; taking account of these wishes the council draws up and submits to the parents a proposed programme of future studies or training for their child. The parents' final views are considered by the guidance council which sits during the summer term; it includes the head and several other teachers, one of whom is the child's class teacher, a doctor, school social welfare officer and guidance counsellor.

When the parents feel the decision of the guidance council is unacceptable, an appeal committee, including the *inspecteur d'académie* and a CIO director, examines the case. If their advice still differs from the parents' wishes, an examination is set for the child and the results assessed by a committee external to the *collège*.[10]

This kind of alternative to public examinations, although superficially very appealing in relieving the pupil of anxiety and failure, is in fact only a 'cosmetic' reform. If *orientation* protects the pupil from the vagaries of the individual examiner, its judgment is also that much harder to refute.[11] It introduces a set of rigorous, pre-established norms to replace the arbitrary power of the individual judge. On the surface it is more 'just' and 'objective'. In practice, the effect of replacing 'the very private and intuitive procedure' (Branthwaite *et al.*, 1981) of marking scripts with 'positive' collective counselling is to provide a different but even more effective basis for selection. It is the Ministry's expressed intention that

> Through his school-life, he will be subject to a continuous observation on the part of his educators which will allow teaching to be better adapted to his needs, help him to know himself and to prepare himself for educational and later career choices.[12]

In practice, however, 'L'orientation est subie non choisie' (i.e. is submitted to, not chosen) (*Le Monde de l'Education*, March, 1981). The individual is rarely motivated to resist the decision which is the end product of a continuous and benign surveillance. 'Etre orientée' is now synonymous with failure (Prost, 1983, p. 135). As Herzlich (1980) suggests

> *orientation* thus largely functions as a mechanism of successive exclusions, to the detriment of the least favoured social categories . . . it is said 'what one wants': they say, if one can . . .[13]

That this is indeed the case was officially recognized in the recent Le Grand Report on the 11–16 (*collège*) stage of comprehensive education. A situation in which opportunities for diversified further education opportunities are frequently restricted; in which pupils lack knowledge of different vocational opportunities and in which educational decisions are effectively a form of selection based on school marks makes *orientation*, in the view of the Le Grand Report, both during school and on leaving, 'a continuous process of selection by educational failure designated as intellectual failure'.[14]

In this respect *orientation* operates in much the same way as the intelligence test used to — its particular value being that its apparently scientific objectivity made it an excellent means of justifying selection. Thus *orientation* conceals under a pretence of 'equal but different' a process of sorting and selecting pupils according to their academic level for different scholastic and ultimately occupational routes, which has not changed in any fundamental way except in being considerably more educationally and socially acceptable.[15]

The solution to this problem proposed in Le Grand Report is a move from summative to formative evaluation with an associated greatly increased emphasis on the provision of personal tutoring and careers *awareness*, as well as guidance.

Although the opposition this proposal has provoked among teachers is characteristically French, the French experience of trying to abolish examinations in favour of *orientation*, selection in favour of 'differentiation', has much to teach us. I have therefore dwelt at some length on this particular alternative to public examinations because it provides a very salutory lesson for other countries, such as England, who show signs of moving in the same direction.

### The 'Pupil Profiles' Movement

In the last few years, the idea of profile assessment based on very similar principles to the French *dossier* has been rapidly gaining ground. Although the idea of a 'profile' involving the assessment of one or more of the following — basic skills, subject achievement, personal characteristics and personal achievements — is on the whole more radical in its conception than the French *dossier* and although the 'profile' is still largely seen as a supplement to, rather than a replacement of, public examinations as in France, the two movements have much in common. Both are concerned with providing alternative goals for those pupils who are not talented academically; with removing the spectre of failure. In England, there is now a significant body of educational opinion looking for a realistic and meaningful assessment target for all pupils — particularly those excluded from public examination success. More recently the idea has been gaining ground in government and other policy-making circles who see a potential for profile assessment in reinforcing a more broad-based, vocationally-oriented curriculum and in helping youngsters to get jobs through providing relevant information for employers.

On 28 November 1983, the Secretary of State for Education and Science, Sir Keith Joseph, pledged £10m of government money to support the development of Records of Achievement for all school-leavers. Such records were to contain assessments of skills, personal qualities and achievements beyond the usual subject attainments. The two reasons for this initiative to which Sir Keith drew particular attention were

(i) to acknowledge 'the totality of what pupils have done in order to improve their motivation and help schools identify their needs more closely';

(ii) to provide a testimonial respected and valued by employers and colleges for 'there is evidence that some pupils who are at present poorly motivated would aspire to higher standards of attainment if they know that their achievements and efforts would be formally recognized'. (DES, 1983, p. 3)

The DES initiative in this respect is the culmination of nearly a decade of rapidly growing interest in 'pupil profiles' which followed the publication of a pioneering Scottish research study in this area (SCRE, 1977). In 1972, the Headteachers Association of Scotland, concerned with the lack of relevant and achievable goals for a whole new school population created by the recent raising of the school-leaving age to 16 (ROSLA), set themselves the task of considering

the form and range of items of information needed to produce, for all secondary pupils, a comprehensive picture of their aptitudes and interests so as to enable responsible guidance staff to give them the best possible advice on future curricular and/or vocational choice and on appropriate social and leisure activities; and offering them a common form of statement, which would be generally comprehensible and which would be available to them when appropriate.

The following objectives were agreed: '(i) to enhance pupils' self-knowledge; (ii) to provide users with useful information; (iii) to orientate teachers towards a guidance model; (iv) to support the school in its programme of total education' (SCRE, 1977).

The conclusion they came to was very similar to that expressed at the same time in England in the Schools Council's document (1977), *The Whole Curriculum 13–16*, namely that

> What are increasingly required in the secondary school are not so much terminal measures of achievement to be used for selection purposes as kinds of assessment which provide teachers, parents and pupils with guidance. We are particularly anxious that the examination system should not perpetuate a divisive curriculum. We believe that all pupils should be offered a documentary record at the completion of their secondary schooling. This record should be a balanced account of the pupils' attainments, interests and aspirations. The document should be externally validated and underwritten by appropriately authorised bodies. We would see these bodies as offering a comprehensive assessment service which would in time supersede the present system of examining at 16+.

Enthusiasm for this idea has inspired a veritable explosion of practical initiatives in England, if not in Scotland where the advent of a comprehensive 16+ examination has largely served to deflect such concern for the present. Bodies ranging from individual schools; groups of schools; local authorities and examination boards to national bodies such as the Schools Council, the Manpower Services Commission and the Further Education Unit of the DES have all been active in their attempts to devise such a record. There is now an agreed *national* profile for Wales (Jones, 1983). The recent explicit commitment by the DES to such provision is thus a characteristically English example of policy-making reflecting what is already virtually a *fait accompli*. It now seems likely that most secondary schools will be adopting some kind of profile certificate for 16+ school-leavers over the next few years. There are signs too that again following continental practice such alternatives to public examinations are beginning to receive support as the basis for university entrance (Broadfoot, 1984b).[16]

There is thus an urgent necessity for some hard thinking and research directed at discovering whether profiles do indeed meet the claims made for them. Unlike public examinations, which have by and large grown like 'Topsy', profiles represent a genuine and educationally-inspired attempt to face up to the problem of what examination-based selection and the associated curriculum distortion do to the process of schooling. Nevertheless it is clear from the French experience that such apparently 'benign' initiatives may still involve pupils being sorted according to their academic performance with judgment being made by teachers even more exposed than examination markers to all the potential bias of any social situation. Not only is it likely that the assessments will be subject to the well-known disadvantages of continuous teacher-assessment such as the halo effect, social-class bias, and personal antipathy,[17] it is also likely that many pupils will continue to regard the process of schooling as something imposed on them, still be able to judge their performance in comparison with their peers and still protect themselves from the experience of failure by regarding their real life as something apart from school.

Hargreaves (1984) argues that such problems are not just the result of the insensitive use of profiles but are actually inherent in their conception. Should teachers

> mediate employer values by encouraging pupils to record only those activities and achievements which call to mind such things as loyalty, dependability and leadership — scouting and guiding, playing in the school orchestra, running the fishing club, for instance? And how do they react to those pupil activities which might not chime so sweetly in the ears of employers — to Rastafarianism, feminism, peace campaigning or the like? Do they discourage pupils from recording activities and achievements of these kinds — and what would be the consequences of this denial of experience for pupils' sense of worth and motivation? (p. 10)

In a telling study of pupil deviance, Schostak (1983) argues that all too often pupils' individualism is defined as deviance because the institutional inflexibility makes schools unable to respond to it constructively. Worse still, in the eyes of at least one writer, is the situation where the record is not controlled and owned by the pupil. In such a situation, Stansbury (1984) suggests

> What would be left could be rather nasty — the negotiated record, summarized and distilled by the teacher and sent away to some authority to be validated, copied and returned. Little snippets of private information revealed in all innocence and sifted out, stored away and copied. A record of the

private life of every child and of much more about family and friends. A record to contemplate in 1984.

Several writers have made an explicit link between such discursive assessment and Bernstein's (1977) concept of invisible pedagogy (see, for example Broadfoot, 1984a; Hargreaves, 1984; Ranson, 1984), in which more informal progressive teaching methods (including more informal evaluation procedures), whilst superficially more liberal and democratic and thus more acceptable to the recipient, conceal a potential for social control considerably greater than more traditional 'visible' pedagogy. It is the strength of such procedures, their humanity, that is also their danger. Their very acceptability, their concern with the whole person and their use of flexible, covert standards in place of explicit overt assessment, allow in practice a much greater degree of intrusion into the pupil's life. To the extent that aspects of pupils' lives do not conform to prevailing school values — their interests, their home background, their values — it is more than possible that they will be subject to a negative evaluation, an evaluation, moreover, that, whilst it is probably rarely, if ever, made explicit, has a profound influence on teachers' expectations and thus, as so much research shows,[18] on their eventual achievement.

However, whilst it is true that any attempt to broaden the basis for assessment so that it offers the possibility for all pupils to achieve something worthy of note carries with it the corresponding danger of greater intrusion into their lives, the various profile initiatives are very far from being homogeneous and have different implications in this respect. As Hitchcock (1983) suggests, it is possible to identify at least four generic types of profile — grids, criterion checklists, comment banks and more extended forms of pupil self-recording. The first of these, typified by the SCRE Profile Assessment System and the City and Guilds 365 pro-formas, has recently come under heavy criticism (see, for example, Stronach, 1982). Despite attempts to offer only positive 'levels of achievement', it is now widely recognized that the provision of different levels of achievement criteria which may range from 'can use simple tools such as a screwdriver' to 'can wire a micro-circuit' fool no-one, and indeed often need to be pitched so low as to be perceived by pupils as insulting. On top of this there are the difficulties specifying appropriate criteria for the different levels of achievement which are neither vague at one extreme nor banal at the other. There is no scope for selecting the items for comment and usually little scope for negotiation between teacher and pupil. In short, whilst 'grids' have a ready appeal for employers, they embody many of the same problems as exams. Their priorities, like those of public examinations, are to judge pupils against pre-ordained criteria and, in so doing, provide for a measure of comparability and thus selection. Pupil achievements must be tailored to the record.

In the other major forms of profiling, by contrast, much more emphasis is put on fitting the record to the pupil's achievements. Criterion checklists — as pioneered by Evesham High School for example (Duffy, 1980) — involve the pupil initiating an assessment on some fifty or more individual objectives such as 'can swim 50 yards' or 'can show a visitor round the school', whose attainment is witnessed on his 'Personal Achievement Record'. Whilst this approach has achieved great popularity among schools[19] and has the support of many local employers, it still has the disadvantage of finding achievement criteria of a suitable range of difficulty and preciseness. Even more seriously, such recording takes place largely outside the normal curriculum and thus can do little to affect the quality of the educational relationship during the main business of teaching and learning, although the need for a change in this respect is one of the main arguments for profiles.

This criticism that it does not impinge on the official curriculum can also be made of pupil recording such as Don Stansbury's 'Record of Personal Experience' or Richard de Groot's 'Pupils' Personal Recording', which has proved over the space of ten years or so that it can be a powerful motivating force for the lower-achieving pupil with whom it is most often used. Nevertheless this form of recording shows little sign of providing a real alternative to examinations. It resolutely resists any attempt to introduce an outsider's judgment — as opposed to a validation — on the pupils' record. Thus it does not readily provide an alternative means of meeting those social needs hitherto fulfilled by examinations — the attestation of competence, the provision of some control over what is taught, the regulation and legitimation of selection and a criterion for accountability.

By far the most popular type of profile at the present time is the verbal description, increasingly associated with the formulation and use of a 'comment bank'. Under this approach used, for example, in the Welsh national profile, a large number of descriptive statements are provided within various categories such as numeracy, social relations and language skills. Each comment is given a code number, allowing the teacher to build up a profile rather in the manner of an 'identikit' picture. The ensuing statement, which can readily be produced by means of a computer, reads like a traditional report or reference though in this case the clichés and well-worn phrases of habit have been greatly refined and polished to provide a more discursive, if still inevitably stereotyped, picture. While it has much to recommend it in terms of practicability and comparability, growing familiarity with the range of comments is likely to mean, as with 'grid-style' profiles, an increasing tendency to emphasize quantitative rather than qualitative differences between pupils.

Sadly, even such a brief analysis of the pursuit of records of achievement illustrates the impossibility of designing an assessment procedure which is both motivating to the whole range of individuals and at the same time provides for society's more general requirement that the education system sort, select and justify. Not only does the introduction of any basis for comparison between pupils, however disguised, bring with it the demotivating effects of failure, any attempt to provide a more broadly-based assessment also poses technical problems of comparability on a scale that makes the unremitting efforts of examination boards in this respect pale into insignificance (Nuttall and Goldstein, 1984). Although the very small amount of research currently available (see, for example, SCRE, 1977) suggests teachers can produce comparable assessments in any one school, any attempt to produce profiles which have a wider currency is likely to be fraught with difficulty unless the profiles are so rigid in format that they in turn lose their point.

### Graded Tests: Another Alternative?

One way of overcoming the problems inherent in profiles without losing their potential benefits as an alternative to examinations is to have a 'multi-record'. For example, the current initiative at the Oxford Delegacy to institute the Oxford Certificate of Educational Achievement has three parts — the traditional 'E' or Examination component, the 'P' or Profile component and a 'G' or Graded Test component. It is hoped that such multi-mode assessment will combine the advantages and disadvantages of each different approach, thus maximising both motivation and comparability.

Indeed it is no accident that the 'graded test' movement has also burgeoned in the last few years. As Mortimore and Mortimore (1984) show in their comprehensive critique of examinations, graded tests are the other side of the profiles coin. As the tendency has grown for profiles to be less concerned with subject attainments and more with skills and personal qualities, to be discursive and negotiated in format, so the idea of graded tests has gathered momentum. Such tests modelled on the graded approach to examining, widely used in sport, music and the arts, were first developed in mathematics and modern languages where the advantages of a series of short-term objectives and the ready possibility of designing appropriate tests made these subjects fertile ground for such development. Although this approach to assessment has now assumed a more general credibility,[20] research to date suggests that existing modes of curriculum organization do not lend themselves readily to the institution of the individualized learning and assessment timetables presupposed by such tests (Harrison, 1983; HMI, 1982). In addition, whilst it is not necessarily the case that graded tests should be criterion-referenced and thus bring with them major dangers of 'curriculum ossification' (Macintosh, 1984), it is likely that the provision of a series of competency-oriented 'mini-exams' would lead to a greater measure of curriculum rationalization — not to say control — than exists at present (Pennycuik, 1983).

Thus graded tests present yet another assessment dilemma. This time the equation would appear to be one in which the price of the motivation the institution of such short-term goals provides is the sacrifice of larger less readily-assessable curriculum objectives. Part of the solution to this dilemma is a measure of compromise, restricting the use of graded tests to a minority of appropriate subjects, combined with a profiling system that is flexible and useful, but not too comprehensive. These can help to undo some of the damage caused by traditional examinations. But whether used singly or combined neither procedure can get to the root of the problem. As the French experience suggests, any genuine attempt to overcome such fundamental problems can be nothing less than a challenge to the relationship between schools and society which has been built up over the last century. It must be concerned with divorcing the process of schooling from the process of selection. If school achievement continues to be used as the basis for occupational selection, most of the potential alternatives to public examinations will make only superficial improvements in the malaise of the non-academically-gifted pupil for whom the bitter pill of failure cannot be so masked. It is only the removal of selection and hence invidious competition which can make a genuine difference in encouraging intrinsic rather than extrinsic motivation in schools.

## Some More Radical Developments: The Move Away from Selection

The British are famous for compromise and it is in the 'anarchic incrementalism'[21] of British educational organization that some solution to this dilemma may be beginning to emerge. In an education system which allows them considerable freedom, individual teachers and schools are developing their own answer to the problem of selection in the face of the effects which daily confront them. In a resumé of some of these developments, Burgess and Adams (1980) bring together proposals based on radical alternatives which have yet to become widely accepted. Recognizing that higher education and employment largely depend on examination certificates at the present time they argue that

> examinations dominate the schools, trivializing the curriculum and precluding young people from sharing responsibility for their own education, examinations which are unsatisfactory as predictors of academic success and are largely irrelevant to the needs of employers offering as they do no description of what has been tested nor any statement of the young person's unexamined competences, attributes, interests or purposes.

It should be obvious, suggests Gray (1981), that 'in a system where the average leaver obtains barely two "O" levels and assorted CSE awards, examinations can scarcely be sufficient educational objectives for all schools'. The problem is a vicious circle in which the current importance of examination success and the associated public pressure, together with the difficulty of assessing more diffuse progress and qualities, means it is all too tempting for a school, particularly in the present political climate of parental choice, falling rolls and school accountability, to concentrate on helping its 'bright' pupils achieve extra 'O' levels, than to search for other criteria of success.

To break this vicious circle, Burgess and Adams propose a 'statement' which every 16-year-old would receive on leaving school showing his or her experience, competence, interests and purposes as the culmination of the previous two years' work. Central to this proposal is that the young people *themselves* would have the initiative in creating their programme of work so that the content of the curriculum, the recording of its outcome and the measurement of achievement is planned, agreed and pursued jointly by pupils and teachers, individual pupils deciding their own objectives. The advantages of this approach, Burgess and Adams suggest, are, firstly, that it will 'personalize' education, making students think through for themselves what they need and want to learn. Secondly, it offers the chance of changing what schools actually offer by encouraging teachers to recognize those characteristics and achievements currently neglected. Thirdly, it will encourage a new relationship of collaboration between pupils and teachers. Fourthly, the statement finally produced will be a direct communication from the pupil himself, not the inevitably biased and incomplete summary based on a teacher's evaluative interpretation. Central to the proposals of Burgess and Adams is the involvement of the pupils themselves in both the organization of their learning and the eventual production of a statement describing its outcomes. Because of this the statements are necessarily idiosyncratic so that it is not possible to compare one pupil's achievements with another's at second hand.

Clearly, implementing this scheme would have major implications for the organization of the learning process and the elaborate structure of subjects, lessons and curricula with which we are currently familiar. These changes are not impracticable and would be regarded as highly desirable by many teachers who deplore the fragmented contact which is all the current system of secondary school organization at least permits. That movement in this direction is possible is well-illustrated by Withers' account in this volume of the Victoria Secondary Teachers' initiative in instituting alternative certification procedures. Nearer home, a similarly radical change is overtaking 16+ curriculum and assessment provision in Scotland where up to a thousand different course modules — to be offered in both schools and colleges as appropriate, each with its own built-in criteria of successful completion — will provide for each student the possibility of an individualized curriculum and certification procedure (SED, 1984). Replacing public examinations in England in this kind of way would require more commitment to fundamental change than is yet apparent, as well as a more centralized policy-making system. In particular, it would require both a willingness and an ability — currently both lacking — to tackle curriculum change on a scale equivalent to that resulting from the advent of the public examination in the nineteenth century when it in its turn radically altered the then existing organization and content of the curriculum. But, if it is true, as Dale and Pires (1984) suggest, that school credentials are only very loosely related to getting jobs and that it is largely their *assumed* relevance that perpetuates the extreme importance accorded to them within the education system, then there is indeed scope for change. What is required is a great deal more research into the actual and potential relationship between educational credentials and jobs in order to identify the fundamental cause of the examinations malaise and the right priorities for alternative forms of assessment.

Firth (1969) suggests that part of the commitment to public examinations is that they provide an important *rite de passage* in contemporary society. Actually the contrary is true. In contrast to almost every simple society, the *rite de passage* of public examinations is not concerned with the necessary competencies for adult life; nor is it expected that every adolescent will successfully pass the test. This particular qualification ritual is entirely inappropriate as a completion of the compulsory stage of schooling and indeed was never intended to be. Thus any genuine alternative to public examinations must not be simply another, more fashionable, way of doing the same thing. It must be the product of an explicit recognition that a good deal of what is wrong with the contemporary process of schooling is a direct result of the undisciplined growth of public examinations. To replace such examinations simply with alternative techniques, without at the same time getting rid of the associated and much more fundamental problems of an impersonal, knowledge-oriented curriculum arbitrarily divided into subjects which follow each other in a timetable whose main rationale is managerial, is not to solve any of the fundamental disadvantages of public examinations. There is nothing in itself wrong with assessing educational performance. Indeed, it is an integral and vital part of teaching. Nor would it be right to rule out all public examinations. It may be that they still provide the best, albeit inaccurate, way of regulating entry to the professions. What is wrong is the failure, until now, to bring together both the technical and the educational criticisms of public examinations in conjunction with careful consideration of what the goals of compulsory schooling should be. We have been so busy discussing how to prevent the cart going before the horse that we have failed to notice that we are no longer on the road.

### Notes

1 See for example Macintosh's account of examination developments in this volume.
2 The examples given are an arbitrary selection from a wide range of

alternative courses and qualifications offered within the very different educational traditions of further education whose increasingly close links with the school system, represented by the control of the new CPVE by the City and Guilds and BTEC, may be one of the principal factors in paving the way for examination reform.

3  Various estimates have been made of the probable extent of such inaccuracies. The review by Branthwaite *et al.* (1981) of the research evidence suggests the correlation of marks given between different markers is only around 0.44 and only 0.37 when the same markers mark the same scripts after a lapse of time. For a recent graphic description of such inaccuracies see Price, J. (1984) 'Absolute standards', *Times Educational Supplement*, 20 January, p. 24. Research in other countries has produced similar results. See, for example, Pieron, H. and Langier, H. (1927) *Valeur sélective du certificat d'études — comparison de cet examen avec une épreuve par tests*, Conférence Internationale de Psychotechnique IV Paris, Comptes Rendus.

4  A term used by Dore, R.P. (1976) in *The Diploma Disease*, Allen and Unwin, to describe the situation in which, as opportunities to gain qualifications expand, so the greater number of aspirants for jobs pushes up the level of qualification that can be demanded by the employer.

5  SSRC-funded project 'Constants and Contexts in Educational Accountability: a Comparative Study', Final Report 1981.

6  The 10 + 3 proposals are described in *The Curriculum for the Ten-Year School*, Delhi, NCERT. Current thinking about assessing is expressed in Srivastava, H.S., Singh, P. and Anand, V.S. (1979) *Reforming Examinations*, NCERT.

7  Although this is the official policy, the option to sit for the traditional certificate examinations is still widely exercised by parents unconvinced that their child will be able to get a job without such certificates.

8  The advent of the socialist government has served to strengthen rather than rescind this policy, despite teachers' opposition to any increased 'pastoral' dimension to their role. See for example 'Appelez-moi Maman on la face cachée du tutorat', *Ecole et Socialisme*, no. 26, May 1983.

9  'Ce qu'il faut éviter, avant tout, c'est l'orientation par l'échec ... Il n'y a pas de métier qui corresponde à une échec, mais il y a des métiers qui correspondent à des dispositions diverses ... l'orientation ne peut cependant être le fait de l'école seule. Elle doit être le résultat d'une collaboration entre les enfants — concernés au premier chef, les parents — qui sont responsables d'eux, et l'école.' (*Le Monde de l'Education*, March 1981.)

10  The *actualités service* of the *Service d'Information et de Diffusion — Rentrée Scolaire, 1977: ce qui change* — describes in detail the *dossier* and the process of *orientation*.

11  Many of these ideas were first suggested to me by Dr. G. Berger of the University of Paris-Vincennes, in an interview conducted in connection with the SSRC-funded project 'Constants and Contexts in Educational Accountability: A Comparative Study'.

12  'Toute au long de sa scolarité il sera l'objet de la part de ses éducateurs d'une observation continue qui permettra de mieux adapter l'enseigne-

ment à ses besoins, l'aidera à se connaître et à bien préparer son orientation scolaire et professionnelle ultérieure.'

13 'L'orientation fonctionne ainsi en grande partie comme un mécanisme d'exclusions successives, au détriment des catégories sociales moins favorisées ... on dit ce qu'on veut: ils disent si on peut ...'

14 'Cette situation générale fit de l'orientation au collège et à sa sortie, un processus continu de sélection par l'échec scolaire désigné comme échec intellectuel.'

15 There are interesting parallels here with the tripartite rationale of the 1944 Education Act.

16 See the speech by Sir Frederick Dainton, former Chairman of the UGC in his presidential address to the North of England Conference, January 1984, in which he called for 'global, school-based assessment including profiles to end universities' reliance on "A" levels'.

17 For a view of some of the research evidence in this respect see Nash, R. (1976) *Teacher Expectation and Pupil Learning*, London, Routledge and Kegan Paul.

18 See for example, Rogers, C. (1982) *A Social Psychology of Schooling*, London, Routledge and Kegan Paul.

19 A recently published survey by Malcolm Bowring at Evesham High School reveals that the school has received literally hundreds of enquiries about its scheme which have resulted in many schools modelling their own 'PAR' schemes upon it.

20 A great deal of development work is now going on in this area in local authority consortia, examination boards and at the NFER.

21 A phrase used to describe the process of innovation in British education by Fowler in his article, 'The changing nature of educational politics in the 1970s', in Broadfoot, P., Brock, C. and Tulasiezicz, W. (1981) (Eds) *Politics and Educational Change*, London, Croom Helm.

## References

BLACK, H.D. and BROADFOOT, P.M. (1982) *Keeping Track of Teaching*, London, Routledge and Kegan Paul.

BOURDIEU, P. and PASSERON, J.C. (1976) *Reproduction*, London, Sage Publications.

BRANTHWAITE, A., TRUEMAN, M. and BERRISFORD, T. (1981) 'Unreliability of marking', *Educational Review*, 33, 1, pp. 41–6.

BROADFOOT, P.M. (1979) *Assessment, Schools and Society*, London, Methuen.

BROADFOOT, P.M. (1984a) 'From public examinations to profile assessment: the French experience' in BROADFOOT, P.M. (Ed.) *Selection, Certification and Control*, Lewes, Falmer Press

BROADFOOT, P.M. (1984b) 'They do it differently abroad: examinations' in WATSON, K. (Ed.) forthcoming, Croom Helm.

BURGESS, T. and ADAMS, E. (Eds) (1980) *Outcomes of Education*, London, Macmillan.

DAVID, P. (1981) 'Multiple-choice under fire', *The Times Educational Supplement*, 27 November.

DEPARTMENT OF EDUCATION AND SCIENCE (1983) *Draft Policy Statement on Records of Achievement*, London, HMSO.

DUFFY, M. (1980) 'The Evesham personal achievement record: A logbook of personal achievement', *Education*, 1 December.

DUNSTAN, M. (1966) 'Sources of variation in examination marks', in HEYWOOD, J. and ILIFFE, A.H. (Eds) *Some Problems of Testing Academic Performance*, Lancaster, University of Lancaster.

EGGLESTON, J. (1984) 'School examinations: some sociological issues', in BROADFOOT, P.M. (Ed.) *Selection, Certification and Control*, Lewes, Falmer Press.

FIRTH, R. (1969) 'Examinations and ritual initiation', *World Year Book of Education*.

FRASER, W.R. (1971) *Reforms and Restraints in Modern French Education*, London, Routledge and Kegan Paul.

GRAY, J. (1981) 'A competitive edge: Examination results and the probable limits of secondary school effectiveness', *Education Review*, 33, 1, pp. 25–35.

HARGREAVES, A. (1984) 'Motivation versus selection: A dilemma for records of achievement', mini-paper for conference on Research Needs in Pastoral Care, University of Warwick, February.

HARRISON, A. (1983) *A Review of Graded Tests*, London, Methuen Educational.

HARTOG, P. and RHODES, E.C. (1935) *An Examination of Examinations*, London, Macmillan.

HER MAJESTY'S INSPECTORATE (1982) *A Survey of the Use of Graded-tests in Modern Languages*, London, DES.

HERZLICH, G. (1980) editorial *Le Monde de l'Education*, May.

HITCHCOCK, G. (1983) 'Profiles: a critical appraisal', unpublished MEd. dissertation, University of Bristol.

HOLMES, E. (1911) *What Is and What Might Be*, London, Constable.

HUSBANDS, C.T. (1976) 'Ideological bias in the marking of examinations', *Research in Education*, 15, pp. 17–38.

INGENKAMP, K. (1977) *Educational Assessment*, Slough, NFER.

JESSELL, J. (1980) 'Minister ignores wide support for BAC reform', *The Times Educational Supplement*, 22 February.

JONES, J. (1983) *Pupil Profile*, Cardiff, Schools Council for Wales.

LE GRAND, L. (1982) *Pour un collège démocratique*, Rapport au Ministère de l'Education Nationale présenté par M Louis Le Grand, Ministère de l'Education National, Paris.

MACINTOSH, H. (1984) 'Testing for careerworthiness', *Times Educational Supplement*, 20 January.

MORTIMORE, J. and MORTIMORE, P. (1984) *Secondary School Examinations: The Helpful Servants not the Dominating Master*, Bedford Way Papers 18, University of London Institute of Education.

NUTTALL, D.L. and GOLDSTEIN, H. (1984) 'Profiles and graded tests: The technical issues' in MORTIMORE, J. (Ed.) *Profiles in Action*, London, FEU.

ONISEP (1979) 'L'entrée en sixième: qu'est-ce qui ce passe?', Ministère de l'Education Nationale, Paris.

OTTOBRE, F.M. (Ed.) (1979) *Criteria for Awarding School-Leaving Certificates*, proceedings of the 1977 conference of the International Association for Educational Assessment, Oxford, Pergamon.

PENNYCUIK, D. (1983) 'What is a graded test?', University of Southampton, mimeo.

POWELL, J.L. (1973) *Selection for University in Scotland*, Edinburgh, University of London Press for SCRE.

PROST, A. (1983) 'Les lycées et leurs études au seuil du XXIième siècle', Rapport au Directeur des lycées presenté par le Groupe de Travail National sur les seconds cycles, Service d'informations, November, 1983.

RANSON, S. (1984) 'Toward a tertiary tripartism: new codes of control and the 17+' in BROADFOOT, P. (Ed.) *Selection, Certification and Control*, Lewes, Falmer Press.

SCHOOLS COUNCIL (1977) *The Whole Curriculum 13-16*, London, Evans/Methuen.

SCHOSTAK, J. (1983) *Maladjusted Schooling*, Lewes, Falmer Press.

SCOTTISH COUNCIL FOR RESEARCH IN EDUCATION (1977) *Pupils in Profile*, Edinburgh, Hodder and Stoughton for SCRE.

SCOTTISH EDUCATION DEPARTMENT (1984) *16s-18s in Scotland: An Action Plan*, Edinburgh, HMSO.

SOLBERG, W. (1979) 'The case for school-leaving examinations', in OTTOBRE, F.M. (Ed.) *Criteria for Awarding School-Leaving Certificates*, proceedings of the 1977 conference of the International Association for Educational Assessment, Oxford, Pergamon.

STANSBURY, D. (1984) 'Lies, damned lies and profiles', *Times Educational Supplement*, 10 February

STRONACH, I. (1982) 'Made-to-measure', Resources for Learning Unit, Jordanhill College, Glasgow.

WANCHOO, V.N. and RAINA, T.N. (1979) 'India: The State of Rajasthan', in OTTOBRE, F.M. (Ed.) *Criteria for Awarding School-Leaving Certificates*, proceedings of the 1977 conference of the International Association for Educational Assessment, Oxford, Pergamon.

*Section 2*

# Exams in Context: Values and Power in Educational Accountability

*Stewart Ranson, John Gray, David Jesson and Ben Jones*

*Institute of Local Government Studies, University of Birmingham and Division of Education, University of Sheffield.*

## Introduction

The exam stakes are high. They condense much of the purposes and experience of traditional schooling and focus diverse interests. Pupils and students, after several years of endeavour, have their capacities and life chances assessed in a series of short examinations. Schools frequently believe they should judge the quality of their achievements when the examinations boards publish their results in August, while parents and communities use exams to test their confidence in local schools. Society turns to examinations to 'cool-out' inflated aspirations and to sort out young people for the layered demands of the labour market.

In short, both individual and social interests are expressed through the examination system. When, in the 1970s, questions began to be asked about the purposes and qualities of schools, attention focussed inevitably upon their exam performance. Exam results featured strongly in the ensuing debate about accountability. For many they were a means of evaluating not only the performance of individual schools but, more significantly, the whole series of post-war reforms in education which had led to the creation of comprehensive schools.

The extent to which exams should be central to the accounting of educational achievement has been fiercely contested, reflecting deep divisions about the conception and government of education. In introducing the parliamentary debate on the 1980 Education Act, Dr.

Boyson suggested that the publication of examination results was essential to the Conservative party's concern to 'provide full(er) information on schools so that parents can make their choice of school . . . an informed choice' (*Hansard*, 5 November 1979, p. 157).

Mr. Kinnock, the then Labour spokesman on education, challenged the divisiveness of publishing exam results. The Labour government, in their 1978 Bill, had proposed to improve the information made available to parents, but specifically to exclude exam results. Mr. Kinnock contrasted the legislative proposals of the two parties: 'that which was intended for the constructive purpose of informing parents and the general public about the facilities of a school and the opportunities it offered has now been turned into an entirely destructive power which will divide society and end in the deprivation of parts of our education system . . . Publication . . . will [cause] demoralization because those who are not part of the successful league team will feel that their efforts are not recognized because they cannot be demonstrated in the precise but often misleading form of examination results' (*Hansard*, 11 December 1979, pp. 822–3).

The Parliamentary Standing Committee sat all night and the vote was carried. Schools now found themselves required by law to publish their results. The information they were to place in their prospectuses (breakdowns of the entries and passes subject-by-subject) was probably the simplest and most straightforward for them to produce — but it was also likely to be difficult to interpret and potentially misleading. A form of educational accountability which was anathema to many in the profession had become a reality. The 1981 summer examination results became a matter of public record.

The intention of this chapter is to focus upon the debate about examination results as a means of illustrating some of the central issues in educational accountability. Forms of accountability serve to express a deeper order of values and power. This is particularly well demonstrated in the case of examination results.


## Breaking the Mould: The National Debate about Exam Results

September 1978 was to prove a crucial month in the debates about publication. The particular occasion was an address by Dr. Rhodes Boyson, then a junior opposition spokesman on education, to a conference of the National Council for Educational Standards (NCES), a right-wing educational pressure group.

During his speech Boyson released and commented on the 'A' level results for comprehensive schools in Manchester. He had gathered these, he said, without the cooperation of the local education authority. In the process he compared the Manchester results with those of neighbouring, selective Trafford. Pupils in Trafford, he claimed, had three times as much chance of getting an 'A' level as those in Manchester, and five times as much chance of obtaining a grade A. At the same time he accused the then Secretary of State, Mrs. Shirley Williams, of supporting a 'cover-up' by refusing to publish results from comprehensive schools (*The Times Educational Supplement*, 22 September 1978).

This much was familiar — merely the latest in a series of comparisons of the results of one form of organization or another that had peppered the 1970s. But Boyson went further and singled out several *individual schools* for comment.

This was an essentially new development which broke the mould of previous national debates. Since Boyson promised similar exercises, on a quarterly basis, for other authorities, starting with Sheffield, Oxford and inner London, a furious and hostile debate was the likely outcome.

The speech was roundly condemned on all sides, as Boyson must have anticipated. The Chairman of Manchester's Education Committee predictably described it as 'quite monstrous'. 'It was unfair to compare (inner-city) children ... with the children of middle-class managers and skilled workers living in the city suburbs'. But he was also criticized, although in more temperate terms, by the Conservative chairmen of the two major local authority associations (the Association of County Councils and the Association of Metropolitan Authorities). One commented that the 'question was much more complex than simply comparing examination results'; the other stressed that 'one must compare like with like' (all reported in *The Times*, 19 September 1978).

It soon emerged that Boyson had not cleared his speech with Norman St. John Stevas, the main Conservative spokesman on education. The official Conservative attitude towards the publication of exam results was that 'they should be made available but not presented in the form of a "league table"' (*ibid*). Elsewhere, St. John Stevas was reported as maintaining that 'examination results should be seen only in the social context of the school concerned' (*Times Educational Supplement*, 6 October 1978).

Other statements of policy followed. The President of the Secondary Heads Association (SHA) outlined the doubts of the profession about publication: '. . . exam results on their own tell very little about the quality of a school . . . the social composition of a school's catchment area still remains the most important influence on academic success . . . unless this and related factors such as the range of IQ are taken into account, raw statistics of exam passes or failures are largely meaningless' (*Times Educational Supplement*, 6th October 1978). The SHA's policy, he asserted, was to ensure that results were published 'only at the discretion of schools themselves, only for proper educational purposes, only in ways which seek to avert their misinterpretation by the public, and which preclude meaningless comparisons between schools in different circumstances'.

Finally, in response to the allegations of a 'cover-up', a spokesman from the Department of Education and Science commented: 'It is entirely a matter for headteachers and local authorities as to whether they publish the exam results of individual schools. We publish in our annual statistics the results of various types of school. We do not go into the details of individual schools' (*Times Educational Supplement*, 22 September 1978).

In brief, just a year before the topic was to become the subject of parliamentary legislation, the profession was united in its condemnation of results being published.

### The Debate about Comprehensive Education

Politicians of both major persuasions, however, had begun using exam statistics to assess the achievement of schools. Since the first Black Paper in 1969 accused the Labour government of attempting to 'destroy a fine and tried educational system' (Cox and Dyson, 1969, p. 3), comparisons of exam results have featured prominently in the debates about the relative merits of selective as opposed to comprehensive forms of school organization.

In the summer of 1974 the Manchester Education Committee released some statistics which were immediately seized upon by critics of the comprehensive system as evidence of 'failure'. Three months later, the Chairman of Sheffield's Education Committee was using exam results to trumpet the successes of the city's comprehensive schools (*Times Educational Supplement*, 25 October 1974). The following year brought further controversies, which culminated in a round of claims and counter-claims provoked by an analysis entitled

*The Great Comprehensive Gamble.* In it, R.W. Baldwin, then Chairman of the governors at the highly selective Manchester Grammar School, again attacked the performance of the comprehensive system (Baldwin, 1975).

Although early in 1979, with a Labour government in power, prospects of government legislation were still distant, more comparisons were produced. The London Borough of Richmond had been the first local authority to release results school-by-school on its comprehensive system; it had also experienced some problems of 'sensationalizing' media treatment (*Times Educational Supplement*, 21 December 1979). Oxfordshire had also taken this particular plunge (*Daily Telegraph*, 10 April 1979). Baldwin, meanwhile, was keeping up the pressure; using a somewhat more 'like-with-like' strategy than Boyson had employed the previous year, he compared Manchester's results with neighbouring Trafford's and still found them wanting (*Daily Telegraph*, 1 February 1979). A month later he produced further comparisons between bright children in comprehensives and the former grammar schools (*Daily Telegraph*, 9 March 1979).

The publication of an analysis of the 'A' level exam results for the Inner London Education Authority, which Boyson had promised, kept the pot simmering (Cox and Marks, 1981), although, interestingly, the further analysis by the NCES of Sheffield's results did not emerge. However, it is no exaggeration to say (a) that in every single year since 1974 there has been some controversy or other in the educational press about the relative merits of the comprehensive system; and (b) that these have focussed almost exclusively on examination results.

The debates were further fuelled by a row over a DES-funded report by the National Children's Bureau on the attainments of pupils attending different types of (reorganized) secondary schools (Steedman, 1980). Cox and Marks attacked the study's conclusions on methodological grounds but combined this with other questions about motives and bias; rebuttals followed (Steedman *et al.*, 1980). An interesting feature of this particular study was that it covered many more outcomes than tested attainments in the basic skills of reading and mathematics but these were largely ignored. There was also an implication that the 'real' evidence in the form of exam results were still awaited (see Steedman, 1983).

Although many more schools had become 'comprehensive' during the course of the decade, the continued existence of selection in many parts of the country made it possible to argue that the examination results being reported were not really the products of a fully-fledged comprehensive system. By the early 1980s, however, there were sufficient comprehensive authorities around for this 'defence' to come under strain. In 1983, several studies were produced which suggested very different conclusions about what had been happening.

Early on in the year a study of Scottish comprehensives was reported (Gray, McPherson and Raffe, 1983). Scotland had implemented comprehensive reorganization earlier than England. The study suggested that in terms of examination results there were few, if any, differences between the 'comprehensive' and 'selective' sectors. This pattern of small or non-existent differences between the two sectors was confirmed, some months later, by the National Children's Bureau study of exam results in selective and non-selective schools (Steedman, 1983); its publication date, however, conceals the fact that its data were collected almost a decade earlier. The annual report on examination results in the ILEA appeared to confirm that 'standards had been maintained' for the first cohort (the 1977 intake) to pass through a fully comprehensive system (Byford and Mortimore, 1983, p. 3).

The controversy, however, was reserved for the NCES analysis of the exam results first made public by the 1980 Education Act (Marks, Cox and Pomian-Srzednicki, 1983). It claimed that the selective system had achieved considerably superior results, even after differences in social class composition had been taken into account. This study, too, was criticized on methodological grounds; and an episode developed during which the DES's own statisticians were brought into the debate. A parallel analysis of DES data for all the local authorities in England for the same years, conducted by two of the authors of the present chapter, reached the conclusion that there were no differences between the results of those authorities which had gone 'fully comprehensive' and those which had 'retained selection to a greater or lesser extent' (Gray, Jesson and Jones, 1984).

This more recent debate, then, is merely the latest in a long succession which have focussed, almost invariably, on exam results as the single measure of account and, quite frequently, the sole criterion for discussion.

## Understanding and Interpreting Accountability

It is clear, from the previous discussion, that some parties to the debates have seen publication of results by schools as the most significant means of strengthening accountability to the communities which they serve. Whether this is a reasonable expectation or an adequate strategy will depend upon one's understanding and interpretation of this densely packed concept. Clarifying what *we* mean will contribute to our analysis and explanation of exams as the emerging form at school accountability.

To be accountable is to be 'held to account' but also to 'give an account' (cf. Sockett, 1976 and 1980a; Stewart, 1984). These elements reveal the distinctive social characteristics bound up in the accountable relationship; accountability structures relations of control which are designed to enhance purposes and values that are (believed to be) central to particular institutions.

'To be held to account' defines a relationship of control. It implies rather formal ties between the parties, one of whom is answerable to the other for the quality of their actions and performance (cf. Lello, 1979). Being called to account in this way suggests, moreover, that what has been accomplished will be evaluated and judged:

> Being accountable may mean ... no more than having to answer questions about what has happened or is happening within one's jurisdiction... But most usages require an additional implication: the answer when given, or the account when rendered, is to be evaluated by the superior or superior body, measured against some standards or some expectation, and the differences noted; and then praise or blame to be meted out and sanctions applied. It is the coupling of information with its evaluation and application of sanctions that gives 'accountability' or 'answerability' or 'responsibility' their full sense in ordinary organizational usage. (Dunsire, 1978)

These elements have been distinctively present in the recent development of accountability in education. LEAs and schools have increasingly been called upon to inform their public about a broader spectrum of their activities: they may be called to account for the cost of providing the service and thus their efficiency in the use of contracting resources; within schools, teachers have been asked to submit their curriculum and teaching practice to inspection and public report; and, most significantly, as we have described earlier in the chapter, schools have been required by law to account for their performance by publishing their exam results.

The public account of educational performance is, therefore, being enlarged as attention is being directed to each stage of the schooling process. The intention, however, as Dunsire stresses, is to evaluate performance against 'standards' of achievement. This may mean using CIPFA (Chartered Institute of Public Finance and Accountancy) statistics or Government Audit Commission efficiency manuals to evaluate comparative performance between LEAs on improving unit costs; or drawing upon the detached frame of reference of HMI to evaluate more objectively the quality of the teaching process within schools; while national standards of exam performance can be adduced to evaluate the achievement of individual schools or LEAs.

Implicit in the processes of evaluation is a judgment about performances and the potential application of sanctions. Parents can withdraw their children and select an alternative school if results begin to falter; the LEA can redefine its priorities and thus the distribution of resources to schools; while the fees provided by industry and commerce allow them to hold colleges to account and, if necessary, withhold confidence and finance.

This stress within the accountability framework on evaluating comparative performance can lead to a discussion between the parties about the validity of the 'standards' applied. The party held to account may question whether the expectations imposed on them are reasonable and strive to redefine what are fair comparators for the purposes of evaluation. Beliefs about the justness of the sanctions applied will depend upon the consensus achieved about appropriate standards.

The evaluative nature of accountability may tend, therefore, to encourage a discussion about purposes. Those called to account will be inclined to assert that their performance can only be judged in relation to the objectives which they have set themselves. Schools will argue that in evaluating their achievement it is reasonable to take into account the context in which they are working — the buildings, the resources available, the social characteristics of the community they serve, and the qualities of the young people they teach.

The parties to an accountable relationship, driven to argue about the standards which a school should attain, will thus seek to clarify the understandings and knowledge claims which should be taken into account in determining 'standards'. They will also begin to make explicit the values which shape their view of schooling and constitute their expectations of effective performance. The duty to tell a story or to give an account, stimulates an account of the 'assumptive worlds' which have inspired and lent meaning to action.

Thus those who can call others to account are able to use the controls available to them to protect and enhance their educational values. As Pateman (1978) has argued cogently, 'preferences among different possible forms of accountability in education relate to and serve different orderings of socially available values'. Thus the professional community of teachers remains committed to the value of the personal development of young people; elected members of the Education Committee search for an improvement in efficiency and value for money; industry promotes basic skills and employability; parents argue for the right to select the school of their choice; while the government articulates the implications for schooling of society's changing needs.

Each of these 'partners' in the education service hope to hold the others to account to the values which they espouse. For much of the post-war period, nevertheless, there was considerable agreement about the purposes and values which should inform the development of the education service. Common objectives shaped formal relations. There was, apparently, in education a remarkable degree of mutual answerability.

Such interdependence and unity of assumptions is not, however, a necessary feature of accountability. It is equally feasible to expect competing assumptions and values. Since the 1970s the implicit consensus has begun to fall apart, as the partners came to disagree about the direction of the service, the content of the curriculum, the value of the comprehensive reforms and the standards which these schools were achieving.

As the dominant values came to be challenged so did the existing forms of accountability which those values constituted. Alternative values and forms of accountability were asserted and implemented. The 1980 Education Act is one of the more visible expressions of this trend.

## The Changing Forms of Accountability

The demand during the 1970s to hold education to account was, in practice, a demand for a different form of accountability. During the decades of post-war growth the service had incorporated internal and professional procedures of accountability which served agreed values and beliefs about the evaluation of educational performance. Demands to extend the scope of accountability were designed not to supplement but to subordinate the existing tradition to new forms of public accountability to the consumer which would incorporate the publication of examination results as their keystone. We need to consider these two competing modes of professional and 'market' accountability in more detail.

### Professional Accountability

The professional account focusses upon the processes of schooling and thus upon the quality of the whole educational experience young people are being offered: 'via the curriculum, teaching, grouping for instruction, informal group membership, pastoral care and so on' (Hoyle, 1979). When the account turns to the standards young people are achieving in schools the professional eye reviews performance in public examinations but also other aspects of educational achievement. The professional view is that exams constitute an important but narrow indicator of school achievement and that other dimensions of activity need to be taken into account when evaluating standards: the whole cultural, social and creative aspects of school life should be assessed (cf. Shipman, 1978; Rutter *et al.*, 1979). A more comprehensive account is even more important, professionals argue, for each student. Exams cannot adequately summarize educational progress and need to be complemented by 'profiles' or 'records of achievement' which allow a much broader spectrum of personal qualities to be taken into account (Burgess and Adams, 1980).

Professional values, therefore, emphasize the scope of educational achievement and a belief in the unfolding potential of young people whose progress at any one point in time should be recognized as reflecting the quality of the relations and expectations which teachers can create within the classroom. The professional mode of accountability is thus grounded in assumptions about the complexity of the educational task of developing students' capacities over time.

Given these complexities of educational process, the professionals argue that the necessary requirements of being held to account are best undertaken internally by teachers or by advisory and inspectorial colleagues who understand the nature of the task and the extent of progress. Only the skilled professional can judge sensitively the context within which schools are working and the objectives it is reasonable for them to work towards. Evaluating standards presupposes an understanding of context and, if sanctions are warranted, then professional peers are best suited to determine the improvements required, without damaging the quality of the relations within the school.

To expose a delicate plant to a continual glare may damage its growth. Professionals argue that certain forms of public scrutiny can have similar effects upon schools. To focus an account of their performance upon examination results which are then published in the market place would be to distort and to disrupt educational progress. These arguments were articulated strongly by the Labour Party's education spokesman during the committee proceedings leading up to the 1980 Education Act. The publication of examination results would not 'provide an accurate judgment of the real performance of a school and the way in which it served its pupils'. To avoid misleading interpretations considerably more 'criteria and qualifying details' would be required. These would include an understanding of the aspirations and traditions of the school, the particular type of education that the school sought to provide, the extent of parental assistance over and above the LEA's resourcing of the school, together with a view of the social and economic context in which the school was located. Because schools served recognizably different populations of pupils with different needs, the publication of results, it was argued, would be 'destructive' and 'divisive'. Publication would then be at odds with the nature and purposes of education itself and could only lead to the 'demoralization of pupils, teaching staffs, parents and communities' (Hansard, 11 December 1979, pp. 822–5).

The professional response to the demand for greater educational accountability has been to deflect attention from exams and in some cases, to encourage schools to evaluate their own performance. A number of LEAs — notably the ILEA, Oxfordshire and Solihull — have been developing procedures for professional 'self-evaluation' in schools:

> The object of applying some form of systematic self-appraisal is to assist in the clarification of objectives and priorities, to identify weaknesses and strengths and ensure that due attention is given to all aspects of school life. (ILEA, 1977)

> This document is intended to be: (a) an aid to teachers, individually or collectively, and schools in examining the value of what they do; (b) a starting point for discussion and further questioning whenever a school as a whole, or a department within a school, considers it appropriate to take stock of what it is achieving. Any initiative aimed at improving

the quality of learning, teaching and pupil achievement in schools needs to start by a critical analysis of existing practice. (Brighouse, 1979)

This idea of self-evaluation, which allows the school to account for achievement in terms of its own objectives and internal processes, has gained much support from the community of educational research (cf. Bridges, 1980; Elliott, 1980; Pateman, 1978). For Macdonald (1978), however, the internal 'self-report' should not conclude the accounting but form the basis of a dialogue with governors, parents and the general public. Here the professionals would be able to provide an interpretative analysis that would shape the ensuing discourse of public accounting.

### Market Accountability

The proponents of this model, in contrast, argue that the professional strategy of internal accounting distorts the essential purpose of institutions looking outwards to the public beyond their boundaries. Schools should be answerable to parents, employers and their local community: to those who receive and consume the schools' service.

The focus of this account, it is claimed, should be upon attainment and performance rather than process. When we buy a cycle or a washing maching we are not interested in problems of production, only in the quality of the final product. If we are dissatisfied we can always choose another brand and sanctions implied in such a shift of preferences provide the necessary signals to producers to improve their standards. The quality of institutional performance is best tested in the market place of individual consumer choices. Schools, no different from factories, can equally benefit from the test of the market.

Once more the Parliamentary debate upon the 1980 Education Act is of interest because it illustrates the competing views about the purposes of education and the ways in which the differential quality of schooling might be evaluated. For the government, it became clear, that 'market forces', through the expression of parental choices, would provide the prime determinant of what was judged to be 'good'. For the market to function efficiently, it was important that parents have the information necessary to make informed choices. Two contributors to the debate expressed this view in different, but related, ways.

Mr. John Carlisle (not related to the then Secretary of State,

Mark Carlisle) argued that 'for too long bad schools have been able to hide behind mediocre exam results and poor academic achievement' (*Hansard*, 5 November 1979, p. 99). They were kept in business, he suggested, because LEAs operating in a monopolistic manner, kept their numbers up through changes in catchment areas and admission limits. Informed parents exercising informed choices would soon ensure their demise. Pursuing the market model, he went on to suggest that:

> Schools sell a product — the ability to educate. That product should be pushed forward, as with any product in a shop window, to make children fit for adult life. Sales literature for a school must by statute be honest and contain all relevant facts about a school. That is an essential part of the offer made to parents. *Examination results speak for themselves.* However, the percentage of failures and passes should be included in that literature. A school should also advertise the general appearance of the staff and pupils. (*Hansard*, 5 November 1979, p. 100, our emphasis)

Sir John Eden, earlier in the debate, had acknowledged that choosing between schools was a 'complex' matter, but was still insistent that examination results had a part to play:

> ... some parents will be influenced by the buildings and facilities. Others will look closely at the type of education, the sort of work that is done by the school, the standard of teaching which is encouraged ... and the degree of involvement of teachers both in the classroom and outside it. That is much more difficult to ascertain *and it cannot be seen by examination standards alone, even though they serve as a guide and as an indicator.* (*Hansard*, 5 November, 1979, p. 74, our emphasis)

The 1980 Education Act made the publication of examination results central to the account which schools must offer their public. It provided, it was claimed, the single common currency that could be carried into the market place to test school standards. Parental affirmation or sanction, registered in their selection of particular schools, was now regarded as the best instrument for holding schools to account: consumer sovereignty was to replace the potentially undemocratic imposition of professional will.

Stewart Ranson et al.

## Interests and Power in Accountability

With the 1980 Act a new mode of accountability had gained ascendancy. It emphasized an external account to the public. There was much to be commended in such a development. Schools had been criticized, with some validity, for being too insular so that, when concern was expressed about behaviour or the shape of the curriculum or about standards, the professional practice of internal review seemed unduly secretive. A closed world needed to gain the confidence of its several publics. Yet the legislation endorsed a specific form of public accounting. We need to grasp this development at different levels of analysis.

Accountability, as we have argued, is a distinctive institution of control constituting and serving particular sets of values and beliefs about the purposes and structure of schooling. As with other forms of institutional development (cf. Giddens, 1976; Archer, 1980; Ranson *et al.*, 1980), structuring is neither neutral nor inevitable but socially created, reflecting the strategic choices of those groups which have gained sufficient power to redesign organizations in ways which secure their dominant values.

The market mode of accounting, with its focus and controls upon the publishing of examination results, has been encouraged by an alliance of interests — parental pressure groups, the private sector, the political right — with particular beliefs about education. Their concern has been to protect and enhance a more traditional, academic schooling with a curriculum directed to passing public examinations at 16 and 18. The potential influence of exams upon the curriculum is well known (DES, 1979). Knowing that they will be held to account for their exam performance, there will be a tendency for schools to concentrate their teaching and resources upon preparation for exams. Indirectly, the stress upon exams will tend to reinforce the teaching of basic subjects and more formal styles of teaching. How strong these tendencies will be will depend on the circumstances of individual schools. There are already limits. Many schools are presently heavily committed to an *examined* curriculum for their fourth and fifth-year pupils. Changes in assessment procedures are also possible. But the dangers, real or supposed, are widely recognized and feared.

The publishing of exam results signals and structures a traditional academic schooling. More particularly it signals relative performance between schools in achieving good academic results. It is a signal to parents in general, and to some parents in particular to differentiate between schools and to select the academically successful. Publishing exams stimulates competition between schools — a school market.

This analysis however, focussing as it does within education, only allows a partial explanation of the emerging forms of market accountability. An adequate understanding of the attachment to publishing examination results lies in identifying deeper social interests. We need a level of analysis which explores the changing relations education has with other social institutions — in particular, schools serve to select and differentiate young people for the layers of the labour market (Gray *et al.*, 1983; Ranson, 1983; Shipman, 1984). Shipman has recently analysed with some force the role of public examinations in mediating the demands of employment as well as selecting and sorting students. We should, he claims:

> avoid seeing the dominance of qualifications as more than a symptom. The underlying problem is the dovetailing of education into the division of labour. (p. 161)

In particular, academic qualifications determine access to higher education, to the professions and thus to privileged income, status and influence in society. The publishing of results signals to parents the success, or lack of success, of individual schools in gaining access for their students to such economic and social privileges.

Ironically, as our programme of research has begun to show, the information on exam results provided by the Act does not, in itself, tell one very much about the actual performance of the schools themselves; nor is it very informative about the prospects for the offspring of any individual parent. Given the very strong relationships between the intake a school receives and its subsequent output in terms of examination results, the main inference that can be drawn from such exam accounts is that the school has had a more or a less advantaged intake (Gray, 1981). Some parents may find this useful, if indirect, information when making their choice of schools. But statistics on entries and pass rates cannot be meaningfully interpreted in the absence of the contextual information, whose potential inclusion was the subject of the fierce debates described earlier.


## Conclusions

Demands for greater accountability in education during the 1970s reflected diverse concerns about the performance of schools which were not the sole province of any one political party. There are recognizable educational reasons why 'opening up' schools to their various publics might be considered desirable and strategies which were more sensitive to the circumstances of individual schools could have been implemented. The particular strategy selected to hold education to account, however, was a distinctive form of public accountability. It emphasized one narrow indicator of educational achievement and insisted upon its publication in order to promote greater consumer choice and competition between schools.

The information to be published on examination results was, in practice, that which it was most simple and most straightforward for schools to produce but it was by no means as simple and straightforward to interpret. Indeed, all one can say with any confidence is that pupils at some schools may obtain more exam passes than pupils at others. One cannot say why or attribute causes with any confidence, although the temptation to do so may be present. For that relatively small group of parents anticipating high levels of exam success such statistics *may* be helpful. But, for the majority, the main conclusion to be drawn from such information is a broader one that relates not so much to schools' actual performance as to their ethos. Schools with larger number of exam passes signal, thereby, their 'academic' status in comparison with others.

Much educational policy over the past two decades has been devoted to ensuring that secondary schools develop a common framework of purpose and provision, within which 'academic' forms of schooling may play a part but not a dominant one. The publication of exam results serves as a symbolic reminder that this policy has not yet been fully implemented.

## Acknowledgments

The authors of this chapter are all members of the Contexts Project which has been funded by the Economic and Social Research Council to investigate 'the use and interpretation of examination results as measures of school performance'. They are grateful to the ESRC for their support but the views expressed in this chapter are their responsibility alone.

## References

ARCHER, M. (1979) *Social Origins of Educational Systems*, London, Sage.
BALDWIN, R.W. (1975) *The Great Comprehensive Gamble*, London,

Harvester Press.

BRIDGES, D. (1980) 'Accountability and the politics of the staffroom', in SOCKETT, H.T. (1980b) *Accountability in the English Educational System*, London, Hodder and Stoughton.

BRIGHOUSE, T. (1979) *Starting Points in Self-Evaluation*, Oxfordshire County Council.

BURGESS, T. and ADAMS, E. (Eds) (1980) *Outcomes of Education*, London, Macmillan.

BYFORD, D. and MORTIMORE, P. (1983) *School Examination Results in the ILEA, 1982*, Inner London Education Authority (RS871/83).

COX, C and MARKS, J. (1980) *Real Concern*, London, Centre for Policy Studies.

COX, C. and MARKS, J. (1981) *Sixth Forms in ILEA Comprehensives: A Cruel Confidence Trick?* Esher, National Council for Educational Standards

COX, C.B. and DYSON, A.E. (Eds) (1969) *Fight for Education: A Black Paper*, London, Critical Quarterly Society.

DEPARTMENT OF EDUCATION AND SCIENCE (1979) *Aspects of Secondary Education*, London, HMSO.

DUNSIRE, A. (1978) *Control in a Bureaucracy: The Execution Process*, Vol. 2, London, Martin Robertson.

ELLIOTT, J. (1980) 'Who should monitor performance in schools?' in SOCKETT H.T. (1980b) *Accountability in the English Educational System*, London, Hodder and Stoughton.

GIDDENS, A. (1976) *New Rules of Sociological Method*, London, Hutchinson.

GRAY, J. (1981) 'Are examination results a suitable measure of school performance?' in PLEWIS, I. (Ed.) *Publishing School Examination Results: A Discussion*, London Institute of Education, Bedford Way Papers, no. 5.

GRAY J., JESSON, D. and JONES, B. (1984) 'Predicting differences in examination results between local education authorities: does school organization matter?', *Oxford Review of Education*, 10, 1, pp. 45–68.

GRAY, J., MCPHERSON, A.F. and RAFFE, D. (1983) *Reconstructions of Secondary Education*, London, Routledge and Kegan Paul.

ILEA (1977) *Keeping the School Under Review*, London, Inner London Education Authority.

LELLO, J. (Ed.) (1979) *Accountability in Education*, London, Ward Lock Educational.

MACDONALD, B. (1978) 'Accountability, standards and the process of schooling' in BECHER, T. and MACLURE, S. (Eds) *Accountability in Education*, Windsor, National Foundation for Educational Research Publishing Co.

MARKS, J., COX, C. and POMIAN-SRZEDNICKI, M. (1983) *Standards in English Schools: an Analysis of the Examination Results of Secondary Schools in England for 1981*, London, National Council for Educational Standards.

PATEMAN, T. (1978) 'Accountability, values and schooling', in BECHER, T. and MACLURE, S. (Eds) *Accountability in Education*, Windsor, National Foundation for Educational Research Publishing Co.

RANSON, S. (1984) 'Towards a tertiary tripartism: New codes of social control and the 17+ in BROADFOOT, P.M. (Ed.) *Selection, Certification and Control*, Lewes, Falmer Press

RANSON, S., HININGS, B. and GREENWOOD, R. (1980) 'The structuring of organizational structures', *Administrative Science Quarterly*, 25, March.

RUTTER, M., MAUGHAN, B., MORTIMORE, P. and OUSTON, J. (1979). *Fifteen Thousand Hours: Secondary Schools and their Effects on Children*, London, Open Books.

SHIPMAN, M. (1978) *In-School Evaluation*, London, Heinemann Educational.

SHIPMAN, M. (1984) *Education as a Public Service*, London, Harper and Row.

SOCKETT, H.T. (1976) 'Teacher accountability', *Proceedings of the Philosophy of Education Society of Great Britian*, 10.

SOCKETT, H.T. (1980a) 'Accountability: the contemporary issues' in SOCKETT, H.T. *Accountability in the English Educational System*, London, Hodder and Stoughton.

SOCKETT, H.T. (Ed.) (1980b) *Accountability in the English Educational System*, London, Hodder and Stoughton.

STEEDMAN, J. (1980) *Progress in Secondary Schools*, London, National Children's Bureau.

STEEDMAN, J. (1983) *Examination Results in Selective and Non-selective Schools*, London, National Children's Bureau.

STEEDMAN, J., FOGELMAN, K. and HUTCHISON, D. (1980) *Real Research: A Rebuttal of Allegations*, London, National Children's Bureau.

STEWART, J. (1984) 'The role of information in public accountability', in *Current Issues in Public Sector Accountancy*, London, Phillip Allan.

# A Critique of the APU

Caroline Gipps
*University of London Institute of Education*

Following a seminar on accountability and education held at Cambridge in September 1977, the Social Science Research Council (now the Economic and Social Research Council) set aside a sum of money for research on accountability. Slightly less than half the funds were awarded to a team at the Institute of Education to carry out a three-year project, one of the main tasks of which was to evaluate the work of the Assessment of Performance Unit (APU). The other task was to investigate the extent and impact of LEA testing programmes. In carrying out the research the team interviewed LEA advisers, heads and teachers, both about LEA testing and about the impact of the APU's work. We reported on the LEA testing at the end of 1983.[1]

This chapter is based on our report on the APU.[2] In writing the report we had access to APU committee papers and minutes as well as APU personnel, and we are indebted to the DES/APU for their cooperation. Like others, we had access to all the published material on the APU — publicity material, reports, etc. — but we did not have access to test items. Nor were we given access to any information on schools or LEAs involved in the APU's testing programme since this was confidential information. As well as reading minutes and documents we interviewed over forty people involved at some time or another with the APU. This interview material was invaluable in shaping our understanding of the history of the Unit and in clarifying the problems facing those whose job it was to make decisions about the paths along which the APU was to go.

For readers who are not familiar with the APU, we start with a brief description, incorporating some of its history. We then bring the history up to date and give our evaluation of the APU's work.

## What is the APU?[3]

The APU is a unit within the Department of Education and Science. It is headed by a senior HMI, the professional head, and a senior civil servant, the administrative head. They report to an Under-Secretary and ultimately to the Permanent Secretary at the DES. The Unit oversees the surveying of performance in maths and language at 11 and 15, science at 11, 13 and 15 and first modern foreign language at 13. The Unit is also considering the possibility of monitoring design and technology, and a decision is expected on this in the spring (1984). Given the emphasis on practical skills in Sir Keith Joseph's Sheffield speech,[4] a topic such as design and technology would be high on the agenda for monitoring, but the cost of the exercise might militate against it. Aesthetic and physical development were also considered for monitoring; it has now been decided that these are not suitable for national assessment, but the discussion documents produced by the exploratory groups are available for use by LEAs. Plans to assess two highly contentious areas, personal and social development and the performance of West Indian children, have also been dropped. These decisions were taken as a result of widespread consultation both within and without the APU committee structure.

The actual test development and surveying is contracted out to the National Foundation for Educational Research (NFER) for maths, language and modern language and to the University of Leeds and Chelsea College, London, for science. Each of the development teams has a steering group to advise them, and these groups are composed of teachers, advisers, researchers, lecturers and HMI, all of whom are nominated by the DES. All the steering groups are chaired by HMI attached to the APU. There is also a Statistics Advisory Group made up of DES, NFER and outside statisticians and researchers, which advises the Unit on the technical aspects of its work.

Over all these groups and teams sits the Consultative Committee with approximately thirty members, of whom about two-thirds are appointed by teacher and LEA associations or represent parents, industry and research. The other members, drawn from the HMI and DES, are nominees of the Secretary of State, while the Chairman is an academic. Thus the Consultative Committee is the only group representative of outside interests. Its role was defined in an early APU publicity leaflet as one of examining the broad outlines and priorities that are proposed for the Unit's work and bringing its influence to bear on them.[5]

There also used to be a Coordinating Group which, as its name implies, coordinated the work of the various groups and reported to the Consultative Committee rather as an executive would. Of the seventeen members, ten were HMI or DES personnel and one was from the NFER, while the remaining six were chosen by the DES from schools, colleges, universities and LEAs. This group was disbanded in early 1980.

## How the APU Began

To understand the APU fully, it is necessary to go back over fifteen years and look at the APU's precursors.

In the late 1960s several strands came together which were to encourage, within the DES, an interest in national monitoring. First, there was growing interest in subjecting the education system to systematic study of its objectives and evaluation of its achievements. At the same time, there was increasing discussion about trends in educational standards. Critics of the reorganization of secondary education were claiming that standards would fall[6] and there was also concern about 'underachievement' of particular groups, especially ethnic minorities. The NFER had carried out a series of reading surveys from 1948 to 1964 which showed steadily improving performance but there was little information in other areas, especially mathematics. Finally, there seems to have been an increasing concern around 1970 that the DES (as distinct from HMI) was excluded from involvement with the educational curriculum, despite funding the system and ultimately being held accountable for it. Since the Schools Council and the teachers themselves retained control over the curriculum, DES involvement with testing presented itself as a means of obtaining direct evaluation of the performance of the system and consequently a means of achieving some say in curriculum content.

All these strands came together in 1970 with the setting up under the DES planning branch of a working group on the measurement of educational attainment (WGMET).[7] It consisted of two administrators, two HMIs and four academics. The working group reported at the end of 1971 and its main conclusions were that 'regular measurements of educational attainment are desirable', that 'measurement is feasible', should 'be done by sampling' covering 'the main educational stages and school subjects' and should be 'a partnership between testing bodies, the Schools Council, LEAs and the DES'. The group recommended an early start, and arising from this, a feasibility project at the NFER (Tests of Attainment in Mathematics in Schools) was commissioned by the newly-formed DES Policy Group B in 1972. This project became the precursor to the APU maths monitoring programme. In 1974 an interim report from the project indicated that large-scale maths monitoring was clearly feasible and could be undertaken by the NFER.

Also in 1972 the Committee of Enquiry into Reading and the Use of English, the Bullock Committee, was set up. This had a Monitoring Sub-committee which included two administrators, one HMI, two NFER representatives and four educationists and academics. The outcome of the discussions of this Sub-committee formed Chapter 3 of the Bullock Committee report.[8] The recommendations went much further than the 1970 group's report and strongly recommended a national system of monitoring, using 'light sampling' and item banking techniques, both of which it was felt could overcome 'curriculum backwash' problems. The report attached great importance to a monitoring system which could make statements about trends in performance.

Thus by the end of 1974, when the APU was formally announced, there had been a strong series of recommendations in favour of national monitoring in the areas of maths and reading.

The intimation that the APU was on its way came in April 1974 in a speech by the then Secretary of State for Education, Mr. Reg Prentice, to the National Association of Schoolmasters' Conference.[9] In August of the same year came the first official announcement in the White Paper *Educational Disadvantage and the Educational Needs of Immigrants*.[10] This paper announced the setting up of an Educational Disadvantage Unit (EDU) within the DES, the purpose of which was to influence the allocation of resources in the interests of those suffering from educational disadvantage which, given the focus of the White Paper, was generally understood to mean ethnic minority groups. The EDU was to develop, *in conjunction with the APU*, criteria to improve identification of this educational disadvantage. It was in an annex to this paper that the APU's terms of reference and tasks were set out formally for the first time.

The Unit's terms of reference are:

To promote the development of methods of assessing and monitoring the achievement of children at school, and to seek to identify the incidence of under-achievement.

The tasks laid down are:

(i) To identify and appraise existing instruments and methods of assessment which may be relevant for these purposes.

(ii) To sponsor the creation of new instruments and techniques for assessment, having due regard to statistical and sampling methods.

(iii) To promote the conduct of assessment in cooperation with local education authorities and teachers.

(iv) To identify significant differences of achievement related to the circumstances in which children learn, including the incidence of underachievement, and to make findings available to those concerned with resource allocation within government departments, local education authorities and schools.

However, publicity material produced by the APU between 1977 and 1980 carried quite a different message: the APU's role was to monitor in order to provide information on standards and how these change over time. There was no mention of underachievement, the circumstances in which children learn, or resource allocation.

Clearly, both from its early publicity material and from the way it has approached its task, as well as its pre-history, the APU's main aim was to monitor standards. Why then was it announced in the way that it was: 'disguised' by a concern about the educational disadvantage of ethnic minority groups? Both the Great Debate, which started in 1976 when Callaghan gave his Ruskin College speech, and the accountability movement which also sprang up in the mid-1970s, were a culmination of an increasingly questioning attitude in the early seventies among commentators, and sections of the general public too, towards the outcomes of the maintained education system. Thus, given the climate at the time when the APU was announced, any proposal to monitor standards nationally would have been strongly resisted by the teaching profession which was feeling under attack. However, assessing the needs of disadvantaged children is less questionable professionally and so the announcement of the APU, presented as part of a programme for dealing with disadvantage and underachievement, created little dissent among educationists.

Why then did dissent appear later? What led up to the publication in 1979 and 1980 of several articles criticizing the APU and its likely effects? These are interesting questions for, as sociologists like Broadfoot[11] have argued, in the past the *efficiency* of assessment has been the main area of concern, not its purpose and effects. With the advent of the APU, however, this has changed, for the criticisms have centred on its wider effect although the efficiency of the programme has been questioned too.

The first reason is that by 1975 it had become clear that the APU was not assessing underachievement and disadvantage as originally announced, but was going to become a full-scale national assessment programme concerned with standards. Why was a national assessment programme considered to be dangerous? Though few observers believed that the more extreme aspects of the American accountability-through-testing model — such as basing teacher dismissals or school closures on test scores — would come into play in this country, when the APU showed that it aimed to monitor standards there was some concern that the APU was intended as an instrument to force accountability on schools and therefore teachers. Though ostensibly concerned with children's standards, this was interpreted as dealing with teachers' competencies. However, by adhering to the principle of light sampling the APU has gone a long way towards allaying fears over its intentions. Also, because only a small number of children is tested at any time and the names of children are not known to researchers, there is no way in which results can be used to judge individual schools or teachers.

The next concern, however, was that LEAs might be encouraged to indulge in 'saturation' or 'blanket' testing with a view to making judgments about the effectiveness of institutions. In the 1977 Green Paper, *Education in Schools*,[12] it was suggested that tests suitable for monitoring in LEAs were likely to come out of the work of the APU. LEAs were then urged to wait for this test material but, if they could not wait, to monitor using only a light sample of children.[13] Against this advice, many LEAs introduced their own blanket testing system whereby they tested every child in the target age group rather than the 10 per cent recommended by the DES.

The other big worry was about the APU's effect on the curriculum. Is it possible to have a national system of assessment and not affect the curriculum in some way? In order to develop test items it is necessary to take a model of the curriculum. Will this model then become the dominant model for the curriculum? There was indeed some concern in the early days that the APU was an attempt by the DES to bring in an assessment-led curriculum. The way that it was thought this might come about is essentially an indirect one, by which the APU's curriculum model would provide a frame-work for local authority assessment and thereby a means for introducing a core curriculum.[14] The pressure on LEAs to monitor their standards has already been discussed, and the danger envisaged lay in the possibility that through 'item banking' procedures and in particular the LEA and Schools Item Bank (LEASIB) project at the NFER it would be possible to link local testing programmes to the APU's national monitoring programme. APU findings would provide a baseline of performance and a core of items from which LEAs would be able to develop their own tests and examine the performance of their pupils. The range of APU items would then provide the common core of a national curriculum. As it happens there are technical problems associated with item banking and it is now apparent that LEAs will not have access to APU-style tests via LEASIB. However, the use by LEAs of actual APU test items is currently being discussed and, while it is still some way off, this link is considered by some observers to be potentially more dangerous, because it is more direct, than the LEASIB link.

## The APU in 1984

The initial cycle of five annual surveys ended in 1982 for maths, 1983 for language and 1984 for science; the last of the three annual surveys in modern language will take place in 1985. Maths, language and science will then be monitored once every five years; a decision about the future of modern language monitoring has yet to be made. This rolling system of monitoring with maths, language and science taking it in turns will have the function of updating the national picture and identifying trends, while limiting the burden on schools and reducing costs. Each of the teams will produce a retrospective report at the end of their cycle of annual surveys; though the first of these reports is not yet available, it is understood that they will present composite information for the five years and the different ages tested.

The total running costs of the APU in the 1983/84 financial year are expected to be about £1.4m, about £1.2m of which is attributable to monitoring and research.[15] Part of these costs are met by the Education Departments of Wales and Northern Ireland, the remainder (about £1m) being a charge on the DES, and representing about 40 per cent of its research budget. On the basis of the APU's programme as currently planned, DES costs are expected to fall to a little over £500,000 per annum from 1986/87 onwards when all annual monitoring will be completed, but there will be some fluctuations, especially in the years when science is monitored owing to the high cost of practical testing and the three ages involved.

The impact of published reports, particularly on teachers, has been poor and this was a major theme of our 1982 evaluation. In November 1982 the decision was made that more emphasis be put on dissemination. Thus there is a series of occasional papers and there is a regular newsletter; the DES has produced a booklet on the writing performance on 15 year olds;[16] and the Association for Science Education, acting as the APU's agent, is publishing a series of pamphlets on science performance aimed at the classroom teacher.[17] The policy on published major reports is that, from the beginning of 1984, these will be produced in limited number by the DES and will be free; reports will no longer be published (at considerable expense) by HMSO. Instead the emphasis is now on short, easy-to-read pamphlets and booklets on specific areas aimed at a specific audience. The APU has also commissioned independent evaluations of maths and language reports. The maths evaluation is based at the Cambridge Institute of Education, the language evaluation is being conducted by an ex-ILEA inspector. (An evaluation of the science work is expected to be commissioned in the summer of 1984.) It is expected that these independent evaluations will result in pamphlets and documents for in-service training of teachers. There has been continuing discussion within the Unit, its committees, groups and teams over the nature and extent of the background variables which should be measured. Information of this sort is essential for the interpretation of findings and to provide data of value to policy-makers, that is, to fulfil part of its fourth task — identifying differences of achievement in relation to the circumstances in which children learn. The Statistics Advisory Group has advised against the collection of several proposed variables because of problems of measurement, while the Consultative Committee has been consistently against the collection of home background information from either parents or children. The outcome of a research project based at Leeds, commissioned by the DES to look for a 'surrogate' measure of home background, is awaited. Meanwhile, the current situation is that school-based measures are being collected by the teams in their surveys. However, composite measures of background (both social and educational) have limited potential for explaining performance at an individual or group level. And, as Nuttall[18] has pointed out, there can be little doubt that, in any case, information on classroom processes and detailed curriculum information is vital for interpretation of the survey results. The collection of such data is not compatible with survey techniques but requires more intensive study. In the fallow four-year period between surveys, the teams will have an opportunity to make in-depth studies which were promised when the work was first commissioned. At this point, however, only in-depth analysis of *existing* data is involved; although in-depth studies involving the collection of *new* data are possible, this option has not yet been taken up by the teams.

With regard to making test items available to LEAs and making the data available for secondary analysis by outside researchers, the APU is in favour of both these in principle. However, things are still at the discussion stage. There are problems, of course, about opening the item banks: the DES is concerned not to encourage more blanket testing by LEAs and with some of the test items the marking is extremely sophisticated and training is required. As for the data, the APU accepts that these are a major research resource which should be opened up but with arrangements which safeguard the interests of the monitoring teams.

## An Evaluation of the APU

What then has been the impact of the APU? Have the early fears been realized? How far has the APU fulfilled its tasks?

The first task — to appraise existing instruments and methods of assessment — has varied according to the curriculum area involved. The maths team was always intended to base its work on an assessment of the TAMS material. The language team, on the other hand, following Bullock, would never have used existing tests; as for the science team, there was really nothing available for it to consider using. The discussion documents produced by the Aesthetics and Personal-Social groups, however, include extensive reviews of existing methods of assessment.

It is in dealing with the second task — to sponsor the creation of new instruments and methods of assessment — that the APU can be seen to have had its biggest success. There is no doubt that the teams have produced exciting new material and done pioneering work in the assessment of practical skills in maths and science and in the assessment of oracy. The APU has also broken new ground in sponsoring the assessment of pupils' attitudes as part of the national surveys.

The third task — to promote the conduct of assessment in cooperation with LEAs and teachers — is rather puzzling. If the DES had meant it to mean persuading LEAs to allow the tests to be carried out in their areas and teachers to administer them in the classrooms, then the Unit has certainly succeeded, though the school refusal rate has become worryingly high. If on the other hand, as seems more probable, this task meant something more active on behalf of the LEAs, for example, LEASIB, then this has not materialized in workable form, though it may with the proposed availability to LEAs of APU items.

On the fourth task, a start has been made on looking at performance in relation to some background measures. However, many of the measures used, for example, pupil/teacher ratio and region of the country, are really of little direct use to policy-makers. More relevant variables which would relate the circumstances in which children learn, for example, size of teaching group, qualifications and experience of the teacher, resources available (particularly for science) and aims of the programme of work, have been used in the later surveys but often are not as relevant as they might appear since, for example, the particular teacher responsible for the class at the time of testing may have been less influential on the children's attainment than other teachers earlier in their education. Moreover, there can be little doubt that this type of information is not best collected via large-scale surveys but in studies of an in-depth type. It is quite clear that any attempt to look at low achievement will have to be via in-depth studies. As for making the findings available to those concerned with resource allocation, as we have said, the findings are of little value to policy-makers and, as they were reported up to mid-1983, of little value to LEAs. However, there is a considerable amount of data which could be 'mined' for its lessons to teachers and this is what the Unit, with its new dissemination policy, is aiming at. Within the Unit the emphasis seems to have shifted away from a concern with information relevant to policy-making and resource allocation towards a concern with detailed test information which could throw light on children's cognitive development.

On the Unit's other aims as outlined in their publicity material rather than in the terms of reference, namely, to provide information on standards and monitor changes in performance over time, there has been little progress. The two are related and no consensus has been reached on how to analyse trends over time. This problem has dogged the APU for several years now (see both Nuttall's chapter in this volume[19] and Goldstein's 1983 article[20] for an admirably clear discussion of the issue) and is by no means a uniquely British problem. The National Assessment of Educational Progress in the USA has also grappled with it[21] and relies on using a number of items that are common from one survey to the next to indicate change, rather than using the controversial Rasch technique. The problem with this method is that the core of items which is used regularly cannot provide a wholly representative sample of the items used in any particular survey and so the information thus provided on changes in performance over time is inevitably limited. The APU teams are also using some common items from one survey to another, for example, in maths half the items were common in the first and last annual surveys. At the end of its five-year period of surveying, each team will produce composite measures of performance over the five years which serve as a baseline (or standard) with which to compare performance measured subsequently in the five-yearly surveys. By then, the question of how to analyse trends in performance may have been answered in part. Certainly the Unit, although it said much about standards in the early days, has not attempted to define 'standards' in the sense of acceptable or looked-for performance, and will instead rely on describing measured performance over a period of several years — a far less contentious and more acceptable task — and on comparing relevant changes between groups, for example, sexes, over time. The DES, however, is not quite so circumspect: the pamphlet on the writing performance of 15-year-olds was launched as a contribution to the debate on standards 'to trigger a public debate about the content of English teaching and the standards needed' (*Times Educational Supplement*, 2 December 1983, p. 3).

What about the early fears? Teachers' concerns that national monitoring, though ostensibly to do with children's performance, could be interpreted as dealing with teachers' competencies have proved to be unfounded. The Unit's adherence to light-sampling techniques, insistence on anonymity and inclusion of teacher union representatives on the Consultative Committee have all helped to allay teachers' fears. The extent to which the APU has carried the teachers with it can be illustrated by some findings of a teacher-interview survey we carried out late in 1982: approximately 70 per cent of the primary and secondary heads interviewed (120) were in favour of national monitoring,[22] with accountability and the need to keep a check on standards to the fore in their comments.

The other concern was about its impact on the curriculum. Would the four-topic core curriculum monitored result in undue emphasis being placed on these subjects? Would what was tested one year become the curriculum in future years? The answer to the second question is no, because the APU's sampling and testing policies have prevented this happening, and if the answer to the first question is yes, then the impact of the APU on the development of a core curriculum cannot easily be separated from the influence of other factors in education. In 1982, when we published our evaluation of the APU, we felt that any impact there might be on the curriculum would be via the curriculum models adopted by the test development teams; the teams were aware of this and operated on a wide curriculum model so that any impact would be widening not narrowing, and positive not negative. Indeed in 1982 there was a certain ambivalence on the part of the APU towards its role vis-à-vis the curriculum. The APU had been accused of being a Trojan horse to bring in an assessment-led curriculum; this, however, was a slightly paranoid view of the role of central government in the educational system without sufficient awareness of the constraints on it through the countervailing power of bodies such as the National Union of Teachers. But the Unit, in order to allay fears, maintained that it would not attempt to influence the curriculum via back-door methods. That ambivalence about its curriculum role has now gone and one of the Unit's current major aims is to milk its very detailed survey findings in order to improve curriculum content and delivery — that is, teaching. This is being done via its new policy on reports, the independent evaluations and the commissioned occasional papers referred to earlier. Both APU staff and monitoring teams have given considerable time to in-service courses in LEAs, for which there is great demand particularly in the area of practical testing.

Of course, there have been considerable changes in the education scene since 1982 and the APU, with the information it can provide on levels of performance, is particularly relevant to discussions about raising standards set off by Sir Keith Joseph's Sheffield speech.[23] Though there are no formal links between the APU and the two new bodies, the Schools Curriculum Development Committee (SCDC) and the Secondary Examinations Council (SEC), that have been established by the DES to replace the Schools Council, the APU data will be fed into their committees for their early deliberations. Two particular areas of input are likely to be in helping to define grade-related criteria and in suggesting modes for the 16+ exams.[24] Of course now the DES has the SCDC, composed of its own nominees (in contrast to the Schools Council whose members were nominated by all the partners in the education service), it no longer needs the APU as a means of having some say in the curriculum.

It is instead in the area of providing detailed information to guide teaching practice that the APU's profile now seems to be highest. The incidence of low achievement, changes over time, policy decisions concerning resource allocation, making test items available to LEAs — these are all still on the agenda but one senses that they are no longer considered to be paramount. These areas are of course potentially far more problematic, particularly given the way the APU carried out its tasks up to 1982. The Unit's achievements, given the scope of the task and the newness of the ground to be covered, should not be undervalued but our view is that given a more careful structuring of early plans and more rigorous forward planning throughout, the Unit could have made more progress than it has. We know that the DES never gave the APU guidance about which policy questions to address. The aim seems to have been simply to develop a national system of assessment that functioned and was acceptable with little thought as to what specific questions it might answer. Indeed it was not until June 1981 that a list was made public, for the first time, of questions the Unit hoped to be able to answer. When the list was analysed, given the way the APU programme turned out, it was possible to provide answers to only a handful of these questions. Why did the Department or the Unit not list more clearly at the outset the policy questions to which they wanted answers? It is possible that the APU was intended solely as a monitoring exercise giving information on overall standards and nothing else. It is possible that the story of the APU is just an example of lack of forward planning. It is also possible that it was a more deliberate policy of leaving all options open in order to gain maximum cooperation from interested professional and lay people. We have concluded that the last two factors both played a part.

In 1982 the APU's future was reviewed within the DES and several crucial decisions were made:

— the dissemination policy was modified so that short, easy to read, cheap publications would be aimed at particular groups in society;
— data would eventually be made available to other researchers for secondary analysis;
— quinquennial monitoring was to be adopted in order to reduce the cost and burden on schools and to allow in-depth analysis of results by the research teams;
— definitive statements about changes in performance over time could not be made for the immediate future.

We believe that these decisions were necessary and for the good. The current moves to disseminate its findings to improve the curriculum — by, it must be admitted, anything but backdoor methods — can be given a cautious welcome (and certainly the demand from LEAs and teachers for courses and conferences seems quite considerable). However, its future impact on the curriculum is uncertain and much will depend on the APU's links with the two new organizations (the SCDC and the SEC) and how these bodies attempt to control the curriculum.

To draw back from musings about the future to comment on the APU at present, we must conclude that, though the APU's work has not to date served policy-makers, it has promoted valuable test developments which serve a broad curricular approach. As a consequence the results of the surveys have a great potential for alerting teachers to areas of weakness in teaching content and method. With the Unit's changing emphasis towards dissemination of interpreted findings this potentially beneficial influence could be released.

## Notes

1 GIPPS, C., STEADMAN, S., BLACKSTONE, T. and STIERER, B. (1983) *Testing Children: Standardized Testing in Local Education Authorities and Schools*, London, Heinemann Educational Books.
2 GIPPS, C. and GOLDSTEIN, H. (1983) *Monitoring Children: An Evaluation of the Assessment of Performance Unit*, London, Heinemann Educational Books.
3 Whenever we use the term 'APU' we are referring to the DES-based secretariat. Committees, groups and teams are always named individually.
4 Report of Sir Keith Joseph's speech to the North of England Education Conference, 6 January 1984 in *Education*, 13 January 1984.
5 DEPARTMENT OF EDUCATION AND SCIENCE (1976) *The APU — An Introduction*, London, Department of Education and Science.
6 COX, C.B. and DYSON, A. (1969) *The Fight for Education*, London, Critical Quarterly Society.
7 REPORT OF THE WORKING GROUP ON THE MEASUREMENT OF EDUCATIONAL ATTAINMENT (1971), London, DES.
8 DEPARTMENT OF EDUCATION AND SCIENCE (1975) *A Language for Life* (The Bullock Report), London, HMSO.
9 LAWTON, D. (1980) *Politics of the School Curriculum*, London, Routledge and Kegan Paul.
10 DEPARTMENT OF EDUCATION AND SCIENCE (1974) *Educational Disadvantage and the Educational Needs of Immigrants* (Cmnd 5720), London, HMSO.
11 BROADFOOT, P.M. (1979) *Assessment, Schools and Society*, London, Methuen.
12 DEPARTMENT OF EDUCATION AND SCIENCE (1977) *Education in Schools: A Consultative Document* (Cmnd 6869), London, HMSO.
13 DEPARTMENT OF EDUCATION AND SCIENCE (1978) *Assessment in Schools* (Reports on Education No. 93), London, DES.
14 PRING, R. (1980) *APU and the Core Curriculum*, Curriculum and Resource Centre, University of Exeter School of Education.

15 Letter from Jean Dawson, Administrative Head of the APU, 12 March 1984.
16 DEPARTMENT OF EDUCATION AND SCIENCE (1983) *How Well Can 15 Year Olds Write?*, London, DES.
17 See, for example, *APU Science Report for Teachers: 1, Science at Age 11*, Hatfield, Association for Science Education.
18 NUTTALL, D.L. (1983) 'Monitoring in North America', *Westminster Studies in Education*, 6, pp. 63–90.
19 NUTTALL, D.L. 'Problems in the measurement of change' (in this volume).
20 GOLDSTEIN, H. (1983) 'Measuring changes in educational attainment over time: Problems and possibilities', *Journal of Educational Measurement*, 20, 4, pp. 369–77.
21 See note 18.
22 See note 1.
23 See note 4.
24 Personal communication, Arthur Clegg, Professional Head of APU, 16 February 1984.

# Testing in the USA

Archie E. Lapointe
*National Assessment of Educational Progress*

The period 1982 to 1984 has witnessed a rather significant revolution in education in the United States of America. During the past few years a general context of discontent with the products of our educational system developed as policy-makers at the state and federal levels considered issues of youth unemployment, increasing evidence of deteriorating basic skill performance on the part of school children, and the levels of achievement of young men and women entering the military services. All of these observations were occurring during a period of diminishing enrollments, the closing of individual school buildings and large reductions in the number of teachers employed.

Finally, there was continuing concern over performance on the college admission tests (the Scholastic Aptitude Test and the American College Testing Program) both of which had seen significant score declines over a prolonged period.

All of these elements provided a ready context for action.

The catalyst for this revolution was Dr. Terrell H. Bell, the Secretary of Education under President Reagan. Early in the administration of the new President, Dr. Bell called together an impressive group of lay people and scholars to consider the condition of American education. They spent a year hearing testimony and considering the elements of the problem. Their report, entitled *A Nation At Risk* (1983), was to become one of a series of reports on the quality of American education that appeared within a short period of time. Six of them were to command considerable attention (Adler, 1982; Boyer, 1983; Finn, *et al.*, 1984; Messick, *et al.*, 1983; National Science Board, 1983; and Plisko, 1984).

The theme of all of these documents was that American education needed serious attention, with the most significant problems being identified at the secondary school level. American children were not being provided the quality education guaranteed them by the Constitution nor was the substance of their exposure to learning fair return for the investment of tax dollars. The theme of one report, *The Paiedeia Proposal* (1982) by Mortimer Adler, was that the USA had met half of its Constitutional commitment by assuring access to education to all children and the country should now address the second issue: providing each student the same quality and the same content. Several of the criticisms had to do with the fact that performance declines were occurring while expenditures for education were increasing at a rapid rate.

At the same time, the conservative administration of Ronald Reagan was attempting to move as many governmental responsibilities back to the individual states as possible. Education has traditionally been a state responsibility and there exists an equally strong tradition of resisting any attempt of the Federal Government to influence or control the curriculum or to generate national testing programs. Also the national or federal participation in education funding has always been at a very low level, usually 10 per cent or less. Most of the funding for education comes from local municipal governments (typically 50 per cent) and the second largest portion of education funding comes from the state treasuries. So it was an appropriate move to focus on the states as more and more people and all sectors of society looked for reform and improvement.

The criticisms of teachers and of the education establishment generally are well documented in several other places and it is not necessary to explore them here. The fact that there was general disillusion with the educational establishment provided opportunities for the lay sectors of the society to think about, comment upon and in many cases take action about the condition of education.

This was especially true in the case of elected politicians. Each of the fifty state governors saw this as an important issue that touched the lives of large numbers of constituents. State legislators as well perceived this as an important item around which they could mobilize opinion and take action. And they did.

Indeed a year after the publication of *The Nation At Risk*, the Federal Department of Education published a second document called *The Nation Responds* (1984). It is a series of descriptions of what each of the fifty states has done in response to the points outlined in the initial report. This is a rather impressive registry of actions taken at several levels within states and school districts to address the concerns described in the first report. Most of the fifty states have created their own commissions of one kind or another. In some cases a single state has created several commissions to look at different aspects of the curriculum or of the local institution. Many of the states have enacted new laws increasing standards for education and/or for secondary school graduation. Several of the states have strengthened their state-wide testing or assessment procedures. Over half of the states have addressed the question of teacher qualifications and have imposed, or are attempting to impose, tests that will measure the qualifications of entering teachers and/or practising teachers.

A large percentage of these decisions involve testing in one form or another. Broad categories of questions and related actions can be described as follows:

— How good or bad is local/state educational system?
  Test children and find out how they are achieving.
— How effective have the reforms of the past been?
  Compare test results of today to those of the past.
— How can we assure students will leave school with adequate skills?
  Test at several grade levels during their education and insist on performance.
— How can we improve the value of a secondary certificate or diploma?
  Award one only after students can pass a test.
— How competent are our teachers?
  Test them and find out.
— How can we assure that only competent people will become teachers in the system?
  Test all applicants to assure that they have good skills and are competent.
— How will we know if the reforms being instituted now will have been effective?
  Test now and again in a few years to determine if they have made a difference.
— How does a district or state compare to others of like characteristics?
  Use similar assessment techniques so that results will be comparable.

Many of these decisions are being turned into laws enacted by each state and several of the states are taking the additional difficult steps of increasing taxes to support these new programs.

As in every educational era, there seem to be a set of themes that underlie these events. 'Competency' remains an important word both in terms of describing what children know and can do as well as what teachers should bring to their profession. 'Higher order skills' as a phrase is being used more and more to describe a part of learning that requires more significant attention. 'Computer competence' and 'education for a technological society' are also heard more and more as the objectives of modern education are described.

A consistent theme that runs through all of these issues is the notion of *accountability*. The states and the Federal Government have consistently increased the expenditures for education during the past twenty years. Local communities, states and the Federal Government have invested large sums of money for general and specific programs to improve certain aspects of the system. Many of these have had to do with equity and providing basic services to specific groups of children, for example, minorities, non-English-speaking children and handicapped youngsters. However, large percentages of these annual budgets were devoted to improving instruction and to making materials and teachers available to improve work in the basic skills of reading, language and mathematics.

Media commentators, the legislators, and parents want to know what has happened as a result of these expenditures and efforts and why is the current concern over the condition of education so serious. What has the American public gotten for its money?

One natural response to this query is to test children, teachers and the system and find out the current status. A second answer is to continue to test over time to see if things are changing. Is the situation getting better or are declines continuing? Do trend lines in the data indicate that problems are growing?

Indeed most local school districts as well as most of the fifty states have well-established and long-standing testing programs of one kind or another. Various interested parties examined the information being generated by these tests and looked for specific answers to their questions. In many cases they found them lacking in specificity or that they were inappropriate in content. If the test results did provide information about growth or about achievement vis-à-vis specific objectives or criteria, often times it was difficult to interpret those results in terms of what students *should* know or *ought* to be able to do.

The responsibility for setting educational standards in the

United States is clearly not that of the Federal Government. Legally, the states have that charge and in most situations they pass it along to the local communities. Local school superintendents as well as state agency officials all face the same dilemma: each community represents such a great diversity of populations, of minorities and of parental interests, that it is usually very difficult if not impossible to develop a set of standards upon which all citizens of a school district or state agree.

Therefore, for example, test results that indicate that a group of children are able to achieve at certain levels with regard to certain criteria leaves the reader with a fundamental question of significance. Are these results acceptable? Could they be improved? Are we doing as well as other communities in the state or as well as other states in the nation? Are we as a nation doing as well as countries with whom we are competing? Inevitably it becomes important to turn these data into statements of performance that can be compared or juxtaposed to a set of standards.

One possibility, when faced with this kind of situation, is to compare one's results to those of others. Competition is a traditional and useful technique of most Western societies. Most of the testing that has been developed in the United States relies upon comparisons to some kind of 'norm' that reflects average or overall performance for a group of children or adults. So the notion of comparisons seems like a reasonable first step in interpreting performance statistics.

However, just as there is no national or standard curriculum in the United States, there is no national test. Nor are there any standards that are common to all states nor to school districts that administer tests. Indeed most of these objectives or standards decisions are made on local or state bases to satisfy specific and idiosyncratic sets of specifications. States and school districts want to test the content that they feel is important to their publics. They, therefore, select tests from commercial test publishers or create committees that develop tests that are specific to their objectives. As a consequence the results tend not to be comparable across school districts nor across states. Indeed many states have found that within their own boundaries it is impossible for them to compare the results of local school districts one with another. American society has always prided itself on this kind of diversification. Individuality has encouraged and permitted a kind of innovation that has proven to be very useful as we have looked for new solutions to old problems.

At another level Congress and the Federal Department of Education, looking at the fifty states, could find no bases for comparisons. The reasons for this situation again are understandable. The characteristics of the populations within each of the fifty states, the variety of objectives of those states' educational programs and the range in the amount of state resources devoted to providing educational services for young people are so great that on the face of it it would seem to make little sense. On the other hand, it can be argued that children grow up and move from state to state and that since the Federal Government is paying some portion of the educational bill, it has a responsibility to guarantee that all of its citizens are receiving a minimal educational opportunity. Added to this is an overall national concern that has to do with the quality of the human resource available to the country in order to permit us to achieve certain national objectives in science, health, defense, etc. Finally, there was a recognition on the part of the federal officials that competition has traditionally been a spur to states to try harder to achieve certain objectives. It was felt that if reasonable comparisons in education can be made, they could be an effective way to encourage positive action.

In the absence of such available comparative data the Federal Department of Education created what became known as 'the wall chart'. This was an attempt to compare educational achievement in the fifty states using available data. These data included SAT and ACT college entrance scores, information about the amount of money spent per pupil by each of the states, and certain information about dropouts and other characteristic data that were already available. The states were ranked according to these statistics and the results generated a great deal of debate. States found themselves on the bottom of the list for the wrong reasons. For example, a state in which only 4 per cent or 5 per cent of their graduating secondary school students take the college entrance test was compared against a state in which 60 per cent or 70 per cent of their students take the same test. Clearly the data are not comparable. Similarly the dropout rates of states with practically no minority populations were compared to those of states that have significant portions of their populations that are non-English-speaking.

Reactions to the 'wall chart' were vocal and negative. Several people suggested that some adaptation of the National Assessment of Educational Progress (NAEP) be used to permit the states to compare themselves one to another. It was felt that this measurement of outcomes of instruction would be a more appropriate set of characteristics to compare. It has also been suggested that a set of 'educational indicators' that would include achievement results but also information about the quality and experience of teaching staffs, about dropouts, about funding for education, etc. would provide a broader and more accurate picture that would permit more reasonable comparisons. This debate continues and will probably not achieve resolution for some time.

In the meantime the mosaic of testing practice that exists across the fifty states and the thousands of local districts in the country continues to be a feature of education in America. Those states that have imposed minimal competency testing programs are discovering the strengths and weaknesses of those kinds of actions. As results are taken seriously by school boards and by school administrators, teachers and administrators are preparing more carefully for the tests and in fact in many cases are 'teaching to the tests'. In almost all situations, however, results on these minimum competency tests do show improvement of student performance. It seems realistic to assume that they have had an impact on curriculum.

Other kinds of more general tests similar to those that have traditionally been used and are available from commercial test publishers continue to predominate. A study by the Center for the Studies in Evaluation at UCLA recently indicated that most test results continue to go unused by teachers and school administrators and as a result have little impact on school programs (Rudner, *et al.,* 1983).

Finally, an over-riding issue of concern to test publishers is the quality of their normative data. It is becoming increasingly expensive and difficult to collect sufficient information on a large enough sample of students during the test development process to generate norms that are of high quality. Test publishers must ask the co-operation of school districts for which this represents a significant intrusion and a burden they are less and less willing or able to accommodate. The publishers are concerned about this problem and are working with the testing directors of the large cities and states to find solutions.

In sum, the amount of testing done of American school children at the present time is greater than at any time in our history. These tests include the traditional publishers' offerings, tests developed by individual states and large school districts to reflect their own instructional objectives and minimum competency testing programs created to monitor state programs. Participation in the national programs for college entrance tests (the SAT and the ACT) continues to grow in spite of declining total populations of young people.

There is an increasing sophistication on the part of the lay public in interpreting test results and as a result there is a growing demand for results that can be intelligently and easily interpreted and related to the questions they feel are important.

## The National Assessment of Educational Progress

In July of 1983 the responsibility for the administration of the National Assessment of Educational Progress (NAEP) was transferred from the Education Commission of the States (ECS) to the Educational Testing Service (ETS) in Princeton, New Jersey. The grant has historically been awarded for five-year periods and the responsibility for NAEP had rested with the Education Commission of the States for about twelve years. During that time the instruments and the procedures associated with NAEP were developed and perfected by ECS and had acquired general and wide respect. The quality of the work performed at ECS has been outstanding and their success in getting the cooperation of schools has been unusually good.

Five major testing organizations competed for the grant and the decision to award it to ETS was made in March 1983 with the official transfer date in July of that same year. ETS in its proposal made a commitment to maintaining the high quality standards traditionally associated with NAEP and to ensuring the dissemination of NAEP results to wider and broader publics. In addition it proposed several new and innovative design features that would enhance both the data collection and psychometric characteristics of the assessment.

The new design proposed by ETS includes several features:

1  Putting NAEP on a 24-month cycle
   This essentially involves a commitment to collect data from the field once every two years rather than every single year. This permits the expensive field data collection process to be utilized with maximum efficiency. Each time data are collected from schools four curriculum areas will be assessed. Reading will be assessed every two years. Mathematics and writing will be assessed every four years and other curriculum areas will complete the third and fourth curriculum areas that will be assessed when space is available. In addition special probes will be conducted in conjunction with regular assessments or during the off years.
2  BIB Spiralling
   The technique of Balanced Incomplete Block spiralling of

assessment booklets represents a powerful feature in terms of the optimization of data analysis. This technique, though costly to implement because of the printing considerations (a large number of booklets each with small print runs), depends on the number of pairs of items that are answered by individual children. Analyses of common data permit reliable interpretations of their significance when matched with other pairs of answers so that a wide range of correlations are possible.

3   Background and attitude questions have been increased so that ten times as much information is asked of students as in the past. In addition to the typical socio-economic and personal background questions asked of all students, children are asked information about their experiences in subject matter courses, how they are being taught, what kinds of leisure activities they are involved in, how they feel about the curriculum area being assessed, etc., etc. As many as 350 different questions were asked during this last assessment of reading and writing and because of BIB spiralling, performance achievement can be related to any of these characteristics.

4   In the past, schools were allowed to exclude certain students from the assessment for whatever reason they deemed appropriate. While it is essential they be permitted to do this, NAEP never had a picture of what kinds of biases might be introduced into the sample of these exclusions. As of 1983/84, exclusions are still possible and permitted but each one must be explained. This practice now permits the complete description of all students; those who have answered the questions on the national assessment and those who have been excluded.

5   A teacher questionnaire has been designed and is administered to a sample of the teachers whose students complete the assessment. These are questions concerning the teacher's background, experience, training and personal techniques of teaching. Teachers are also asked questions parallel to those asked of their students about the programs being assessed. Performance data from student answer booklets can be related to these teacher characteristics.

6   Finally school characteristic questionnaires are sent to the principals of the schools in which the assessment takes place. Principals or their designees are asked to characterize the school buildings, to describe the types of programs that are

ongoing and to describe the school climate. Once again the student achievement can be related to the answers supplied on these questionnaires.

Important promises were made in the ETS proposal concerning the dissemination of NAEP data and information. In addition to the traditional reports and newsletters, ETS stated that it would make available in an aggressive way information useful and appropriate to school building principals, to teachers, to parents, to school board members, to state legislators and to the Congress. It envisages using the traditional print media and the network of professional associations as well as capitalizing on mass media tools whenever these are available or would prove to be effective.

A further commitment has to do with facilitating the use of NAEP by the various states and large city school districts. The expensive development of objectives and test items should be made available to the states for their own assessment purposes. This would permit a higher quality product than they otherwise would be able to afford. In addition, utilization of these test items permits comparisons of their results to results achieved by national and regional populations.

The National Assessment has a tradition and history of conducting special probes to collect information about various populations or in specialized curriculum areas. ETS plans to continue this practice and has one such special probe identified and in the planning stage for children of limited English-speaking ability.

Another new feature of the National Assessment has to do with the addition of an adult assessment that has been funded for the year 1984/85. This activity will collect background and attitude information as well as cognitive information about literacy skills from a sample of young adults ages 21 to 25 from across the country. The sample will be expanded to permit the collection of statistically significant data from blacks and Hispanics which represent two important segments of that population.

Rather than attempt to define literacy as a point on a scale above or below which people can function, the assessment will profile all the competencies of that sample and describe the entire range of skills and abilities. It is the intention to include this adult assessment as an ongoing part of the project.

In these various ways, then, NAEP is responding to the concerns of the community and providing the maximum amount of information to answer the key questions about standards and how they might be improved.

*Archie E. Lapointe*

## References

ADLER, M.J. (1982) *The Paiedeia Proposal: An Educational Manifesto*, New York, Macmillan.

BOYER, E.L. (1983) *High School: A Report on Secondary Education in America*, New York, Harper and Row.

FEDERAL DEPARTMENT OF EDUCATION (1984) *The Nation Responds.*

FINN, C.E., RAVITCH, D. and FANCHER, R.T. (Eds) (1984) *Against Mediocrity: The Humanities in America's High Schools*, New York, Holmes and Meier.

MESSICK, S., BEATON, A., and LORD, F. (1983) *A New Design for a New Era: National Assessment of Educational Progress Reconsidered*, Princeton, NJ, Educational Testing Service.

NATIONAL COMMITTEE ON EXCELLENCE IN EDUCATION (1983) *A Nation at Risk: The Imperative For Educational Reform*, Washington, DC.

NATIONAL SCIENCE BOARD COMMISSION ON PRECOLLEGE EDUCATION IN MATHEMATICS, SCIENCE AND TECHNOLOGY (1983) *Educating Americans for the 21st Century: A Plan of Action for Improving Mathematics, Science and Technology Education for all American Elementary and Secondary Students so that their Achievement is the Best in the World by 1995*, Washington, DC.

PLISKO, V.W. (1984) *The Condition of Education: 1984 Edition*, Washington, DC, National Center for Education Statistics.

RAVITCH, D. (1983) *The Troubled Crusade: American Education, 1945–1980*, New York, Basic Books.

RUDNER, L.M. *et al.* (Eds) (1983) *Testing in Our Schools*, Proceedings of the NIE Invitational Conference on Test Use, Washington, DC, National Institute of Education.

# Educational Assessment in the Canadian Provinces

*Les D. McLean*
*Educational Evaluation Centre,*
*The Ontario Institute for Studies in Education*

The loose confederation of provinces called Canada is impossible to describe succinctly, and nowhere is that difficulty greater than in education. Since education is exclusively a provincial responsibility, any description has to be a mixture of provincial accounts. Readers are asked to be tolerant of the necessary repetition of the names of provinces.

The provinces are alike in one respect ≏ provincial assessments of educational achievement have been started or modified since the early 1970s in response to public demand for greater accountability on the part of schools. The term 'accountability' first gained prominence in the education lexicon in the USA and was adopted in Canada soon after. Activity was evident enough that the Canadian Teachers' Federation convened a conference in early 1980 to formulate a response to this growing movement.[1] The mood of the conference was critical and suspicious. In his summation, the Secretary General of the Federation noted that assessments are not all bad if they are limited to what they 'can properly and helpfully do'. Following this faint praise, however, he said,

> But along the way it was almost as if we stopped being afraid of the return of rather naive and superficial and bad standardized testing. I think that danger does exist, and I think that we may be lulled into a false sense of security by the skills of the professional evaluators who can sell system assessment programs, and in doing so, often our resistance to what may lie beyond. (Goble, 1980, p. 35)

Provincial graduation examinations were administered in all provinces until the late 1960s. Ontario dropped theirs in 1968 and Alberta in 1973. Only Quebec and Newfoundland retained compulsory school-leaving examinations up to the present, going only so far as reducing the contribution of the exams from 100 per cent of the graduation mark to 50 per cent. There has been a return to standardized testing elsewhere, as Goble feared, but there is difference of opinion whether it is naive, superficial and bad. It is testimony to the power of examinations, any examinations, that educators are unable to assure the public by any other means that adequate standards are being maintained.

## Reintroducing Provincial Testing

There had been strong educational and social arguments for dropping province-wide testing ≃ the narrowing effect on the curriculum, the manifestly different effect of standard tests on different social and ethnic groups. Schools should tailor evaluation to the local curriculum and to their student population, it was argued. If provincial tests were to be reintroduced, therefore, the agreement, or at least the acquiescence, of teachers was desirable. Various committees and commissions were therefore struck.

British Columbia (BC) was off the mark early, with a ministerial Joint Committee on Evaluation in 1974. A Technical Advisory Committee set out plans for a BC Assessment program in a 1 July 1975 report. Management was then turned over to the Ministry of Education's new Learning Assessment Branch. The Alberta Minister's Advisory Committee on Student Achievement (MACOSA) was appointed in November 1976, and functioned as overall adviser and manager until 1981. Ontario's Work Group on Evaluation and Reporting was appointed in November 1976.

These committees and commissions had an important political function and were so constituted ≃ ministry officials, staff from faculties of education, administrators and, always, representatives of the unions (the teachers' federations). Sometimes the citizenry slipped in via the Home and School organization, but they usually had to wait to serve on committees reviewing the results of the 'assessments' recommended (to no one's surprise) by the advisory committees. The purpose of these assessments was to be program evaluation. No students or schools were to be identified. In some provinces, only provincial level results were published.

The Work Group on Evaluation and Reporting in Ontario recommended a different approach. Collections of assessment instruments were to be assembled, linked closely to the curriculum as set out in provincial guidelines, and these collections were to be made available to teachers for their use. The Ministry might also use them on a sampling basis to do program evaluation. Work was started on the first 'Assessment Instrument Pools' in 1978 and the first pools were published in 1980. The first provincial achievement survey was carried out in 1981.

Before considering the more formal testing programs that followed these initiatives in some provinces, we take a close look at assessment as carried out in all provinces except Newfoundland and Prince Edward Island. In Saskatchewan, an assessment was done only once (in 1977/78, in grades IV and X).

## Assessment Methodology

At a minimum, an assessment requires (i) collection or construction of a set of measuring instruments relevant to a domain of content; (ii) design and selection of a representative sample of students; (iii) assignment of instruments to students according to a design in which each student often responds to a small proportion of the instruments; (iv) recovery, coding, scoring, checking and entry of student responses to a computer; (v) estimation of group means and derivation of descriptive indices, with standard errors; (vi) interpretation of the results for decision makers, parents and the general public; and (vii) reporting of the results and interpretations.

Provinces have gone about these tasks in different ways and have supplemented them to various extents. In addition to collecting written compositions, most provinces included some item forms other than multichoice. Ontario's instruments in English and mathematics asked predominantly for a constructed response. Often all students were tested, rather than a sample.

Various scores were derived and scales used, and the results have been interpreted by panels of teachers, parents and officials (BC and Alberta). Most provinces collected data on attitudes to school and learning at the same time as they measured attainment. Provinces differed greatly in the extent to which they identified educational jurisdictions in publishing assessment results. The actual printing, distribution, scoring, analysis and report writing were contracted to university teams (Alberta, Ontario), private firms plus university

(BC) or conducted by the ministry. A team in the Quebec Ministry of Education began work in 1981 on an ambitious program of provincial assessments, 'end-of-cycle tests'.

## Instrumentation

New Brunswick started its 'Criterion Referenced Testing Programme' in 1977 by purchasing multichoice items from a test publisher. In 1978, however, one finds this section in their report (New Brunswick Dept. of Education, 1979, p. 1):

> In March, 1978, the Department of Education invited over thirty of the province's teachers and supervisors to Fredericton to attend a one-day conference in order to review the results of the 1977 CRT's. On the basis of that review, conference participants developed a tentative list of language arts and mathematics objectives for the fall 1978 CRT's.
>
> In early April 1978, a second group of the province's teachers and supervisors attended a one-day seminar in Fredericton sponsored by the Department of Education. The Seminar had a two-fold purpose; (i) to finalize the selection of objectives for the 1978 CRT's; and (ii) to develop skills in constructing multiple-choice test items.
>
> Those who participated in the April 1978 item-writing seminar planned and coordinated item writing sessions for other teachers in their own districts later in the month. Every school district with at least one English class (26) was asked to create fifteen to twenty multiple-choice test items for a single objective. Each district under the leadership of the Department trained person was responsible for writing items for three to six objectives.
>
> By late April 1978, approximately 1300 items were forwarded to Fredericton where they were assembled into more than eighty 'mini tests'. Each 'mini test' was composed of twelve to twenty multiple-choice items and was given to groups of thirty to sixty pupils in the appropriate grade levels. Classroom teachers who helped in the administration of the 'mini test' were asked to evaluate each item with respect of difficulty and relevance.
>
> On the basis of pretesting, teacher evaluations, and curriculum specialists' recommendations, six items per objec-

tive were selected for inclusion in the final versions of the six CRT multi-choice tests. Well over 95 per cent of the 1978 CRT items were written by New Brunswick teachers and supervisors. The remaining 5 per cent were again purchased from Thomas Nelson and Son in order to retest specific items.

A similar, if not identical, section can be found in reports from most provinces ≏ educators at appropriate levels arrive at agreed objectives and then teacher committees produce items they believe measure the objectives. Items are then given a trial run and technical vetting, usually depending on classical test construction methodology for evidence of acceptable item quality. In the end, an item collection is retained whose primary, and valuable, characteristic is its approval by a teacher committee.

Items with a very high or very low success ratio are examined (BC cites 95 per cent and 20 per cent), as are distractors that attract very few students. Where there are test scores, i.e., where item sampling has not been used, items that have very low correlations with the test score are usually deleted. BC uses five-option multi-choice, the fifth always being, 'I don't know.' An example appears in Figure 1, with results included. The 'I don't know' option all but eliminates the ambiguity of omitted responses, but the incidence and effects of guessing still remain unknown.

*Figure 1: Example of a grade 4 item and results from the 1981 British Columbia assessment*

N5. To find the missing number in 746 + __ = 931 you should:

|  | % of students |
|---|---|
| Subtract 746 from 931 | 42 |
| Add 746 to 931 | 12 |
| Subtract 931 from 746 | 25 |
| Add 931 to 746 | 4 |
| I don't know | 16 |

*Cloze tests*

In the language arts, Manitoba has used a cloze procedure to assess global reading ability in grades 3, 6, 9 and 12.[2] Both multichoice and one-word answer formats were used, the former exclusively in grade 3.

*Writing tasks*

An attempt was always made to give purpose to the written compositions. New Brunswick's 1978 survey in grades 8 and 11 asked
students to write a letter to the local television station manager,
protesting the possible cancellation of a favourite program (transac-
tional). Grade 5 students were to write to a chum who had recently
moved to another school (descriptive-narrative). The next year, all
tasks were narrative. Ontario students in grades 7, 8, 9 and 10 were
given titles and brief explanations, for example, 'Trouble always starts
when ____ is around' (supply an entry for the blank), 'How to shop
for a ___', and some were asked to write a critical analysis of school
vacations. In the Alberta assessment, tasks were varied from narrative
(grade 3), description (grade 6), exposition (grade 9) and argument
(grade 12).

Every language arts assessment included short-answer exercises
as well ≃ multichoice, error correction, sentence combination, spelling
and the like. The ever-present scoring challenge will be discussed in a
separate section.


*Reading passages*

The cloze procedure used in Manitoba was very much an exception in
assessment of reading comprehension. Most assessments employed
traditional instruments — a passage of text to be read followed by a
number of multichoice questions, but there was variety in the choice
of passages and in the length and types of questions asked. The
researchers behind the instruments reveal their beliefs about the
nature of reading in the categories they propose for their questions.

Four 'domains' were advanced in BC: (i) word attack; (ii) word
meaning; (iii) passage comprehension; and (iv) applied reading/study
skills. More items in category (i) were included in the grade 4 assessment, while greater numbers appear in categories (iii) and (iv) in
grades 8 and 12.

The Ontario Assessment Instrument Pool (OAIP) contains
seventy-seven selections from published material. Except for the
poems, they are 300–400 words in length. Each selection is accom-
panied by six to twelve multichoice questions (four options). The
questions are described (in the Pool, not in the instruments) as
directed to one of five objectives — (i) main idea; (ii) author's
purpose; (iii) meaning from context; (iv) inference and (v) significant
detail. New Brunswick stuck with main idea (grades 5 and 8) and

main and subordinate ideas (grade 11). The Ontario items in the inference category explicitly require the student to combine or extend information in the passage itself, for example,

1   According to this passage, the present policy of the Canadian Government toward the Innuit people is
    (a)   to increase pride in the Innuit's own culture;
    (b)   to help them become Canadian citizens;
    (c)   to encourage a return to a nomadic life;
    (d)   to reduce government supported services.

Inclusion of such items underlines an inescapable dilemma in reading assessment — whether to restrict questions as much as possible to discrete skills in hopes that these can be taught where needed or to approximate the actual reading process more closely (with inference, for example) and thereby construct a verbal intelligence test. The dominant choice in the last few years has been the latter.

## Mathematics

While the multichoice question is still dominant in mathematics assessment, 30 per cent of Alberta's questions were 'open-ended', and all but a few of those in the mathematics OAIP require the student to produce an answer and write it down.

The mathematics OAIP is organized in a hierarchy of fifty-five terminal objectives, many of them with one or more enabling objectives. Each objective is defined by an 'item form' from which items are generated. For Ontario's 1981 assessment, six items were generated from each terminal objective form and four from each enabling objective form, yielding more than 600 items.

## Attitudes and plans

Assessments in Canada often rely on Likert-type scales to reveal students' feelings about the subjects being assessed. BC and Ontario both used all or part of the scale, 'Mathematics and Myself', developed for the IEA Second International Mathematics Study, but the other provinces asked straightforward questions: Do you like mathematics?[3] (Alberta). Do you enjoy working in mathematics? (Manitoba). The IEA response scale has five points, with extremes 'Strongly Agree' and 'Strongly Disagree'.

Apart from attitudes and the usual characteristics (age, sex), students were often asked about future plans (quit school, go to college, ...), use of calculators and amount of homework done. Ontario asked about the language spoken at home, and where the student was in school four years prior to the assessment, the latter because length of residence has been proposed as the most important variable for understanding school achievement of immigrants whose first language is not English (Cummins, 1981).

*Sampling*

The public reports never provide enough detail to describe the designed samples for provincial assessments accurately, and information on the executed and achieved samples is rarely released. British Columbia tested in all grade 4, 8, and 12 classrooms in their 1977 mathematics assessment (enrollment in grade 8 was 46,888), but began sampling from large districts in 1981 (BC reports results by district).

A 10 per cent sample was drawn for the 1979/80 reading assessment in Manitoba, where an unusual option system permitted schools to test all students or just a portion. If all students were tested, the provincial ministry got its 10 per cent by means of sealed lists that schools used to select results to send to the ministry. The 10 per cent choice yielded just over 1500 papers in each of grades 3, 6 and 9 and 978 in grade 12. No error estimates were offered for the results by sex, skill area and stream in the summary report that was available. The advantage of mandated testing programs becomes clear when one reads that students in advanced streams devoted 150 minutes of testing time to the mathematics assessment, answering over ninety items.

Ontario has about 130,000 pupils per grade in grades 7, 8, 9 and 10, half of them within 80 km of Toronto (the provincial capital) and the other half scattered over an irregularly shaped area more than 1600 km on one diagonal. Schools were finely stratified (seventeen strata) and a sample of 180 schools selected with probability proportional to size. The number of schools, classes and students was chosen to provide at least 150 responses per item per grade to the 600 maths and 1000 English items. Complex matrix sampling of content was obviously required. Full details have been published (McLean, 1983).

The 1979 Alberta mathematics assessment also utilized complex school and content sampling (10 per cent of schools, 120 items per grade) that is said to be described in detail in the contractor's technical report to the Minister's Advisory committee. The claim is made that a difference in percentage correct of 6 or more points on any item (between grade 3 and grade 6, for example) was significant at the 5 per cent level, an impressive degree of precision, if true. Given the difficulty of calculating standard errors in data from complex samples, the technical report would bear reading.

A marvelously candid quotation from the British Columbia contractor, BC Research, seems appropriate to end this section.

> The sampling procedures used to meet the desired criteria are based partly on technical principles derived from the body of sampling theory and partly on a healthy dose of common sense.

*Analysis*

Interpretations in all reports are based on straightforward estimates of the percentage of pupils giving correct answers to items, objectives or subtests. One has to dig deeply to discover standard errors, the usual practice being to report percentages without any discussion of bias or precision and without mention of weighting. If available at all, such discussions appear in technical reports not usually published.

An exception was mentioned above, under sampling, where the authors of the Alberta mathematics assessment report cited overall error bounds. Reflecting a different perspective on weighting, they wrote, 'No weighting scheme was used or needed to be used in calculating the arithmetic means since the number of items assigned to a given mathematical topic was in proportion to its emphasis in the curriculum at that Division, as specified by the various guides issued by Alberta Education for use by schools.' (Olson, Sawada and Sigurdson, 1979, p. 8.)

It is difficult to believe that the designed, implemented and achieved student samples were so excellent in all cases that no attention to weighting was indicated in calculating the percentage correct estimates. Even if so, the estimation of realistic standard errors would still be difficult. Some mention of the statistical techniques used, perhaps in a footnote or appendix, would allow a more informed appreciation of the results.

Another omission is curious. One topic has clearly dominated the educational measurement literature in North America in the past five years — item response theory (IRT) utilizing logistic latent trait models. One of these, the one-parameter (Rasch) model has been used extensively in district and statewide assessments in the US. None of the Canadian reports mentions use of IRT models, though BC is known to have experimented with the Rasch model and to have calibrated some of their assessment results.[4] Perhaps the failure of the US National Assessment of Educational Progress (NAEP) to jump on the bandwagon had some influence. The first Canadian report appeared before the NFER took its decision to abandon work on the Rasch model in the UK.

*Interpretation and Reporting*

Interpretation panels are struck in BC for each subject assessment. The panels contain teachers, officials, parents and representatives of business, whose job it is to go over the results with the contract team and rate the outcomes as weak, marginal, satisfactory, very satisfactory and strong. Panel members are asked to take into account the difficulty of the item as well as its importance in the curriculum. This proves difficult, as the authors of the 1981 BC report noted (Robitaille, 1981), citing the example reproduced in this chapter as Figure 1. This proved a difficult item for the grade 4 pupils, most of whom would have been 10 years of age, and yet the panel rated the performance as marginal.

New Brunswick and Alberta refer results to similar panels, while Manitoba has their outcomes rated by teachers and officials at regional meetings. Ontario asked the members of its assessment project committees to prepare comments on student performance as recorded in the 1981 assessment, and these comments were included in the published report.

More sensitive than the interpretations is the level of reporting. All provinces carefully guard the identity of students, teachers and schools in public reports, but most provinces calculate results at the school or district level and provide each district with its results, related to the provincial mean. The district, or Board of Education, is the organizational unit for financing, setting curriculum and governance of the schools — the local authority. Governance is normally provided by an elected board of trustees — hence the term 'School Board.' The Ontario Ministry of Education has given an undertaking that 'students, teachers, schools or boards will not be identifiable'.

New Brunswick and BC are provinces that do not publish

results at the district level but instead supply them to the district on a confidential basis. District officials are then free to release results as and if they wish. Knowledge of the existence of such results is usually sufficient to ensure their release. Quebec first announced that they would publish results of their end-of-cycle assessments on a regional basis (as NAEP does), but realization of the sample sizes required to achieve adequate precision led them to abandon the calculation of regional estimates.

## Follow-up to Assessments

Alberta provides an accessible case study, thanks to good coverage of events in the *ATA News*, a weekly publication of the Alberta Teachers' Association. We can find both chronology and colour in this far-from-unbiased source.

The MACOSA report in May 1979 summarized the numerous studies and surveys commissioned by the Committee (including assessments in reading, writing, mathematics, science and social studies) and made seventeen recommendations. Among these were:

1 Provincial examinations should not be reinstituted.
2 Annual province-wide samples of student achievement should be collected — on a three-year cycle for each subject area.
3 Feasibility of a computerized item bank should be studied.
4 Members of the public should join teachers in validating assessment instruments, which should include some topics outside the specified core curriculum. (The first part of No 4 was the only recommendation with which the ATA disagreed.)
5 Regional offices of the ministry should provide school jurisdictions with consultation services.

Public hearings were held and a further report issued in April 1980. Sixty-five per cent of submissions were favourable or gave conditional support to the proposal for annual assessments, while only 5 per cent were opposed. A like number *supported* the reinstatement of provincial exams but almost 30 per cent were opposed. Only 5 per cent had no opinion about provincial exams. Six questions on MACOSA were part of a Gallup Poll about this time, and the results agreed with those obtained in the public hearings. The ATA President was not happy — 'It's unfortunate that the most recent results are being taken to be the most credible,' he said, and challenged the government to justify the heavy emphasis being given to the Gallup survey. 'MACOSA was more thorough, involved representatives from a variety of fields, and made serious proposals on how to solve evaluation problems. Because it was a detailed study, it didn't lend itself to snappy headlines in the press, or a simple emotional reaction' (*ATA News*, 28 April 1980).

Nothing major happened for seven months, as teachers stepped up their campaign against departmental exams. The assessment results, admittedly not very striking, were forgotten. Then, the 17 November *ATA News* carried the headline, 'Provincial Exams are Back.' 'Diagnostic tests will be given in grades 1, 4 and 7, achievement tests annually in grades 3, 6, 9 and 12 (sample basis), and comprehensive exams in grade 12 will be made available to any student *as an option* at the end of each semester.'

Four comprehensive exams were offered: (a) literacy; (b) computation skills; (c) understanding history and social science; and (d) understanding physical and biological science. Students and adults who wrote and passed the 'optional' exams received a Comprehensive Education Certificate. Those who failed were allowed to rewrite.

The Minister's solution appeared to be wonderfully astute. He embraced the actions favoured by the public while stopping short of reinstituting old-style provincial exams. There was concern, however, just how optional the comprehensives were in practice and how much of a steering effect they would begin to exert on the curriculum and on teaching. The Minister made no bones about it: 'The (testing) program will evaluate teachers, school systems, and programs'.

The ATA President praised the government for everything but the comprehensives. 'They will be effectively mandatory for all those going on to higher education,' he said. Because not all students will write them, 'we are not likely to get as big a warp in the curriculum, or as much centralization as we would have had, if competency exams or departmentals had been introduced'. Teachers and students expressed the expected range of concerns (teaching to the test, teacher evaluation, . . .), and social studies teachers expressed concern for the new curriculum they were just in the process of implementing. They felt another change would disrupt things permanently. Some were optimistic, a science teacher suggesting that more teachers would see links among the biological and physical sciences. Only a few were skeptical that tests could be developed with the advertised characteristics.

After the first round of optional examinations it was clear that they were a mistake. Many students wrote them, but participation was uneven and student motivation was low. The teachers' approach ranged from neglect to hostility, and no one was pleased. The Minister quickly made up his mind — he announced that mandatory graduation exams would recommence in January 1984, for students completing their high school program in mid-year. The graduation mark would be half-examination and half-school mark. Six subjects were subsequently examined in an atmosphere more of relief than of hostility. The achievement testing was expected to continue on a sampling basis in grades 3, 6, 9 and 12, with districts being responsible for follow-up activities as and when they identified the need.

British Columbia has a comprehensive plan for follow-up, involving meetings between provincial and local officials to review the district's results and suggest actions. No systematic information is available on the success of these plans, but anecdotal reports speak of a district spending the entire materials budget buying a dictionary for each pupil when their district scored low on dictionary skills. More common was an announced resolve to give 'more attention' to the lagging topic, with no indication which topics would receive less. In parallel with Alberta, British Columbia reintroduced mandatory graduation examinations (counting 50 per cent of the final mark) in January 1984.

## Unresolved Issues

Aspects of assessment that remain problematic include concerns of a technical or methodological kind, conceptual issues not admitting of a technical solution and mixtures of the two.

### Open, Closed or Mixed Pools

If instruments are kept secure (not revealed except on the tests themselves), then they can be reused with some confidence that answers are not simply memorized responses. The disadvantage lies in the difficulty of communicating what is being tested. The difficulty is related to a concern discussed below — clarity of domain definition. Often, the only way to be clear is to reveal the questions. When the objective is to monitor system-wide functioning and influence the system for the better, a fully closed (secure) pool is counter-productive.

If a pool is to be open and assessment results credible, however, the pool has to be large enough not only to rule out memorization but also to avoid giving undue advantage by virtue of partial exposure. Given the scope of our ambitions for schooling, this means very large pools indeed. The open English OAIP for grades 7–10 comes in two thick volumes, for example, and is by no means complete. Many jurisdictions opt for partial release of instruments after use, for example NAEP's release of 25 per cent of their items each year.

### The Utility of Constructed Responses

Modern computers have made it feasible to capture and process large numbers of complex student responses accurately and consistently. The Ontario assessment involved 106 different booklets (counting teacher and student attitude surveys), the achievement booklets containing a majority of constructed responses — numbers and short paragraphs as well as strokes through words and corrections written in above the strokes. About 600 students responded to each achievement booklet. All responses were first entered into a computer, checked and sorted. Unique constructed responses were then printed out for hand scoring and the scores re-entered and matched with responses. The multichoice items were scored by the computer. It was not uncommon to find 100 different answers to a simple mathematics problem among the 600 responses, and sentence completion exercises were even more diverse, as one would expect.

Processing constructed responses in this way has several advantages over hand-scoring from the booklets themselves. First, consistency in marking is easier to achieve because all responses to one item are marked together (they are printed out on one or two pages, with like responses adjacent). The marker(s) can verify immediately how a similar response has been marked previously, a difficult task if hundreds of booklets have to be re-examined. Second, efficiency is high because scorers work very rapidly — identical responses need be scored only once, for example. Third, the responses are preserved so that error and pattern analyses can be carried out.

Although no comparative study has been done, it was clear that the costs of the computer-based system were not greater than a traditional hand-scoring system would have been for such a large volume because the costs of data entry were offset by lower scoring costs. Now that the development costs of the system have been absorbed and the software refined, constructed responses can be captured at a cost comparable to multichoice. The scoring itself is much more efficient, and development of open-response items is less expensive than for multichoice.

It therefore appears that assessments should employ the type of item that best measures student achievement. It is no longer necessary to rely on multichoice items for practical reasons. In a second provincial assessment in Ontario (of senior chemistry and physics) some items originally cast in multichoice form were redone as open response and the solutions coded for direct entry. A valuable lesson was learned with some items that were *too* open. Student performance was sufficiently poor that no insights were gained as to their strengths or weaknesses.

The last point brings us back to the question of utility. Preserving responses is of no value if no one ever looks at them except to score right or wrong (or on a scale). If a straightforward ranking of students is all that is required, then a relatively short multichoice examination is almost surely the most efficient tool. If program monitoring is the goal, then it is hard to make a case for multichoice at all. Whatever one's objectives, the practical option of constructed response opens the choice of evaluation method wider than it was before.

### Units of Analysis and the Measurement of Change

Given good sample designs and careful weighting of responses to compensate for departures from these designs, we can calculate unbiased estimates of the percentage of students in a population who know how to answer a question (or a group of questions). But is that the most useful number? It can be useful to political decision-makers, that much is clear. What it glosses over is the large variability among schools, and sometimes among classes within schools — variability among the units where instruction takes place.

Even if overall monitoring is the objective and improvement of instruction only a distant goal, one can still argue for measurement of performance at the school level because it yields a truer picture of the patterns of achievement. To illustrate the point, Figure 2 contains distributions of means for each of four grades in Ontario schools of student achievement on eighteen items calling for addition, subtraction, multiplication and division of decimals.

The features such plots convey that other statistical summaries

*Figure 2:  Distributions of school means on decimal fraction items from the
OAIP.*

> Note:  Boxes cover the middle 50 per cent of school means and
> crosses mark the median. Dotted lines run to the maximum and
> minimum values except that school means lying more than 1.5
> box-lengths from the end of a box are marked by asterisks.
> Separate plots are given for the four grades in which students are
> about 12 to 16 years of age.

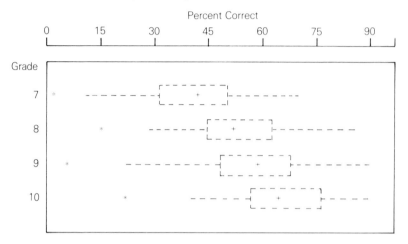

reveal only with difficulty are the large differences in performance
among schools. We know those differences exist and know them to
be strongly influenced by social and economic factors quite out of the
school's control, but the magnitude of the range surprises some
readers. Decision-making should confront the diversity in attainment
when purporting to monitor performance and not always settle for
the cross in the middle of the box.

The challenge of measuring change over time is complicated by
the diversity among schools. The Alberta mathematics assessors
created 'indexes' whose main utility was said to be the measurement
of change at some time in the future. By their definition, an 'index
number' is a p-value and an index is an average p-value, the only
added information being that items are included in the average in
proportion to the degree of emphasis a topic is supposed to receive in
the curriculum (according to the provincial guideline).

The indexes bring out the difficulties of measuring change in
attainment over time. Suppose results of an assessment are interpreted
as unsatisfactory (Index A, for example, is too small). A highly likely
response is a change in emphasis (more time devoted to the topic),
since if teachers knew a better way to teach A they would already be

doing it. By definition, therefore, more items would be added to the set used to estimate Index A. Items would presumably be deleted from sets B and C. Are they still the same indexes? If their estimated values all increase the next time, shall we conclude that attainment is higher? Could it be that the items added (or deleted) were easier (more difficult) than those used in the previous index estimate? How could we know, since better learning will make all items seem easier?

By this reasoning we will have to use the same items at time 2 that we used at time 1, and there will have to be enough of them that teaching to the test will not, to use the ATA president's word, 'warp' the curriculum. Indexes have the same appeal as Rasch-scaled items and the same problems. They are less expensive, however. The BC approach will be described in the next section.

### *Meaningful Curriculum Domains*

If assessments are to serve as a guide in revising the curriculum and teaching methods, the measures must reflect teaching topics, many of which are constructs teachers hold in their heads. It is not at all clear that the present categories comprise the most meaningful topics. At the grade 8 (age 13) level, for example, should we mix fractions and decimals under arithmetic? What about operations with positive and negative integers? Is an English item asking for a correction of errors of subject-verb agreement to be lumped with sentence combination or completion items scored for consistent verb usage? It would appear to this author that we proceed too uncritically to define our domains — and our indexes. A mathematics assessment contract team in BC was more thoughtful.

Realizing that domain definition is crucial to measurement of change, the team wrote the following in the 1981 BC mathematics report. (Robitaille, 1981, pp. 85–6.)

> ... In 1977, the Assessment focussed on three levels of cognitive behavior as the basis for reporting achievement. Three domains — Computation and Knowledge, Comprehension, and Applications — were used as major reporting units, each ranging across various content areas. In 1981, on the other hand, the basis for reporting consisted of a number of domains defined by content: Number and Operation, Geometry, Measurement, Algebraic Topics, and Computer Literacy. Hence, the problem of reporting change was compounded by two differing definitions of the term 'domain'.

This lack of congruence forced the adoption of a new reporting unit for change, the *Change Category*. The number and content of Change Categories at each grade level were dependent upon how many 1977 items were suitable for use in 1981. Such items were selected according to a number of criteria:

* they had to suit the domains defined in 1981, since they were not to be set off in a separate group for change analysis only;
* they had to provide a good cross-section of the content defined for each Change Category;
* their 1977 p-values were to be less than 0.80 in order to allow for the possibility of growth in 1981, that is, to avoid possible ceiling effects.

A further consideration in developing the mechanism for reporting change was the number of items to be used in each Change Category. Because the measurement and reporting of change is a sensitive issue it was felt that there was a need to assign a considerable number of items to each Change Category. For Grades 4 and 8 this number was set at twelve; for Grade 12 it was set at ten since there were fewer items in total to be used at this level. As a result, two or three categories were defined at each grade level. The categories are shown in Table 4–5, along with the number of items in each. These items were not pilot tested as sufficient information on their suitability was available from 1977.

*Table 4–5: Change Categories*

| Grade 4 | Grade 8 | Grade 12 |
| --- | --- | --- |
| Number and Operation (12) | Number and Operation (15) | Number and Operation (10) |
| Measurement (11)* | Geometry and Measurement (12) | Geometry and Measurement (10)** |
| | | Algebra (10) |

*Only eleven items were available in this category.
**Reduced to nine in the Assessment due to a printing error on the final instruments.

The BC report illustrates the best of current practice. Educators have domains in their mind (Number and Operation, Geometry, Measurement) and end up giving operational definition to these domains with 'considerable' numbers of items (ten–fifteen), often items that are on-hand and not demonstrably evil. One notes that items with 1977 p-values greater than 0.80 were not used because of ceiling effects, but no mention was made of possible floor effects.

*Validity*

Validity isn't the main thing, it's everything. This position, eloquently put recently by Messick (1981), has received little explicit attention in the assessment context, and this concluding section can hardly redress the balance. It seems an appropriate topic with which to close, however, since it comprises so many of the issues in assessment.

As Cronbach and Meehl taught us some years ago (1955), one should be concerned with the uses to which measures are put — with the validity of the *interpretations* of the measurement. What a sobering thought. Political decision-makers and educational officials everywhere interpret assessment results as evidence that schools are, or are not, 'doing a good job'. Too seldom do they add the phrase, '. . . of helping students to learn the narrow range of knowledge and skills accessible to our measurement devices'. Against the manifold objectives society has assigned to schools, our assessments loom narrow indeed.

The titles of our reports may promise too much: *British Columbia Mathematics Assessment 1981* (has all of mathematics been assessed?); *Student Achievement in Alberta*. Some are less pretentious: *A Report on the New Brunswick Criterion-Referenced Testing Program; The Manitoba Reading Assessment. Progress from 7 to 10 in OAIP Mathematics* is deliberately enigmatic (what's OAIP mathematics?). *Standards of Numeracy in Central Region*, the Scottish Council thunders. The APU reported, *Mathematical Development: Primary Survey Report*. In the US, NAEP grew bolder recently with *Reading, Thinking, and Writing*.

We have to live with some restrictions to validity due to the narrow scope of our measurement, but what can be done within our scope? Taking a cue from Campbell and Stanley (1966), consider these threats to internal validity: poor samples of students and behavior, errors in data capture, distortions in scoring and analysis.

These errors have cumulative effects and often compound one another.

### *Poor samples*

As noted above, most reports ask us to accept on faith the quality of the sample of students. Given that the essence of assessment is generalization to the student population of the province, and given that designing such a sample requires not only high technical skill but also a good knowledge of schools and access to detailed information (school types and sizes, community characteristics, . . .), both the designed and achieved samples deserve more attention. In Ontario, an independent sampling referee was employed, who produced an eleven-page critique of the sample design.[5]

Content sampling is always a problem. As noted in a previous section, Ontario generated six examples from the item form for each of fifty-five terminal objectives. The range of p-values within grade for the six items indicated that this was adequate for some but not all forms. Few projects can sample items, most having to rely on judgment samples with unknown validity.

Low student motivation can be a threat to the validity of monitoring activities, since success or failure have no consequences for the student. We have a poor sample of student behaviour if students make only a cursory or half-hearted attempt to respond correctly. Normally we just ask the students to do their best and take what we get.

Evidence that the problem can be severe was obtained in an unplanned quasi-experiment in Alberta, when examinations were given two weeks apart in a rural authority. The first was part of a provincial monitoring programme (not affecting student marks) and the second was a graduation examination still retained owing to the small size and restricted resources of the authority. On average, the marks of students writing both examinations were 20 per cent higher on the graduation examination, a difference that could not be explained by the difficulty of the items. The special circumstances make generalization hazardous, but it is clear that student motivation must remain a concern.

Multichoice items pose an extreme threat to the validity of the sample of student behaviour. It would be just too tedious to repeat over and over that the results reflect only such attainment as can be inferred from selection of one of four or five choices, but assessment reports that rely on multichoice questions should be liberally sprinkled with such caveats.

As discussed above, the added expense of collecting and scoring constructed responses can surely be offset, at least in part, by the value of the larger sample of student behaviour they provide. No matter how excellent the sample of student behaviour, however, it will be of no value unless captured with few errors and summarized well in the scoring.

### Data entry errors

No evidence is offered in public reports that the data analysed were a valid representation of students' responses. Again, faith is required. Since data entry errors are more likely to reduce the number of correct responses than increase them (very much more so if responses are constructed rather than multichoice), some note of the measures taken would be reassuring to knowledgeable readers.

Constructed responses pose a special problem. In Ontario, where *all* responses were entered to the computer verbatim (numeratim?) by clerks working at video display terminals, special means of verification had to be devised. In addition to careful training and close supervision, quality control was provided by a computer program with which the nature (letter or number) and length of each entry was anticipated and controlled. Many types of errors could therefore not be made at all (a number for a character and vice versa, a word if single letter was appropriate, . . .).

Data volumes were so great, however, that full verification would have been a forbidding expense. An analysis (McLean, 1981) indicated that a small proportion of certain kinds of errors would make no practical difference to the achievement estimates, so a verification procedure was devised based on the sequential probability ratio test (Wald, 1947). Use of random sampling permitted certification of each clerk's batch (one-two hours work) by checking less than 1 per cent of the entries. Spot checks on whole batches confirmed that the scheme worked well.

### Distortions in scoring

Scoring is a form of data reduction that always means a loss of information. Holistic scoring of English compositions (assignment of a single number to each composition) is an extreme but understandably common example. Reduction is not necessarily distortion, however, and various steps are normally taken to reduce bias. The same set of compositions is placed in every scorer's pile to allow calibration of scorers for consistently high or low marking and detection of odd patterns. Based on nine such 'embedded' compositions, four of twenty-five Ontario scorers were identified as applying some sort of different standards from the others. Their scores were therefore set aside before calculating summary statistics.

When there are several hundred booklets to score, distortion in scoring short answer responses can arise from inconsistent application of standards. Ontario's computer-based scheme was discussed above. Other jurisdictions employ various checks, all of them very costly but unavoidable if bias is to be kept at a low level. Where individual student scores must be retained (such as in graduation examinations), scoring standards must be even higher.

*Poor analysis*

The problems of sample weighting and error estimation have been mentioned, the first risking biased estimates and the second erroneous conclusions. More serious errors are likely to be made in analysis of data from classrooms and schools as if they were simple random samples of students (see, for example, Aitken, Bennett and Hesketh, 1981). Space limitations prevent even a cursory discussion under this heading, but poor data analysis can be a serious threat to the validity of our results, and hence our interpretations. From reading many reports, this author thinks it probable that some contractors spend hundreds of thousands of dollars putting together a high quality data set and then only a few thousand on the data analysis.

## Summative Evaluation — Do Assessments Help Schooling?

With one or more rounds of surveys behind them, several provinces are no doubt assessing their assessments. One program director asked this author if assessments 'made any difference at all', the tone of voice conveying clearly that he didn't think so. The Alberta Minister of Education went ahead with even more testing than his advisory committee had recommended, but concrete plans to utilize results fed back to the schools are conspicuous by their absence. The implication seems to be that everyone will know what to do when they receive the monitoring (or examination) results.

Knowing what to do is especially difficult in first language instruction. Interpretation of the results from the New Brunswick Writing Assessment Program was contracted to an independent educator — the Chief Reader. He described the reality teachers face this way:

> The broader, deeper and more subtle elements in language development are not so susceptible to direct instruction and to meticulously sequenced curriculum programs. A first language simply does not develop in this manner, and growth in a first language depends on a great many variables, not only beyond the range of the English classroom but beyond the range of the school itself. (Roberts, 1980, p. 3)

What the Chief Reader might have added is that broad, deep and subtle elements not so susceptible to direct instruction are even less susceptible to mass measurement.

The popularity of mathematics as an assessment topic would lead one to think there was great progress to be made in that area, but such is not the case. We do not appear to be any closer in mathematics than we are in mother tongue to linking our measurement to our teaching methods. Research on teaching and research on evaluation are carried out by different groups working in different worlds, two solitudes that rarely touch or greet each other.[6]

This review thus has to end on a note of suspended judgment tinged with pessimism. Assessment is flourishing in the Canadian provinces, from sea to sea, but rarely do they have a systematic process in place for discussing the results and planning follow-up actions. Assessment results are useful to political leaders, however, who oversee still-large expenditures on schooling at a time of falling rolls. Perhaps we on the operational end should not be too critical. We have no claim to a profession, however, until we try even harder to increase and extend the validity of our measures, to get close enough to the realities of teaching and learning that our results are directly relevant to classroom processes.

## Appendix: Addresses for Assessment Information in Provincial Ministries of Education

Alberta Education, Planning and Research Branch,
11160 Jasper Avenue
Edmonton, Alberta, L5K 0L2.

British Columbia Ministry of Education,
Learning Assessment Branch,
7451 Elmbridge Way,
Richmond, BC, V6X 1B8.

Manitoba Department of Education,
Measurement and Evaluation Branch,
307–1181 Portage Avenue,
Winnipeg, Manitoba, R3G 0T3.

New Brunswick Department of Education,
Evaluation Branch,
P.O. Box 6000,
Fredericton, N B, E3B 5H1.

Ontario Ministry of Education,
Research and Evaluation Branch,
Mowat Block,
Queen's Park,
Toronto, Ontario, M7A 1L2.

Québec Ministère de l'Education,
Direction générale du développement pédagogique,
1035, rue de la Chevrotiere,
Québec, G1R 5A5.

## Notes

1 Canadian Teachers' Federation (1980) *Province-wide Student Assessment Programs — The Teachers' Response*, Proceedings of a national seminar, Winnipeg, Manitoba, Ottawa, Canadian Teachers' Federation.
2 Every fifth word was deleted from each passage, regardless of grammatical category. Grade 3 students are predominantly 8 years of age; grade 12 or its equivalent is the last year of secondary school in all provinces except Ontario.

3 *Percentage responses by grades*

| Options | | | Grades | |
|---|---|---|---|---|
| | 1–3 | 4–6 | 7–9 | 10–12 |
| A  No, I'm afraid of it | 3 | 2 | 4 | 6 |
| B  No, I hate it | 11 | 12 | 17 | 19 |
| C  Yes, a bit | 39 | 58 | 59 | 56 |
| D  Yes, very much | 47 | 28 | 20 | 19 |

4 The British Columbia unit of calibration was dubbed the Brit.
5 The referee concluded that given proper weighting, unbiased estimates of means could be produced, but that provision for error estimation was inadequte.
6 Love consists in this,
   that two solitudes protect,
   and touch and greet each other.
        Rainer Maria Rilke

## References

AITKEN, M., BENNETT, S.N. and HESKETH, J. (1981) 'Teaching styles and pupil progress: a re-analysis', *British Journal of Educational Psychology*, 51, 2, pp. 170–86.

CAMPBELL, D.T. and STANLEY, J.C. (1966) *Experimental and Quasi-Experimental Designs for Research*, Chicago, Rand McNally.

CUMMINS, J. (1981) 'Age on arrival and immigrant second language learning in Canada: A reassessment', *Applied Linguistics*, 2, 2, pp. 132–49.

CRONBACH, L.J. and MEEHL, P.E. (1955) 'Construct validity in psychological tests', *Psychological Bulletin*, 52, pp. 281–302.

GOBLE, N. (1980) 'Summation — What Next?' in *Province-Wide Student Assessment Programs — The Teachers' Response*, Ottawa, Canadian Teachers' Federation.

MACOSA (1980) *Student Achievement in Alberta*, Edmonton, Alberta, Alberta Education.

McLEAN, L.D. (1981) 'The effects of entry errors', Toronto, Ontario Institute for Studies in Education, Educational Evaluation Centre (mimeo.)

McLEAN, L.D. (1983) *Report of the 1981 Field Trials in English and Mathematics — Intermediate Division*, Toronto, Ontario Ministry of Education.

MESSICK, S. (1981) 'Evidence and ethics in the evaluation of tests', *Educational Researcher*, 10, 9, pp. 9–20.

NEW BRUNSWICK DEPARTMENT OF EDUCATION (1979) *A Report on the New Brunswick Criterion-Referenced Testing Programme — 1978*, Fredericton, New Brunswick, Evaluation Branch, Department of Education.

OLSON, J.T., SAWADA, D. and SIGURDSON, S.E. (1979) *Alberta Assessment of School Mathematics — Condensed Report*, Edmonton, Alberta, Alberta Education.

*Les D. McLean*

ROBERTS, B. (1980) *The 1979 New Brunswick Writing Assessment Program: Summary Version*, Fredericton, New Brunswick, Evaluation Branch, Department of Education.

ROBITAILLE, D.F. (Ed.) (1981) *British Columbia Mathematics Assessment 1981 — General Report*, Victoria, BC, Learning Assessment Branch, Ministry of Education.

WALD, L. (1947) *Sequential Analysis*, New York, Wiley. (The Ontario Institute for Studies in Education application is described in MCLEAN, L.D. (1981) 'Data quality control', Toronto, OISE Educational Evaluation Centre, mimeo.)

*Section 3*

# Problems in the Measurement of Change

*Desmond L. Nuttall*
*The Open University*

The essence of education is change, the acquisition of mental processes, skills and attitudes that were not present before, or the development and improvement of existing ones. It follows that the assessment or measurement of this change is important in education, both to chart the development and to match teaching strategies to the individual's changing needs. A good example of instruments designed for this purpose are the checklists focussing on children's development in scientific thinking developed by Harlen *et al.* (1977). This formative use of assessment is becoming more widely recognized and promoted, as Black's chapter in this volume demonstrates.

But the measurement of change is fraught with problems, especially in the common research strategy using pretest — post-test designs yielding gain scores (see, for example, Harris, 1963). Cronbach and Furby (1970) go as far as to argue that 'gain scores are rarely useful, no matter how they may be adjusted or refined' (p. 68) and offer some recommended procedures that obviate the need to estimate change scores for individuals. The reanalysis by Aitken, Bennett and Hesketh (1981) of Bennett's (1976) study of teaching styles and pupil progress avoids the use of gain scores, and by working at the level of classrooms rather than individuals largely circumvents the key problem of the unreliability of the pretest and post-test scores. But the focus of most longitudinal studies is on the individual; in such cases, statistical modelling taking into account the errors of measurement as set forth by Goldstein (1979a) and Kessler and Greenberg (1981) becomes essential.

This chapter is principally concerned, however, not with the problems of measuring change in individuals, but in the performance of national educational systems and sub-systems, a subject that has been gaining prominence on both sides of the Atlantic over the last fifteen years or so (Husen, 1979). In Britain, there has been a persistent campaign, most obviously in the Black Papers on education and fully documented and evaluated in The Open University (1981a), to discredit so-called progressive methods of education by pointing to an alleged decline in standards of educational performance, especially in reading and mathematics.

Such allegations, coupled with the wider issues of accountability and effective policy-making based on sound information, have led to the establishment of national (or regional) testing programmes designed to collect information about educational performance and to chart changes in the levels of performance. The idea of measuring change was not ostensibly important in the establishment of the Assessment of Performance Unit (APU) in England and Wales: the Unit's terms of reference are 'to promote the development of methods of assessing and monitoring the achievement of children at school, and to seek to identify the incidence of under-achievement'. The tasks amplifying these terms of reference make no reference to the measurement of change but, as Gipps points out in her chapter in this volume, the publicity material produced by the APU in its early years carried the clear message that the APU's role was to monitor in order to provide information on standards and how these change over time.

There was never any doubt that the National Assessment of Educational Progress (NAEP) in the USA should measure changes in educational attainment over time (Forbes, 1982). The evaluation of NAEP by Wirtz and Lapointe (1982) reaffirms the importance of this particular aim, and links it to public expectations:

> The Assessment also identifies changes in student achievement levels over periods of time, characteristically four-year or five-year periods. There are some who challenge the reliability of such comparisons and others who question their value. Whether something is better or worse than it used to be seems less important than whether the present condition is good or bad, satisfactory or unsatisfactory. Yet the popular attraction of comparisons is plain, and the Assessment's titular claim to measuring 'Progress' reflects a widely accepted value. (p. 8)

In Canada, the provincial assessment systems were heavily influenced by NAEP and the measurement of change is an explicit aim in at least two provinces (Alberta and British Columbia) and probably in most, if not all, as McLean demonstrates elsewhere in this volume.

The emergence of these large-scale assessment systems designed, in part at least, to measure changes in the level of educational performance, has led to a considerable debate in Britain (but apparently not in the USA) about the most appropriate techniques for measuring change, if indeed it is sensible to attempt such measurement at all. There are two basic strategies, the use of the same tests (or items) on the different occasions and the use of different tests, in the latter case spawning a variety of techniques. These strategies are critically examined in turn below.

## The Use of the Same Tests

One of the best-known examples of this strategy is the series of studies of reading comprehension between the 1940s and the 1970s (Start and Wells, 1972). Two tests were used (the Watts-Vernon and the NS6), the second also being used in the first APU survey of language development (DES, 1981), thus linking the older series of studies with the new. Although on the authors' own admission the 1970/71 studies were deficient on a number of counts (caustically elaborated upon by Burke and Lewis, 1975), the apparent decline in scores seen in those studies was sufficient to stimulate the establishment of a Government Committee of Enquiry that reported in 1975 (DES, 1975) and was one of the triggers for the establishment of the APU.

One of the most telling criticisms of the study by Start and Wells is that the tests were becoming increasingly dated in the language used. Words such as 'mannequin' and 'wheelwright' were not uncommon when the tests were developed, but are virtually unheard today. Any decline in test score might therefore not be reflecting a decline in the literacy of schoolchildren when faced with realistic and relevant text but a change in the difficulty of certain of the test items and thus of the test itself. What is ostensibly the same test, relied upon as an unchanging yardstick, is in reality slowly changing its nature. Much social and educational research over time is prone to similar problems: one example is in the changing rates of various types of crime (see The Open University, 1981b). Crime may appear to be increasing, not because the number of criminal incidents alters, but because there is a greater willingness on the part of the public to report them, sometimes just because of changing social attitudes but on other occasions as a result of changing social policy and law (such as the change that allowed rape victims to remain unnamed in court).

In the period up to 1983 when NAEP was administered by the Education Commission of the States in Denver, its strategy was also to make direct comparisons through re-use of the same items (administered in as similar a manner as possible) in successive surveys. (For more detail of the method see Nuttall, 1983.) A high proportion of items are released after each survey, so that the proportion of questions that can be used in more than three successive surveys (spanning twelve or so years) is negligible. As events transpired, NAEP in Denver was never obliged to devise a strategy for measuring changes in performance over longer periods, though some sort of chaining of surveys would, of course, have been possible (the first with the second and third, the second with the third and fourth, and so on). The risk of cumulative chaining error would become progressively greater, but linguistic and social factors are less likely to disturb item difficulty if the 'lifespan' of an item remains limited to little more than a decade.

One drawback of the original NAEP strategy is the limited number of questions on which direct comparisons were possible. Questions were (properly) chosen for release after each survey more or less at random, except where it was obvious that they might date (as was the case with some questions in social studies). There was some risk, nevertheless, that the questions common to two surveys were not representative of the questions in either survey.

The domain defined by the common questions may therefore be narrower than the domain of interest in any given year. This was clearly so in the British Columbian comparison of 1977 and 1981 mathematics surveys, as described by McLean in this volume. The Change Categories, comprising items used in both 1977 and 1981, though carefully constructed, did not themselves represent the whole domain of mathematical achievement that was considered worthy of assessing in 1981. As McLean says, domain definition is crucial to the measurement of change; one might add that changes in domain definition (to be expected in the light of curriculum development) undermine the measurement of change. This point is elaborated below. The use of the same tests (or items) is therefore difficult to defend because inevitable curricular, social and linguistic change will convert what appears to be an unchanging yardstick into a piece of elastic. Moreover, the use of the same tests (which become increasingly dated) may increase the difficulties of allowing national assessment systems to address today's and tomorrow's educational problems in line with their other aims — what one evaluation of NAEP characterized as the dangers of 'an unholy alliance with the past' (quoted by Wirtz and Lapointe, 1982, p. 70). Wirtz and Lapointe themselves warn of the dangers of concentrating too much upon techniques that permit comparisons over time, to the extent that broader educational goals that might lead to the raising of standards are neglected.

## The Use of Different Tests

Beside these important educational objections to the continuing use of the same tests, practical reasons resulting from the release of questions in published reports make reliance upon the same items effectively impossible over any substantial period (as with NAEP).

### Latent Trait Theory

One obvious candidate to solve the measurement problem created by a changing item pool is latent trait theory. For the APU, the one-parameter (Rasch) model was favoured — there being no guessing problem with the items — and strongly advocated by those concerned with the monitoring of mathematical and language development. In the latter case, the rating scale and possible differences between raters necessitated a generalization of the model (DES, 1981). But the criticisms (Goldstein and Blinkhorn, 1977; Nuttall, 1979a; Goldstein, 1979b and 1980) were such as to lead to the virtual abandonment of latent trait models by the APU. Criticisms were at two interacting levels: the technical and the educational. The technical criticisms are now by-and-large well known, and common to most psychological and educational applications. A most thorough and trenchant evaluation of these criticisms is given by Traub and Wolfe (1981), focussing particularly on dimensionality and goodness of fit. Goldstein's (1980) demonstration of estimation bias in the fixed-effects model is also a very telling contribution to the swelling literature of the limitations of latent trait models.

But these technical criticisms pale into insignificance beside the educational criticisms. The essence of the process of education is to achieve change in behaviour, change that is (in practice if not in theory) not identical in each individual. The invariance of item parameters (apart from a scaling constant) implied by the Rasch model sits unhappily with the notion of educational change. This proposition is at its most obvious when the order of difficulty of items is compared across groups receiving different kinds of, and amounts, of teaching.

The APU's testing strategy means that some students will face items on topics that they have never been taught (topics A and B, say). For them, such items will appear relatively harder than items on topics (C and D, say) which they have been taught; for a group of students taught topics A and B but not C and D, the relative difficulty of the items is reversed, and the latent trait model breaks down. Ostensibly, a simple solution would be to apply the model separately within each domain (A+B, and C+D) but in practice the number of possible combinations of topics studied and not studied by different groups of students is so large that analysis by each topic would almost certainly degenerate into analysis item by item — the *reductio ad absurdum* foreseen by McDonald (1981).

The measurement of change over time further highlights the inapplicability of latent trait models in the context of the work of the APU. Not only must the item pool be replenished (to make up for items released to the public) but it must be maintained relevant to the curriculum. This implies that the domain specification is changing, and that some items will be discarded as being no longer appropriate. One obvious operationalization of this concept of item inappropriateness is that the difficulty of the item changes relative to the other items in the pool; in other words, an item that once fitted that latent trait model no longer fits it. This again exposes the inherent contradiction between parameter invariance and educational change. These sorts of considerations led Traub and Wolfe (1981), echoing Goldstein, to conclude

> ... we view as potentially dangerous the practice of applying latent trait scaling over time and over educational programs where instruction varies. (p. 380)

Despite these strictures, the new management of NAEP at Educational Testing Service (ETS) is actively investigating the use of latent trait methods, especially the three-parameter model, for the study of changes in performance over time (Messick, Beaton and Lord, 1983). ETS has been in the vanguard of the development and application of latent trait theory (under the leadership of Lord) and is increasingly using the theory in its vast programme of test equating, especially for new forms of the Scholastic Aptitude Test (Holland and Rubin, 1982). Messick *et al.* (1983) acknowledge some of the technical limitations of the theory, particularly the crucial assumption of unidimensionality, but indicate how with the new procedures for the sampling of items (Balanced Incomplete Block Spiralling) it becomes possible to estimate item covariances and hence to explore the dimensionality of the data in a way that was not possible with matrix sampling. They state that they will 'determine how the exercises in a skill area can be subdivided into subareas that are roughly unidimensional. . . . If a few exercises do not fit this procedure, they will be removed from the IRT [latent trait] analysis and analyzed by conventional methods such as proportion-correct' (Messick *et al.*, 1983, pp. 44–5).

On the educational criticisms of latent trait theory, the ETS proposals are silent and the quotation above suggests that technical considerations like fit to the model — itself a highly contentious issue as the review by Nuttall (1983) shows — will prevail over educational judgments concerning the validity and comprehensiveness of the areas and subareas. Given the debate that has taken place in the UK over the last few years (a debate that is not unfamiliar in the US through papers such as Goldstein's (1983) and personal contacts), the fervent advocacy of latent trait methods by ETS is somewhat surprising. But their position is quite clear: the perceived advantages 'make IRT scaling not only ideal for NAEP purposes, but essential' (Messick *et al.*, 1983, p. 85).

In fairness, it must be said that ETS is not planning to rely exclusively upon latent trait methodology. Messick *et al.* describe two major approaches to trend analysis that will be used. The first is at the level of the exercise or item (implying the reuse of the same ones over time), analysing the interactions 'subpopulation x item x years' which if they existed would negate the use of the Rasch model. The second is at the level of the scale (for example, reading comprehension, computation) and will similarly explore interactions: it is not wholly clear how the scale scores will be derived and latent trait methods might well be used.

This account demonstrates an interesting and contrasting change in attitudes towards the use of latent trait models. In England and Wales they were strongly advocated in the mid-1970s and used in the early stages of the work of the APU, but in response to much criticism their use has all but been abandoned in national and local monitoring. In the USA, the first years of national monitoring eschewed their use (but not apparently for the reasons that they have been rejected for in the UK), whereas in the mid-1980s their use is now being ardently and apparently rather uncritically promoted.

Desmond L. Nuttall

## Generalizability Theory

The APU science monitoring team rejected the Rasch model because of their expectation of high student x item interaction, particularly likely because of their process model of the curriculum and curricular differences between schools. Johnson (1982) cites the study of Hively et al. (1968) in which they found student x item effects (admittedly confounded with other interactions and the residual) accounting for some 45 to 50 per cent of the total variance for various kinds of arithmetic test. In her own work on science tests, she found percentage contributions varying between 45 and 64 for the pupil x question interaction (unconfounded).

Johnson and her co-workers (Johnson and Hartley, 1981; Johnson and Bell, in press) have therefore been advocating an approach based on generalizability theory (Cronbach et al., 1972). As its practical use has not been fully reported yet, it is difficult to evaluate, but two immediate criticisms suggest themselves. The key to the approach is the estimation of sampling variance when different samples of items are drawn from the same pool: but is the universe of items well enough defined (i.e. is the domain well enough specified) and are the items in the pool well enough prepared to allow us to assume that the items in the pool are a random sample from the universe? The more general controversy over this issue is well summarized by Shavelson and Webb (1981). On the one hand Loevinger (1965) argues that sampling cannot be random unless one can catalogue or display all possible members of the population (at least in principle). On the other hand, the concept of exchangeability put forward by de Finetti (1964) allows one to consider simply whether the actual items are exchangeable with other potential items without the necessity to catalogue the whole population. This less stringent criterion may still be hard to meet in the early stages of the development of an item pool, as Johnson and Bell (in press) implicitly acknowledge.

The second criticism concerns changes in the domain specification (and hence the definition of the universe of items) and in item difficulty: generalizability theory, like latent trait theory, cannot cope with changing domains or universes, or with items that change in difficulty for cultural reasons. Johnson and Bell (in press) acknowledge this in their concluding sentence:

But there will always remain a potential risk to unambiguous interpretation of the resulting temporal data if the dynamic question pools from which survey questions are selected are ill-defined *and* allowed to change in nature during updating.

## The Subjective Approach

The complexity of the interpretation of changes in test scores and the wide variety of social, cultural, educational and curricular factors that influence the changes are widely acknowledged. For example, Wirtz *et al.* (1977) pointed to the educational and social changes that complicated the interpretation of the significance of the decline in Scholastic Aptitude Test scores over the last twenty-five years. Austin and Garber (1982) similarly stress the need to view educational test score changes 'within the context of a *changing* educational and social milieu, whereas vocal critics view the context as unchanging' (p. 248). Farr and Fay (1982) begin to propose a way in which the broader changes might be taken into account:

> Any responsible comparison of achievement test scores from different time periods must consider a host of factors that may operate on the groups tested and that may vary across time. Such factors involve educational, demographic, economic and other societal factors which act as uncontrolled variables. Events, situations and attitudes unique to time periods ought to be included and studied among such factors.
>
> Since such factors can interact in highly complex ways, most cannot be mathematically removed from the test scores and, so, must be weighed subjectively. While this should not inhibit recognition of a study's potential importance, conclusions and implications of any trend study are open to question and to interpretation from numerous perspectives. The achievement trend analysis which ignores such factors, however, is much more limited than one which takes them into account. (p. 136)

Subjective judgment has always played a large part in the principal achievement testing activity in Britain, the systems of public examinations. These systems customarily make public all the questions used each year and therefore constantly have to face the problem of relating performance on different sets of questions over time (as well as between the examinations in the same subject set by different boards and schools, or by the same board on alternative syllabuses, in the same year). Typical procedures (and possible solutions to the problems of the maintenance of grading standards) are described by Christie and Forrest (1981).

The basic approach is simply to ask a panel of subject experts (the awarders) to 'carry' a notion of a fixed level of performance (for each level of achievement publicly certified) and to apply that notion to performance on any appropriate set of questions constituting an examination in that subject. On many occasions, when the syllabus remains unchanged from year to year, the sets of questions will be roughly parallel but, when the domain specification undergoes revision, the awarders are obliged to do their best to translate the fixed level of performance to a comparable level of performance defined by new criteria. Translated into the context of the APU, Nuttall (1979a and 1981) has proposed that the method might be applied thus: samples of completed test booklets (objective by objective, or domain by domain) at scores representing the 5th, 25th, 50th, 75th and 95th percentiles would be drawn for each of the years involved in the comparison. The task of the panel of experts would be to judge whether the samples at each percentile point represented a similar or a different standard of performance.

There have been many formal investigations of the comparability of public examination standards, with cross-moderation (that is, the remarking and regrading of work by other examiners) being the method currently favoured. All methods have revealed the complexity of the problem of comparability, one of the most difficult aspects hinging on the difficulty of comparing tests with different domain specifications (Bardell *et al.*, 1978; Nuttall, 1979b; Orr and Nuttall, 1983; Goldstein, in this volume).

One merit of the panel approach is that the panel has the option of declaring the comparison invalid, as happened in effect in one of the most sophisticated British studies of examination standards over time (Christie and Forrest, 1980). The domain specification of chemistry at GCE advanced level had changed so much over the period under review (1963 to 1973) that a direct comparison of standards was impossible. Moreover, on those occasions when a panel considers that direct comparison remains possible, they can make subtle adjustments for change in the content or coverage of the test (and assign less weight to skills or topics that are declining in importance, and more to those that are increasing in importance). A further advantage is that a panel would be likely to detect and draw attention only to differences that are of some educational significance.

Introducing subjectivity into the process of measuring changes in performance thus has a number of potential advantages over more mechanistic, and seemingly more objective, processes, but is, of course, not without its problems. Even professionally trained judges have difficulty in assessing the likely performance of students on tests or specific items as the studies by Thorndike (1982) and Black *et al.* (1984) show; the latter warn how societal and professional expectations can be inconsistent as well as inaccurate. It is clearly necessary for subjective accounts to be as reflexive as possible, to avoid keeping hidden the sort of assumptions that are too readily hidden in technically complex methodologies like latent trait and generalizability analyses.

The use of panels to comment upon the findings of surveys (as opposed to judging changes in performance levels) is already an established practice in North America. Wirtz and Lapointe (1982) praise the relatively recent introduction of this practice at NAEP at Denver, and McLean (in this volume) cites three Canadian provinces — British Columbia, New Brunswick and Alberta — that employ panels. The use of panels to comment upon results raises a final very important issue about attempts to measure change in standards, namely the gathering of suitable data about policy and practice in the schools that might help to explain changes in standard. Gardner (1982) points to the very many competing explanations that were offered for the decline in SAT scores; most of these explanations were conjectural, necessarily so in the absence of hard information about social and curricular changes.

Nuttall (1980) argues that attempts to measure change in performance without measuring changes in important educational variables at the level of local authorities and schools (for example, resource provision, staffing standards) and at the level of classrooms (at the very least using a measure of opportunity-to-learn) is pointless and likely to be fruitless, though even if such concomitant educational changes are measured cause-and-effect relationships will be hard to establish in surveys of this kind. Farr and Fay (1982), Wirtz and Lapointe (1982), Messick *et al.* (1983) and McLean (in this volume) also argue for more efforts to be made to collect educationally important background variables so that the results of surveys can be more easily interpreted and put to use.

## Conclusions

The main conclusion is that the measurement of change in the level of performance of educational systems is not possible as there is no way of establishing an unchanging measuring instrument over any length of time. Indeed, there are dangers in attempting to do so because such a measuring instrument cannot adapt to meet current needs or concerns. Procedures claiming to meet the need for the domain specification to vary over time while reporting results on an unchanging scale have also been shown to be inadequate.

If public expectation obliges some comparisons over time to be made, then a method involving panels along the lines described above offers a more sensitive and adaptable way that might prevent chalk being compared with cheese. Alternative strategies have also been offered by Goldstein (1981 and 1983). The first draws upon experience of longitudinal studies (Goldstein, 1979a) and proposes using the school as the basic unit of analysis, sampling in such a way that a proportion of schools would recur in each time sample. This approach also appeals to Messick *et al.* (1983), though they note substantial practical problems. The second is to chart changes in relative *differences* between sub-groups over the years, rather than to attempt direct comparisons between years. These proposals are currently being refined and developed, and are the topic of a research project at the National Foundation for Educational Research (Gipps, in this volume). But whatever strategy is adopted, the exercise will be pointless unless important educational variables other than performance are also systematically assessed.

At the time of writing (mid-1984), the debate about methods continues but major reports using most of the major approaches discussed in this chapter have yet to be published. The reports of the APU surveys, covering the first two or three years in each field (mathematics, language and science), have said little or nothing about comparisons between years (though the reports reviewing the first five years in which surveys were conducted annually will surely do so). The work of NAEP at ETS and, with a few exceptions, the work of the Canadian provinces (see McLean in this volume) is too recent to have yielded published comparisons over time.

Once these reports begin to appear, the debate will inevitably hot up again. Meanwhile almost all experts in Britain, and most in Canada, take the view that strong assumptions of invariance in the way that items behave or are interpreted are unwarranted in education where change is of the essence of the process, if not its *raison d'être*. Change in the items and the domain specifications must therefore be explicitly acknowledged and subjectively allowed for.

## References

AITKEN, M., BENNETT, S.N. and HESKETH, J. (1981) 'Teaching styles and pupil progress: A re-analysis', *British Journal of Educational Psychology*, 51, 2, pp. 170–86.

AUSTIN, G.R. and GARBER, H. (1982) 'The implications for society', in AUSTIN, G.R. and GARBER, H. (Eds) *The Rise and Fall of National Test Scores*, New York, Academic Press.

BARDELL, G.S., FORREST, G.M. and SHOESMITH, D.J. (1978) *Comparability in GCE*, Manchester, Joint Matriculation Board.

BENNETT, S.N. (1976) *Teaching Styles and Pupil Progress*, London, Open Books.

BLACK, P., HARLEN, W. and ORGEE, T. (1984) *Standards of Performance — Expectations and Reality*, APU Occasional Paper No. 3, London, Department of Education and Science.

BURKE, E. and LEWIS, D.G. (1975) 'Standards of reading: A critical review of some recent studies', *Educational Research*, 17, pp. 163–74.

CHRISTIE, T. and FORREST, G.M. (1980) *Standards at GCE A-Level: 1963 and 1973*, London, Macmillan Education.

CHRISTIE, T. and FORREST, G.M. (1981) *Defining Public Examination Standards*, London, Macmillan Education.

CRONBACH, L.J. and FURBY, L. (1970) 'How we should measure "change" — or should we?', *Psychological Bulletin*, 74, 1, pp. 68–80.

CRONBACH, L.J., GLESER, G.C., NANDA, H. and RAJARATNAM, N. (1972) *The Dependability of Behavioral Measurements*, New York, Wiley.

de FINETTI, B. (1964) 'Foresight: Its logical laws, its subjective sources', in KYBURG, H.E. and SMOKLER, G.E. (Eds) *Studies in Subjective Probability*, New York, Wiley.

DEPARTMENT OF EDUCATION AND SCIENCE (1975) *A Language for Life* (the Bullock Report), London, HMSO.

DEPARTMENT OF EDUCATION AND SCIENCE (1981) *Language Performance in Schools: Primary Report No. 1*, London, HMSO.

FARR, R. and FAY, L. (1982) 'Reading trend data in the United States: A mandate for caveats and cautions', in AUSTIN, G.R. and GARBER, H. (Eds) *The Rise and Fall of National Test Scores*, New York, Academic Press.

FORBES, R.H. (1982) 'Testing in the USA', *Educational Analysis*, 4, 3, pp. 69–78.

GARDNER, E. (1982) 'Some aspects of the use and misuse of standardized aptitude and achievement tests', in WIGDOR, A.K. and GARNER, W.R. (Eds) *Ability Testing: Uses, Consequences, and Controversies*, Part II, Washington, D.C., National Academy Press.

GOLDSTEIN, H. (1979a) *The Design and Analysis of Longitudinal Studies*, London, Academic Press.

GOLDSTEIN, H. (1979b) 'Consequences of using the Rasch model for educational assessment', *British Educational Research Journal*, 5, 2, pp. 211–20.

GOLDSTEIN, H. (1980) 'Dimensionality, bias, independence and measurement scale problems in latent trait test score models', *British Journal of*

*Mathematical and Statistical Psychology*, 33, 2, pp. 234–46.

GOLDSTEIN, H. (1981) 'Measuring trends in test performance over time', paper presented to the APU Invitational Seminar on Monitoring over Time, London, June.

GOLDSTEIN, H. (1983) 'Measuring changes in educational attainment over time: Problems and possibilities', *Journal of Educational Measurement*, 20, 4, pp. 369–77.

GOLDSTEIN, H. and BLINKHORN, S. (1977) 'Monitoring educational standards — an inappropriate model', *Bulletin of the British Psychological Society*, 30, pp. 309–11.

HARLEN, W., DARWIN, A. and MURPHY, M. (1977) *Match and Mismatch: Raising Questions*, Edinburgh, Oliver and Boyd.

HARRIS, C.W. (Ed.) (1963) *Problems in Measuring Change*, Madison, University of Wisconsin Press.

HIVELY, W., PATTERSON, H.L. and SAGE, S.H. (1968) 'A universe-defined system of arithmetic tests', *Educational Measurement*, 5, pp. 275–90.

HOLLAND, P.W. and RUBIN, D.B. (Eds) (1982) *Test Equating*, New York, Academic Press.

HUSEN, T. (1979) *The School in Question*, Oxford, Oxford University Press.

JOHNSON, S. (1982) 'Monitoring science performance: comparability and reliability considerations', paper presented to the Fifth International Symposium on Educational Testing held at the University of Stirling, Scotland, June/July.

JOHNSON, S. and BELL, J.F. (in press) 'Evaluating and predicting survey efficiency using generalizability theory', *Journal of Educational Measurement*, summer 1985.

JOHNSON, S. and HARTLEY, R. (1981) 'Generalizability theory and national monitoring of science performance', paper presented to the APU Invitational Seminar on Monitoring over Time, London, June.

KESSLER, R.C. and GREENBERG, D.F. (1981) *Linear Panel Analysis: Models of Quantitative Change*, New York, Academic Press.

LOEVINGER, J. (1965) 'Person and population as psychometric concepts', *Psychological Review*, 72, pp. 143–55.

McDONALD, R.P. (1981) 'The dimensionality of tests and items', *British Journal of Mathematical and Statistical Psychology*, 34, pp. 100–17.

MESSICK, S., BEATON, A. and LORD, F. (1983) *A New Design for a New Era*, Princeton, NJ, ETS/NAEP.

NUTTALL, D.L. (1979a) 'A rash attempt to measure standards', Supplement to *Education*, 21 September, pp. ii–iii.

NUTTALL, D.L. (1979b) 'The myth of comparability', *Journal of the National Association of Inspectors and Educational Advisers*, 11, pp. 16–18.

NUTTALL, D.L. (1980) 'Will the APU rule the curriculum?', Supplement to *Education*, 6 June, pp. ix–x.

NUTTALL, D.L. (1981) 'Assessing changes in performance over time', paper presented to the APU Invitational Seminar on Monitoring over Time, London, June.

NUTTALL, D.L. (1983) 'Monitoring in North America', *Westminster Studies in Education*, 6, pp. 63–90.

OPEN UNIVERSITY (1981a) *E200: Contemporary Issues in Education, Unit 15, Approaches to Teaching*, Milton Keynes, Open University Press.

OPEN UNIVERSITY (1981b) *E200: Contemporary Issues in Education, Unit 17, Schools and Deviance*, Milton Keynes, Open University Press.

ORR, L. and NUTTALL, D.L. (1983) *Determining Standards in the Proposed Single System of Examining at 16+*, London, Schools Council.

SHAVELSON, R.J. and WEBB, N. (1981) 'Generalizability theory: 1973–1980', *British Journal of Mathematical and Statistical Psychology*, 34, pp. 133–66.

START, K.B. and WELLS, B.K. (1972) *The Trend of Reading Standards*, Slough, National Foundation for Educational Research.

THORNDIKE, R.L. (1982) 'Item and score conversion by pooled judgment', in HOLLAND, P.W. and RUBIN, D.B. (Eds) *Test Equating*, New York, Academic Press.

TRAUB, R.E. and WOLFE, R.G. (1981) 'Latent trait theories and the assessment of educational achievement', *Review of Research in Education*, 9, pp. 377–435.

WIRTZ, W. et al. (1977) *On Further Examination: Report of the Advisory Panel on the Scholastic Aptitude Test Score Decline*, New York, College Entrance Examination Board.

WIRTZ, W. and LAPOINTE, A. (1982) *Measuring the Quality of Education: A Report on Assessing Educational Progress*, Washington, D.C., Wirtz and Lapointe.

# Models for Equating Test Scores and for Studying the Comparability of Public Examinations

*Harvey Goldstein*
*University of London Institute of Education*

It is often felt to be necessary, when different educational or other mental tests are given to individuals, to be able to 'equate' the scores on the different tests. Thus for two tests, for every score x on the one test a single 'equivalent' score y is needed on the other test. In this way we obtain a unique conversion, or transformation, from one scale to the other. It will then not matter which test is actually given to an individual, since all individuals can each be assigned a final score on the same scale. For example, if we wished to change tests over a period of time in order to avoid any one test becoming too widely known and thus easier for subsequent candidates, an equating procedure between the tests would still allow all candidates to be compared. Such a motivation lies behind the procedures adopted by the British public exam boards in their 'comparability' exercises.

It is possible to imagine a number of procedures for producing equivalent scores, for example, by transforming separately the distribution of each test score so that it has a standard normal distribution, which means that any score can be given the equivalent normalized score. Alternatively, a sample of individuals could each be given the two (or more) tests and a suitable empirical relationship between the test scores be used to transform one into another. In the following section some basic requirements needed for test scores to be equatable will be outlined, with a discussion of models which incorporate these requirements. Practical methods of estimating equating relationships will be referred to, and references to more detailed discussions will be given where they are available. A valuable reference is the volume edited by Holland and Rubin (1982) which provides the most comprehensive account of modern test equating theory. The so-called comparability problem in public examination results will be discussed, and some suggestions will be made for alternative procedures.

## The Theory of Test Equating

One of the fundamental assumptions in test score theory is that an individual's observed test score (X) consists of two components, his or her 'true score' (T) and a 'measurement error' (e) which add together to give the observed score thus

$$X = T + e \qquad\qquad (1)$$

where the mean value of e in repeated testing is $E(e) = 0$.

Typically, it is the true scores which we are interested in equating, although some authors have argued in favour of observed score equating (see, for example, Braun and Holland, 1982). A major problem with observed score equating, however, is that where measurement error distributions differ, the equated scores generally will have different population distributions, in particular different reliabilities. Thus, confidence intervals for true scores, or for the proportion of the population selected by a cut score, will depend on the 'parent' test — an undesirable feature.

In practice, once a true score equating function has been derived, it is the observed scores with which the function has to be used. This procedure may be justified on the grounds that an individual's observed score is an unbiased estimate of her or his true score and thus of the equated true score. In fact, other estimates may often be preferred. For example, if estimates of reliability and other population distribution parameters are available, so-called 'shrunken' estimates of true scores could be used. A practical difficulty with such procedures would arise, however, if individuals are able to choose which estimates to use, for example, by choosing to be regarded as a member of one particular sub-population so that their equated score could be maximized. The advantage of the observed score is that it is an unbiased estimate for any given set of circumstances. Potthoff (1982) gives a detailed discussion of methods based on the equating of true scores estimated from observed scores.

Suppose that we have two tests with observed scores X, Y, whose true scores S, T are to be equated. For equating to be possible we require every score S to be equivalent to one and only one score T in a strictly increasing or decreasing order. Thus, in the population, every individual with a given true score, say S, on the first test will have an equated true score, say $T_1$, on the second test.

We can write this formally as:

$$S_1 \equiv T_1 \qquad (2)$$

If we now consider the observed scores X, Y then (2) becomes

$$E(X|S_1) = E(Y|T_1) \qquad (3)$$

where $E(X|S_1)$ stands for the mean value of the observed X for an individual with true value $S_1$; likewise for $E(Y|T_1)$. Equation (3) is referred to as the 'weak' definition of equating. Lord (1977 and 1980) proposes a strong definition of equating. Not only does he require (3) to be true but also, after equating to a common scale, that the distribution of X about $S_1$ is identical to the distribution of Y about $T_1$, in particular that the variances of the corresponding measurement errors are equal. Lord justifies this additional requirement on the grounds of 'equity' by which he means that an individual who is equally happy whether he takes test 1 or test 2 must, rationally, want the measurement accuracy of each test to be equal, arguing that a test with a small measurement error variance should be preferred to one with a large measurement error variance. This assumes, however, that individuals have a particular kind of 'utility function' with a very high 'cost' attached to having an observed score a long way from the actual true score. Alternative utility functions are quite plausible, however. For example, large measurement errors will be associated with large over-estimates as well as large under-estimates and an individual, particularly one with low ability, may well prefer to 'gamble' on turning up a large over-estimate of ability. Lord's condition therefore seems to be too constraining. It is also very restrictive in effectively limiting the types of test which can be equated to those which are strictly parallel. In fact, in the later discussion (Lord, 1980), he is forced to consider practical methods of approximate equating for the majority of tests which do not satisfy his extra condition. It seems more sensible and realistic, therefore, to avoid that difficulty and to take equation (3) as the fundamental definition of equated tests (see also Morris, 1982).

We now need to specify how to operationalize expression (2), that is, to define a 'transformation' of the S scores to the T scores. For example, it might be a simple linear transformation

$$T = a + bS$$

and in general we may write T as a function of S

$$T = f(S) \tag{4}$$

where f(S) defines a monotonic relationship, that is, a relationship that is one to one and preserves the ordering.

Equation (4) can be extended readily to a series of tests. Such a series of related tests forms a 'unidimensional' set in the sense that once an individual is assigned a true score on one test, his true scores on the others are also uniquely defined. Note, however, that each separate test itself need not be composed of a unidimensional set of items, so that the test scores might, for example, be determined by a combination of two or more factors.

While (4) may refer to any monotonic relationship, it is simplest to begin with a linear one. A suitable 'model' for this case is the one known as the congeneric test score model described by Jöreskog (1971), the simplest version of which is

$$X_i = a_i + b_i T + e_i \tag{5}$$

where i refers to a test, X the observed score on that test, T the true score, $e_i$ a measurement error and $a_i$, $b_i$ scaling or equating parameters.

The usual assumptions for this model are

$$\text{covariance } (T, e_i) = E(e_i) = 0$$

and for convenience we can set

$$E(T) = 0, \text{ variance } (T) = 1$$

If $a_i = 0$ and $b_i = 1$ then the tests are known as tau-equivalent and if in addition the variances of the $e_i$ are all equal then the tests are parallel.

The problem of equating then becomes the one of finding good estimates of $a_i$, $b_i$ for each test, since when these are available, if we define

$$X_i' = (X_i - a_i)/b_i \tag{6}$$

then we have for two tests i, j

$$E(X_i'|T) = E(X_j'|T) = T \tag{7}$$

which is simply equation (3) with T being the true score on the common single dimension. Thus (7) satisfies our definition of equated scores and the transformation in equation (6) is known as a linear equating procedure (LP). Note that (7) does not require the measurement error variances to be equal so that we do not require tests to be parallel.

Now the variance of X is $b^2_i/R_i$ and the mean of $X_i$ is $a_i$, where $R_i$ is the reliability of the $i$th test. Thus if we have a good estimate of $R_i$ then we can estimate $b_i$ and $a_i$ by $\{R_i \text{ variance } (X_i)\}^{1/2}$ and $X_i$ respectively. Where several tests are to be equated, efficient 'maximum likelihood' methods are available (see, for example, Werts *et al.*, 1980).

While the linear model (5) is relatively easy to deal with, in practice many relationships are non-linear. In principle (5) could be extended to include non-linear terms, but this would not only complicate the analysis, but it would also be difficult in any one case to know precisely which non-linear terms to include. A more flexible approach is the so-called equipercentile (EP) procedure. The aim of this is to rank in order the true scores on each test in order to obtain the cumulative probability distributions and then equate the equivalent percentile values. If a general non-linear monotonic relationship given by (4) exists, then since the whole population of individuals will be ranked (on their true scores) in exactly the same order by each test, an equating of the percentiles of the cumulative probability functions of the true scores will produce the required result. As with the LP method we do not require equal measurement error variances, but we must take care in the estimation. This is because the mean value of a percentile estimated consistently from an observed score distribution is not equal to the same percentile of the true score distribution. From equation (1) we obtain the usual relationship

$$\text{variance } (X) = \text{variance } (T) + \text{variance}(e)$$

with

$$R = \text{variance}(T)/\text{variance}(X)$$

Thus, a given percentile, say the ninety-fifth, corresponds to different values of the observed and true score distributions, and the observed scores need to be 'shrunk' to correspond to the distribution of true scores. If we assume that the distributions can be described in terms of their means and variances then we simply need to multiply the observed values (measured about the mean) by the square root of the reliability. It is then the percentiles of these shrunken distributions which are equated. Of course, when the measurement error variances are equal, then the raw scores can be equated directly. In order to obtain good 'smoothed' estimates of the cumulative distributions a combination of 'eye-fitting' and automatic procedures such as spline-fitting will usually suffice, although large samples will be necessary in order accurately to locate the extreme percentiles.

More recently, latent trait models have been used for equating. Accounts of the procedure can be found in Marco *et al.* (1980) and Peterson *et al.* (1982). Briefly, these models relate the responses of the constituent items of a test to an assumed unidimensional 'ability' for each individual and to one or more parameters relating to each item. Using either separate random samples or common tests, the item parameters for all tests can be estimated, thus enabling the ability of an individual who responds to any of the tests to be estimated. The use of latent trait models has been advocated for 'vertical test equating' where the performance of groups of markedly different ability is to be equated. Because they deal with items rather than the test scores, latent trait models require special assumptions, such as uni-dimensionality of items, to be made. These, however, give rise to difficulties (Goldstein, 1980) and the use of such models seems problematical. Moreover, Peterson *et al.* (1982) find that not only latent trait but also traditional equating procedures perform badly when the tests to be equated differ in difficulty, which is the case in vertical equating. Morris (1982) demonstrates theoretically that tests containing different ranges of difficulty cannot be equated even weakly and also shows that in general, if tests are multidimensional, equating procedures based on total test scores cannot be expected to work and it will be necessary to equate sets of component one-dimensional subtests where each set depends on a single dimension. It is possible for two tests each to be multidimensional and still be equatable in terms of total scores, but only in the special case where they have the same set of one-dimensional components whose loadings on the total score are related by a single linear function.

Educational attainment tests typically are multidimensional and so in general can be equated only via component one-dimensional subtests. This implies that such components have to be identified or, in other words, knowledge of the dimensionality structure of the test is needed. This is no easy matter and seems to have been little attempted in the context of test equating. Alternatively, if in order to make tests easily equatable, they are constructed to be one-dimensional then this carries implications for their validity. As population changes occur, either through curriculum innovation or for other reasons, so any attempt to maintain a sequence of one-dimensional tests begins to look very problematical (Goldstein, 1983).

## Reference Populations

The previous discussion has referred to the equating of tests for a given population. The empirical equating literature, however, tends to be a little vague about the appropriate reference population for any given procedure. For example, that a procedure for equating two tests works well in one population does not guarantee it will do so in another. Furthermore, an equating procedure can work satisfactorily in a population but poorly in a sub-population — for example, a minority ethnic group. There is then an urgent question of the circumstances under which identifiable sub-populations 'gain' or 'suffer'. This is an empirical issue which has hardly been addressed at all by existing studies. Thus, the most common justification for the use of equating methods seems to be the existence of high (dis-attenuated) intercorrelations between the tests used. Part of the high intercorrelations, however, may well be explained by other factors such as socio-economic group, income, curriculum, etc., so that 'partial' correlations within relatively homogeneous sub-groups may be much smaller.

## Equatability

Much of the equating literature seems to take the view that two tests either are equatable, or they are not. Since, short of studying every member of a population exhaustively, we cannot ascertain whether a procedure is perfect, we need some measure of how good a procedure is. Traditionally, a linear correlation coefficient is used, but this seems inappropriate for equipercentile methods. A rank correlation would be better and the following suggestion provides such a measure and suggests how it can be used to improve the practical application of an equating procedure.

Consider a population of individuals who take test A and test B and assume true scores are available, although in practice observed scores will be used. Then we can define perfect equating such that

$$X_{ia} > X_{ja} \Rightarrow X_{ib} > X_{jb} \qquad (8)$$

where i, j refer to individuals and X to test scores. If we have n individuals arrange the $X_{ia}$ in ascending order and for each of the $^{n}C_{2}$ pairs of $X_{ia}$ scores see whether (8) holds. The proportion of pairs for which it does is our index E. Clearly, if E is near to 1.0 we may be content with our procedures. If not, then we may be able to improve matters by amalgamating or grouping scores on both tests to eliminate cases where (8) does not hold. Of course, this will not always be possible, but one would reasonably expect most inconsistencies to arise from nearby scores so that grouping these will lead to a higher value of E. Algorithms to do this could be programmed readily. Thus, we would produce a hierarchy of E values, from the original minimum value upwards. For any E we would have modified test score scales and when one was reached which was thought 'acceptable' this would give the corresponding procedure for equating the grouped test scores. We can regard the functions which carry each original score to the grouped scales as an expression of the loss of score precision required in order to carry out an 'acceptable' equating.

If E is used to measure equatability then we would want to report this for as many sub-populations as possible before recommending that the procedure is used in the total population. Thus, a high value of E over the whole population might be considerably reduced within sub-populations if the variable defining the sub-population was strongly associated with the test scores.

## Designs for Equating

The first systematic attempt to devise a framework for equating studies seems to have been that of Angoff (1971). He proposed four main designs, and the following summary is based on these, incorporating the models of the previous section. (The case of just two tests is used for illustration.)

1  Each test is given to a different sample of the population. For the LP Method, equation (6) is used to equate to a common scale with $a_i$, $b_i$ estimated using the reliabilities and means as given in the previous section. For the EP Method the 'shrinking' procedure is used separately for each sample.

2  Each test is given to all individuals in a sample, with the administration in one order for a random half and the reverse order for the remainder. This uses individuals more efficiently (by cutting down on the numbers needed) and the 'crossover' design enables allowance to be made for possible practice effects. Angoff's method, while incorporating an adjustment for practice, does not make explicit use of the relationship between the tests, although this can be incor-

porated in the congeneric model (5) to obtain improved estimates. In the non-linear case, efficient EP methods are complicated but estimates based on the separate distributions can be used. The relationship information does, however, allow a check on some assumptions.[1]

3   An additional common test U is given to each group in design (1). The purpose is to increase precision by adjusting for sampling fluctuations in the selection of the groups, using 'regression estimation' procedures for the LP method. Any variable with a fairly high correlation with the scores can be used for U, or indeed a combination of variables can be used. For the EP method, assuming a large enough sample, an iterative non-parametric standardization procedure can be used. Details are given in Bianchini and Loret (1974).

4   A common test U is administered as in (3) but U is now used to predict the true scores, with scores predicted by the same value of U deemed to be equated. Alternatively the tests may be used to predict U, with scores predicting the same value of U deemed equated. These methods seem not to be justified by any general model, but are used in public examination comparability exercises and they will be discussed more fully in a later section.

In evaluating the performance of these designs it is useful to assess how closely the sample data conform to the model. For this purpose we can define the conditional variance of equating (D) as follows:

if $X_1' \equiv X_2'$ then for test 2

$$D_2 = E\{(X_{2j}' - X_2')^2 | X_{1j}' = X_1'\}$$

is the variance of the second test score values about the equated score for all individuals (j) with the same first test score.

## Empirical Studies

The most comprehensive equating study so far has been the Anchor Test Study, commissioned by the US Office of Education and carried out by the Educational Testing Service from 1971 to 1974.

One part of the study, which is not of prime concern here, was a norming study involving 150,000 children. The test equating part of the study involved a stratified random sample of 200,000 fourth, fifth and sixth grade children from the whole of the US and seven tests (with one added later in a supplementary study). One of the tests, the Metropolitan Reading Test, was chosen as the 'Anchor' Test (and was the one which was normed) and the others were equated to the scale and norms for this.

The study design consisted of sixteen replications of a basic design involving twenty-eight schools each given a testing assignment at random. For the seven tests there are twenty-one possible pairs and each test had a parallel form giving another seven pairs. Then within each school the testing was repeated using the reverse order to that first assigned. This resulted in $2 \times 28 = 56$ ordered pairs of tests. The final report is in thirty volumes and describes the results, and a project report (Bianchini and Loret, 1974) of 295 pages gives details of the design and methodology of analysis. Both LP and EP methods were used to obtain equated results.

Several studies have compared latent trait models with LP and EP methods, for example, Holmes (1980), Marco *et al.* (1980) and Peterson *et al.* (1982), but no one method emerges as clearly superior, and few useful simulation experiments seem to have been attempted.

## The Comparability of Public Examinations

The General Certificate of Education boards in England, Wales and Northern Ireland issue graded certificates to individuals for each examination subject. Each board issues grades A, B, C, etc., in a particular 'O' level subject, carrying the implication that a grade A from one board is 'equivalent' to a grade A from any other board. As with test equating, therefore, an implicit equivalence relationship underlies the award of grades. I will begin by describing briefly how two common methods of equivalencing operate and then consider what theoretical underpinnings these may have. A more detailed description of the methods can be found in Bardell *et al.* (1978).

### *Monitor or Reference Tests*

In this method, for each examination paper to be equivalenced, the examination score or, more usually, grade (using a simple scoring system) is regressed on a 'reference' test score. The difference between the intercepts of the regression lines (assuming them to be parallel) estimates the differences in the mean grade scores. These difference scores can then be used as the basis of adjustments to grade definitions in order to equivalence the mean grades with respect to the reference test. A detailed description of the workings of this procedure with examples can be found in Newbould and Massey (1979).

Apart from any theoretical difficulties, several practical difficulties occur with this procedure. Firstly, it may not be possible to adjust grade boundaries to produce coincident regression lines, and this will be so particularly if the original lines are not parallel or show signs of non-linearity. Secondly, the use of a simple scoring system for the grades is rather crude. Although it seems not to have been tried, a direct method of relating proportions of candidates in each grade to the reference test score would be preferable, using, for example, a logit linear model. Thirdly, some account should be taken of the measurement error in the reference test; it appears that only one research study has attempted to do this (Willmott, 1977).

### Cross-Moderation

This has now become the favoured method and since 1978 all nine GCE boards have taken part in cross-moderation exercises at 'O' (Ordinary) and 'A' (Advanced) level.

Subject experts (usually examiners) scrutinize examination scripts to decide whether grades are 'comparable' across boards. This is done either by using a wide range of scripts from each board in order to establish where grade boundaries should be, or by using narrow ranges of scripts centred on grade boundaries determined by each board *a priori*. In the latter case it is often found that examiners from one board find another board too lenient, whereas the other board's examiners find the first board too lenient! This indicates that each examiner is using his or her own criteria, based on particular examination experience, to make judgments. To overcome this, attempts have been made, often involving outside experts, to evolve common criteria for these exercises. Nevertheless, agreement on criteria is not easy, and the result may be a compromise which is not as relevant to any single board as were the original criteria.

The advantage claimed for cross-moderation is that it comes close to the actual examining process, allowing the full use of expert judgment. On the other hand, it tends to be costly so that in practice only relatively small samples of scripts can be compared. It is also, ultimately, subjective and dependent on which examiners or experts are used.

Both the reference-test and cross-moderation methods may be used either to compare different boards in the same subject in one year or to compare different examinations in the same subject for a single board for two or more years. The first application is designed to ensure that every candidate is treated 'fairly' or 'comparably' irrespective of which board's examination is chosen, and the second is designed to ensure that examination 'standards' remain constant over time. The reference test method has also occasionally been used to study comparability between subjects, but in the light of the following discussion this seems especially difficult to justify.

In the previous paragraph words such as 'fairly' and 'standards' have been used somewhat imprecisely, and little attempt has been made to provide a strong justification for the methods, unlike those underlying equating. In the next section I will attempt to outline the logic of a comparability model for public examinations, and then to see whether the procedures used actually satisfy the requirements of the model.

## Models for Comparability

Perhaps the simplest procedure which could be used to attempt to obtain grade or score comparability would be a direct application of equipercentile equating using the cumulative grade or score distribution of each examination. An obvious objection to this is that the students taking the various examinations cannot be viewed as random samples from the same population. To overcome this, both the reference test and cross-moderation procedures attempt to 'adjust' for such student differences. Thus, the reference test is assumed to be a measure of student ability which captures such differences. The difficulty is that there is no simple ability or attainment which can be measured objectively (in the reference test case) or subjectively (in the case of cross moderation). The very point of having different syllabuses is to promote different abilities and attainments. Hence, as well as being different in degree, student attainments are different in kind since different aspects of a subject will have been studied and learnt, corresponding to the different exam syllabuses. Such deliberate diversity precludes representation by a single score on a reference test or by the average judgment of a set of examiners. The argument may be formalized in the following way.

For a given examination subject, consider two boards, A, B, and two syllabuses 1, 2. Syllabus 1 is the appropriate one for board A's examination and syllabus 2 for board B's examination. That is to say, each examination is designed to test attainment in the subject as described in the appropriate syllabus. Of course, in practice there are several boards and often more syllabuses than boards, but this raises no new issues of principle.

Now consider a hypothetical experiment whereby half of the candidates following syllabus 1 are allocated at random to paper A and the other half to paper B, and likewise for syllabus 2. For those candidates from syllabus 1 we compute the mean score difference between paper A and B, say x, and likewise for syllabus 2, say y. Since the allocations are at random, the average ability of the candidates is the same for each examination, so that we have the possibility of using the differences x, y for each syllabus separately, as adjustments to the examination marks, so that on average we can be fair to all candidates irrespective of which exam they take.

Unfortunately, since each examination is linked to a syllabus, we would expect those from syllabus 1 to do less than justice to themselves when taking examination B and vice versa for syllabus 2 examinees so leading to different values of x, y. Thus any supposed difference in examination difficulty is confounded with the examination/syllabus link and indeed x and y may even have opposite signs. In effect, this underlies the apparent contradiction found in cross-moderation exercises mentioned previously. In addition there is the practical difficulty that nominally the same syllabuses in different institutions may, in reality, differ considerably in the emphasis given to various topics, hence making them effectively different syllabuses. Moreover, this hypothetical experiment involves random assignment of candidates which is usually quite impractical. Nevertheless, the above argument will apply to other methods of adjusting for ability differences, such as reference-test and cross-moderation methods. The former uses an objective regression or covariance model to judge which candidates are equivalent, that is, have the same ability, and the latter method judges which candidates are equivalent according to subjective criteria developed by one or more moderators, this time using the internal evidence from the examination answers themselves. For both methods the average score difference for equivalent candidates is used to adjust examination scores. We see, therefore, that there can be little theoretical justification for the usual between-board comparability exercises.

Nevertheless, there is one special case when it would be

appropriate to attempt to adjust for 'ability', namely where for a single examination board there are equally relevant examinations for a syllabus. This might apply over time where comparability was desired from one year to the next. Here, however, there are additional problems related to the fact that syllabuses could change from year to year so that the relevance of a reference test to the examinees may change, as might the moderators' criteria.

Having shown that the current attempts at comparability have no adequate theoretical justification, it is relevant to ask whether an alternative theoretical model exists. Imagine, again, a hypothetical experiment in which individuals are initially randomly assigned to one or other syllabus. This would give, on average, equal distribution of ability at the outset, and if it were possible to ensure equality of education provision, teaching, etc., then if both groups take the same examination, any difference in score distributions would reflect differential relevance of the examination to the syllabuses, apart from sampling fluctuations. If there are now two different examinations, each related to one syllabus, then the difference in scores will reflect both 'relevance' and 'difficulty'. Nevertheless, it could be deemed fair in this case to use this difference to adjust scores, since the two groups of students are assumed to be equivalent. This imaginary experiment does seem to be the strongest sense in which public examination comparability can achieve fairness but, as before, we need to ask how closely the hypothetical experiment can be approached.

Firstly, neither the cross-moderation nor reference-test methods come close, since both rely on assessing examinees at the end of exposure to a syllabus. In principle, it would be possible to attempt to measure 'abilities' prior to syllabus allocation and also factors associated with teaching, etc. In practice no comparability studies along these lines seem to have been carried out, and to do so would involve a time-consuming longitudinal study. In addition to the above factors, moreover, variables such as student choice would have to be measured, since generally the choice of which examination to take is not made at random. In practice we know relatively little about how to measure the relevant factors associated with teaching or student choice. While further research aimed at understanding these is worthwhile, clearly we are far from possessing the knowledge needed to create satisfactory comparability exercises.

It should be noted that the above arguments are not limited to current, largely norm-referenced methods of examining. They apply with equal force to attempts to produce so called 'criterion-referenced' examinations. Even were such attempts successful in producing examinations with any notable advantages, they would not provide inherently a solution to comparability, and could make such problems even more intractable (see Orr and Nuttall, 1983).

## Some Conclusions and Recommendations

This review has been generally critical and pessimistic about the utility of the various equating and comparability methods in use. It has been my intention to try to illuminate the logical foundations of these methods, in order then to evaluate the procedures themselves. In equating, there seems to be a need for some realistic simulations to evaluate the performance of different methods on data with known properties. It is worth pointing out that current interest in the provision of 'graded tests' in English and Welsh schools seems to imply large scale equating procedures in order to establish a working system (Nuttall and Goldstein, 1984.) In comparability, some long-term studies would be useful, but simulations of the conditions of student choice, examination choice, etc., would also be useful.

Where there are several examinations related to a single syllabus, it is possible to make progress towards establishing comparability, or at least deciding what degree of comparability might be attainable. This would seem to be the case with certain examining bodies such as the Business and Technician Education Council, where common syllabuses are separately examined by different institutions, and Nuttall and Armitage (1984) investigate models which make allowance for various student characteristics, including previous attainment. They show that it is possible to use their procedures as screening devices to identify potentially aberrant examinations, so that a more detailed study of these can be undertaken.

If reasonable comparability is not possible, perhaps we should be asking whether attempts to achieve it should not be abandoned. Why not, for example, have simple norm-referencing, whereby every year each set of examination scores is separately standardized using those individuals entering for it, and a common grading system used? This would at least have the merit of being well understood. Objectors to such a system might argue, for example, that this would penalize those children who happened to encounter a particularly 'difficult' paper, but it could also be said that any 'unfairness' introduced by this would be small in comparison to other known sources of variation, such as marking variability. It is also possible that after such a system had been in operation for several years, both those who take examinations and those who use the results might accept the system fairly readily. The students would make their own decisions about their prospects with different examination boards, and the users would make allowances for different 'standards' adopted by the boards. Naturally, the boards would wish to maintain stable 'standards' but those would be incorporated into the setting of the examination papers. Since these papers themselves and the objectives of the syllabuses upon which they are based would be publicly available, the onus for a valid interpretation of the examination results would rest with the user rather than the present somewhat shaky comparability procedures. Furthermore, in those cases where valid exercises might still be carried out, such as overtime for a single board with an unchanging syllabus, these would provide a useful check on examination standards.

## Acknowledgement

This chapter has benefited from helpful comments by Dr. J. Houston, Dr. M. Cresswell and Professor D.L. Nuttall to whom I am most grateful.

## Note

1 In order to satisfy equation (4) a further assumption is necessary, namely that $E\{f(X_i)|S\} = f(S)$, with a similar condition for the other tests. However, this ought to be the case so long as the reliabilities are not too low. Also, this assumption can be examined empirically.

## References

ANGOFF, W.H. (1971) 'Scales, norms and equivalent scores' in THORNDIKE, R.L. (Ed.) *Educational Measurement*, Washington, D.C., American Council on Education (2nd edn).

BARDELL, G.S., FORREST, G.M. and SHOESMITH, D.J. (1978) *Comparability in GCE: A Review of the Boards' Studies*, 1964–1977, Manchester, Joint Matriculation Board.

BIANCHINI, J.C. and LORET, P.G. (1974) *Anchor Test Study, Final Report: Project Report*, Berkeley, Calif., Educational Testing Service.

BRAUN, H.G. and HOLLAND, P.W.L. (1982) 'Observed-score test equating: A mathematical analysis of some ETS equating procedures' in HOLLAND, P.W. and RUBIN, D.B. (Eds.) *Test Equating*, New York, Academic Press.

GOLDSTEIN, H. (1980) 'Dimensionality, bias, independence and measurement scale problems in latent trait score models', *British Journal of Mathematical and Statistical Psychology*, 33, pp. 234–46.

GOLDSTEIN, H. (1983) 'Measuring changes in educational attainment over time: Problems and possibilities', *Journal of Educational Measurement*, 20, pp. 369–78.

HOLLAND, P.W. and RUBIN, D.B. (Eds.) (1982) *Test Equating*, New York Academic Press, New York.

HOLMES, S.E. (1980) *ESEA Title 1 Link Project, Final Report*, Salem, Oregon State Dept. of Education.

JÖRESKOG, K.G. (1971) 'Statistical analysis of sets of congeneric tests', *Psychometrika*, 36, pp. 109–33.

LORD, F.M. (1977) 'Practical applications of item characteristic curve theory', *Journal of Educational Measurement*, 14, pp. 117–38.

LORD, F.M. (1980) *Applications of Item Response Theory to Practical Testing Problems*, Hillsdale, N.J., Lawrence Erlbaum Associates.

MARCO, G.L., PETERSEN, N.S. and STEWART, E.E. (1980) 'A test of the adequacy of curvilinear score equating methods' in WEISS, D.J. (Ed.) *Proceedings of the 1979 Computerized Adaptive Testing Conference*, Dept. of Psychology, University of Minnesota.

MORRIS, C.N. (1982) 'On the foundations of test equating' in HOLLAND, P.W. and RUBIN, D.B. (Eds.) (1982) *Test Equating*, New York, Academic Press.

NEWBOULD, C.A. and MASSEY, A.J. (1979) *Comparability Using a Common Element*, Cambridge, Test Development and Research Unit (mimeo).

NUTTALL, D.L. and ARMITAGE, P. (1984) *A Feasibility Study of a Moderating Instrument*, Report to Business and Technician Education Council.

NUTTALL, D.L. and GOLDSTEIN, H. (1984) 'Profiles and graded tests: The technical issues' in *Profiles in Action*, London, Further Education Unit.

ORR, L. and NUTTALL, D.L. (1983) *Determining Standards in the Proposed Single System of Examining at 16+*, London, Schools Council.

PETERSEN, N.S., MARCO, G.L. and STEWART, E.E. (1982) 'A test of the adequacy of linear score equating models' in HOLLAND, P.W. and RUBIN, D.B. (Eds.) *Test Equating*, New York, Academic Press.

POTTHOFF, R. (1982) 'Some issues in test equating' in HOLLAND, P.W. and RUBIN, D.B. (Eds.) *Test Equating*, New York, Academic Press.

WERTS, C.E., GRANDY, J. and SCHUBAKER, W.H. (1980) 'A confirmatory approach to calibrating congeneric measures', *Multivariate Behavioural Research*, 15, pp. 109–22.

WILLMOTT, A.S. (1977) *CSE and GCE Grading Standards: The 1973 Comparability Study*, London, Macmillan Education.

# The Agenda for Educational Measurement[1]

## Robert Wood
### Flinders University

It is no longer necessary to plead for a distinction to be made between educational and psychological measurement but much remains to be done to elaborate and substantiate that distinction. To argue, as some of us have done, that educational measurement has for too long been under the sway of psychometrics is one thing, to establish what educational measurement is, or rather should be, is quite another.

The term itself tends to encourage people to equate 'measurement in education' with 'educational measurement'. What is needed is a striking word to signal a fresh enterprise. At one time I thought Carver's (1974) 'edumetrics' might do the job but it is an ugly word which does not seem to have stuck. What C.P. Scott is supposed to have said about television comes to mind: 'No good will come of this device. The word is half Greek and half Latin.'

Education has always been vulnerable to psychometric incursions and influence, although less so now than before. Lacking a distinctive and self-confident view about the purpose of testing in schools and about what kinds of tests were suitable and unsuitable, it has, rather like a client state, looked on helplessly as psychometric doctrines and practices have been installed and put to work. Which is not to say that there have not been, at all times, as in all client states, individuals in education ready and eager to embrace psychometric assumptions and beliefs about how children differ, and to suppress curiosity about the children themselves.[2] I should add that the classroom has been, for psychometricians, an excellent source of cheap available data.

But education and differential psychology do not have the same aims. Education is not, as far as I know, a permanent research endeavour, although in certain circumstances and at different times it can be made to yield research data (although not the sort that psychometricians took so freely). Educators, by and large, have to take children and students as they find them. This was the message which emerged from the 'Heredity and IQ' debate precipitated by Jensen (1969), an affair which symbolizes education's growing determination to fend off gratuitous psychometric thinking. At the end of it all even someone like Bereiter, in an article characterized by Jensen as 'an exceptionally intelligent and penetrating analysis', was obliged to state that, with respect to social and racial differences, knowledge of a possible genetic basis is relevant neither to the classroom teacher nor to the educational policy makers.[3] Amen to that.

## Some History

That educational and psychological measurement have long been differentiated in *name* is not in doubt; as early as 1918 Ayres was able to write a *history* of educational measurement; there was Monroe's book in 1923 and the founding of the journal *Educational and Psychological Measurement* in 1941. But was educational measurement ever seen as anything other than the application of psychological measurement in an educational setting? The universal answer up to about 1950 would appear to have been 'no'. Nunnally (1975) revealed more than he knew when he wrote, 'Is there an important place for traditional measures of aptitude and achievement in modern education? In 1950 most persons who were prominent either in psychometric research or in education would immediately have answered 'yes' but now there is a lively controversy about the matter.'

It is possible Nunnally took too sanguine a view. Consider *Educational and Psychological Measurement*, admittedly a journal which in all respects has changed little over the years. If you read the inside front cover you will see that it is, as it always was, concerned first and foremost with studies of individual differences, that is to say, with psychometrics or psychological measurement. Other categories of paper are mentioned but you will search in vain for a definition or description of educational measurement, even one as partial as Carver's (1974) 'measurement of intra-individual differences'. In important respects, the psychometric hegemony persists, or do I read too much into the fact that Robert Thorndike's new book (1982) about educational measurement is called *Applied Psychometrics*?

It could have been different. Levine (1976) draws a picture of 'professional test constructors' consistently overriding the requirement of classroom usefulness — 'test constructors wanted to construct tests with good measurement properties amenable to statistical analysis' — so fitting the educational foot to the psychometric shoe. There was an opportunity in the 1930s when Hawkes *et al.* (1936) pointed out that achievement could have been measured in absolute units, in relation to some absolute standard, or even in relation to some passing grade, but these same people managed to argue themselves out of this idea and the chance was lost.

Nunnally's choice of 1950 as a watershed year is significant because by then a group of American educators had already been working for two years on what turned out to be the *Taxonomy of Educational Objectives*, Vol. 1 (Bloom *et al.*, 1956). That ambitious and singular endeavour had little to say about measurement as such (although it did mention promising ideas like the Tab test, a primitive forerunner of the tailored test) but it was immensely successful — and subsequent denigration has done nothing to diminish this — in dramatizing (and often stimulating) a felt need among educators for an approach to measurement which would be reflective of and responsive to what is peculiar to education, in particular the cycle of planning, instruction, learning, achievement and measurement. The mistake Bloom and his colleagues made, as we can see with hindsight, was to formulate educational objectives in ad hoc and naive psychological language. That this formulation exposed a flank which critics, especially philosophers, savaged is of less concern than that the *Taxonomy* gave the impression that educational measurement was still concerned with psychological constructs, indeed more so than ever. The consequence was that lay people, who had hitherto talked about content or just material to be learned, having perhaps been weaned away from faculty psychology not so long before, now wedded themselves to a new orthodoxy whose categories they did not understand, naïve though these were, and which, in the course of time, they came to reify.

But none of this held up the emergence of educational measurement. By the time criticism of the *Taxonomy* had become commonplace and its unfortunate side-effects had taken hold, a crucial event for educational measurement had long since taken place. This was the publication of Glaser's (1963) seminal paper in which he introduced the notions of criterion referencing and criterion-referenced testing (CRT) and differentiated them sharply from norm-referenced testing, emphasis on which, he thought, had been brought about by the preoccupation of test theory with aptitude and with selection and prediction problems. It is true, as Glaser acknowledged, that others had made this distinction previously[4] but it was Glaser's paper which caught the imagination. It can be said to mark the point at which educational measurement began to detach itself from classical psychometrics.

Since then there has been much embellishment, but little invention. Criterion-referenced testing remains the embodiment of educational measurement; notions like mastery testing (although not mastery learning) and minimum competency testing are only developed versions of the original conception, given a particular twist. There is an irony here. The original conception was borrowed from psychology, to some minds a rather dubious branch of psychology which education ought to have resisted.[5]

The odd thing is — and here is another irony — that a paradigm of learning which in the psychological context is not readily associated with a benign, caring disposition towards the individual is, when translated to the educational context, and by dint of a heavily emphasized contrast with norm-referenced testing, and the evils thereof, turned into an instrument of educational equity or even deliverance for the individual. The persistent tendency to disparage the norm-referenced test reached ludicrous proportions when two educators, English not American (Guy and Chambers, 1973 and 1974), wrote a bizarre article denouncing norm-referenced examinations as a violation of students' civil rights because they are made to show their ignorance. I wonder what they would say now as minimum competency tests, constructed on the most impeccable CRT principles, are being hauled regularly through the US courts by individuals who claim that their civil rights are being violated because the state is withholding learning certificates or diplomas granted as a result of these tests. Evidently there is a less benign aspect to CRT. The point is, of course, that the concept of referencing is ultimately irrelevant.[6] Powerful though it may be in mobilizing emotion, it is subordinate to that of function; that is to say, measures can be used for selection, screening or monitoring whatever the referencing assigned to them (Wood, 1976). We might object that referencing determines test construction policy which in turn rules out certain functions but the fact remains that CRT results can be put to purposes generally associated with norm-referenced testing. The effect is the same, as witness the example above.

## Changing Functions of Measurement in Society

The Civil Rights legislation in the United States shook up the testing scene and it has never been the same since. Whereas psychological tests had been used for forty years without any obvious objection and apparently in the public interest, indeed the rationale for their use was that of promoting equal opportunity or advancement through talent rather than social connections (Resnick, 1981), the use of tests to sort people into predetermined categories now seemed distasteful, even obnoxious, and the whole testing system (or industry, as critics have always preferred to call it) a positive hindrance to the realization of equal opportunity in its now much broadened form. It had been noticed that equal opportunity to sit a test is not to be equated with equal opportunity for continuing education, not to mention other desiderata. The meritocratic principle no longer seemed sound or even admirable.

And the critics were right about the tests. They did have nothing to say about children themselves, only about where they stood in relation to each other on some fictional scale; nevertheless, position on this scale, however uninformative about what you could do, and could not do, was tremendously decisive in the matter of life chances. What was wanted now were forms of assessment which above all closed no doors but also drew attention to problems and strengths an individual might have (Gordon and Terrell, 1981). More generally, the search was on for approaches to measurement which would be reflective of and responsive to what is peculiar to education — learning and instruction and school life — and would also be in the best interests of individuals.

Educational measurement can be seen as an attempt to use measurement constructively in the service of individual children and students, to shift the emphasis away from between-individual differences to within-individual differences (Carver, 1974). But it is a matter of emphasis; clearly it would be humbug to suggest that we are no longer interested in individual differences or are not prepared to attend to them. One well-known American educator in the sixties seemed to be wishing away individual differences, or worse, thought he could remove them.[7]

## Paying Attention to Where the Data Came From

Attempts to differentiate educational from psychological measurement have generally been made in terms of the function or purpose of measurement, and the consequences for the individual of the act of measurement. Further differentiation can, and ought, to be made in terms of the data the two kinds of measurement produce, and the methods of analysis which are appropriate for treating each. Evidently one major difference is that achievement data arise as a direct result of instruction and are therefore crucially affected by teaching and teachers. Any model for analysing such data which neglects to incorporate some sort of teaching effect (never mind other effects which are responsible for variation, like interactions) is simply not credible, yet how often are models built expressly for treating psychological data, sometimes of a most specialized kind, taken over and offered as plausible descriptions of how achievement occurs? The experience with the Rasch model (actually only one of his models and a rather thin psychological model at that) over the past decade is instructive (see Goldstein, 1979, for fuller strictures). For the same reason, and because achievement data are 'dirty' compared to aptitude data, which plays havoc with given notions about dimensionality and traits, it is likely to be a waste of time applying the well-worn psychometric apparatus — reliability, validity, internal consistency, homogeneity, etc. But people go on doing it. No doubt the cause lies in the absence of theory to explain or elucidate achievement, which induces desperation and panic.[8] But it is not clear how enlightenment will come from applying inappropriate models to data.

## An Extreme Proposal

A radical move would be to ignore psychology altogether and that is what McIntyre and Brown (1978) did. Until they came along no one was prepared to argue that educational achievement has nothing to do with psychology and, by extension, that educational measurement has nothing to do with psychometrics. This is such a bold forthright solution that one has to admire it, but it is also so provocative that it cannot be allowed to pass, especially as they go on to call for educational measurement to be abandoned.

Educational objectives, state McIntyre and Brown, have nothing to do with the psychology of thinking:

> When we talk about educational attainment, then we are concerned with whether or not intentions that various kinds of knowledge and ability should be mastered have been realised. Neither questions about patterns of variation among

people nor questions about processes of learning and thinking are relevant to such judgments, there is indeed no way in which psychology would seem to be logically relevant to such judgments.

They continue, 'Furthermore we would stress that it is on an understanding of the processes of thinking involved in these subjects that educational objectives depend, since the criteria which inform educational objectives are intrinsic to the subjects, not to the psychology of thinking' (p. 42).

Taking the last statement first, it presents no difficulty because it is tautologous, the consequence follows from the way educational objectives are defined. And does the definition have to be so heavily subject-bound? How would a cross-disciplinary ability like problem-solving be treated? Perhaps it would not be allowed as an objective. All the same, one knows what they are getting at. The application of Piaget's scheme to 'O' level science courses (for example, Shayer *et al.*, 1975) may have elucidated why students fail but they still failed, which means that educational objectives have not yet been realized. One cannot quarrel with this, given the terms of the argument, but, of course, it is precisely the uncurious character of this conceptualization of attainment which Shayer and others reacted against. The point about their work is that it can, and does, lead to improvements in the way mastery is ascertained, as well as to increased understanding of how a subject should be taught. Ascertainment of mastery is crucial to the McIntyre-Brown formulation. In the first quotation they are clearly right, logically at any rate, about variation being irrelevant, and this process I have dealt with. It is the first sentence from 'intentions' onwards which catches the eye. Allowing that 'knowledge' and 'abilities' must be classed as mental predicates, to use Gilbert Ryle's term, if not psychological constructs, the question arises, 'Can you check whether such predicates/constructs have been mastered without invoking psychological categories?'

This question would have appealed to Ryle. As a matter of fact, the McIntyre-Brown method of argument is distinctly reminiscent of the no-nonsense treatment of psychology meted out in Chapter 2 of *The Concept of Mind* (Ryle, 1949). Compare the second quotation above with this from Ryle.

The competent critic of prose style, experimental technique or embroidery, must at least know how to write, experiment or sew. Whether or not he has also learned psychology matters about as much as whether he has learned any chemistry, neurology or economics.

Like Ryle, McIntyre and Brown want no truck with the 'ghost in the machine', preferring instead to deal with 'intentions'; tricky philosophical ground, one would have thought, on to which Ryle would not necessarily have been willing to follow them. Whose 'intentions' are we talking about? The teacher's, the student's, the parents'? If it is the teacher's, as appears to be the case, is it fair to tie a *student's* mastery to a *teacher's* intentions?

Ascertainment of mastery seems not to be thought particularly problematical; perhaps as Ryle would likely have done, McIntyre and Brown argue that knowledge and abilities can be observed directly, in the spirit of knowing *how* rather than knowing *what*. But judging whether a student knows the difference between a concept and a principle is not at all the same as judging whether a man knows how to shoot (to use one of Ryle's examples). This is true even if one uses the most direct means of ascertaining knowledge, which is presumably oral interrogation coupled with requests to demonstrate; it is patently true if one resorts to using paper-and-pencil tests to ascertain mastery. Evidently the test form interposes itself between knowledge or ability and judgment, and to the extent that it is an imperfect transducer of what the student knows or is able to do, so will the judgment be distorted. The multiple-choice item is particularly questionable in this respect. Robert Gagné (1970) has shown how shaky is the inference from response to mastery. Then there are the arguments concerning recall versus recognition (Brown, 1976) which can only be discussed in psychological terms but which affect judgments as to what is truly *known*: sometimes, too, you find an appeal to psychological reasoning to defend the use of a particular testing technique, for example, Keith Davidson's (1974) defence of the use of multiple choice for testing comprehension in 'O' level English language exams.

It may appear that what has been presented constitutes a more powerful argument against paper-and-pencil tests than against McIntyre and Brown and, indeed, they might retort that they are not interested in what are essentially artifacts of certain forms of testing. However, that would be to evade the point. What was said is true of oral questioning or of any mode of interrogative enquiry, that is to say, of any attempt to understand what is in the other person's head. You have only to read Margaret Donaldson's (1978) descriptions of the difficulties children experience in dealing with the language of questions and engaging in 'disembedded' thought to take the point. It may be possible to purge *content* of psychological contamination but it is hard to see how you can chase it out of educational measurement altogether when it persists in cropping up whenever a judgment about mastery has to be made.

I said that McIntyre and Brown were heard to call for the abandonment of educational measurement. How did this come about? It started with the question, 'Here are data from some tests (or items); what did they measure?' This, of course, is the classic psychometric method of proceeding. Finding no satisfactory answer to their question (and one cannot argue with them for their criticism of dimensionality is faultless), they conclude that there is no such thing as coherent measurement and therefore that quantification in education should be abandoned. I would like to suggest that by posing the question as they did, they were bound to arrive at that bleak conclusion. Ask the 'what' question before testing, as Gagné (1970) has shown,[9] and you have entirely different, and more hopeful, possibilities. What you must have, though, is the willingness to expend enough care on the *single item* to ensure, as far as possible, that unequivocal inferences from response to judgment of mastery can be made. How do you do this? You build in controls which permit the ruling out of alternative inferences; distinctive and distortion-free measurement, he called it. Gagné's ideas for item writing deserve closer study.

If the 'what' question can be tackled, there remains the matter of aggregation, or 'how much'. Finding no answer to the 'what' question, McIntyre and Brown saw no point in asking the 'how much' question. It is a pity Gagné did not deal with the matter of aggregation. For a recent opinion, there is Green (1981) who writes: 'Tests work by the weight of numbers ... of course, each item should be carefully designed and as good as possible, but no single item can ever do very much good or very much harm.'

I would not want to dispute this statement but I do wonder if test constructors are not too ready to fasten on to Green's first assertion and use it to justify their lack of attention to single items. Casual treatment of one item is casual treatment of all items. Gagné said you had to start with the single item and work up — there are no short cuts — but I fear such a severe injunction has often proved too much to take.

## A Programme for Educational Measurement

Generally speaking, and thinking not of how things often are but rather of how they might or even ought to be, it can be said that, compared to psychological measurement, educational measurement:

1 deals with the individual's achievement relative to himself rather than to others;
2 seeks to test for competence rather than for intelligence;
3 takes place in relatively uncontrolled conditions and so does not produce 'well-behaved' data;
4 looks for 'best' rather than 'typical' performances;
5 is most effective when rules and regulations characteristic of standardized testing are relaxed;
6 embodies a constructive outlook on assessment where the aim is to help rather than sentence the individual.

Most of these themes, which are not exhaustive, have already been introduced. Consideration of theme 2 requires that McClelland's (1973) famous article be read or re-read, which would be a good thing to do anyway. Note, though, that it is being argued once again (Schmidt and Hunter, 1981) that tests of certain psychological constructs, notably verbal reasoning, are valid for testing suitability for a wide range of occupations, because the constructs are demonstrably or logically inherent in the expected performances. This is precisely the line of argument McClelland was challenging. The extension of the argument back into the schools — which would be a regression to where we were thirty years ago — has not yet been made explicitly, but that would be a straightforward matter since, of course, the argument is so much easier to sustain in the educational context.

Themes 4 and 5 are linked since it would appear that to implement 4 you would first need to implement 5. But that would not be possible if you were to try to observe the *Standards for Educational and Psychological Tests* (APA, 1974) to the letter. This is what recommendation I2 (p. 65) has to say: 'The test administrator is responsible for establishing conditions, consistent with the principle of standardization, that enable each examinee to do his best.'

A commentary on the *Standards* (Brown, 1980, p. 34) explains why this recommendation is necessary. 'As testing is usually viewed as an evaluative situation by test takers, and as many people have evaluation apprehension, it is necessary to establish optimal testing conditions.' Note the euphemism for 'examination nerves'. Note also the blithe use of the word 'optimal'. Would we want to establish sub-optimal conditions? The issue at stake, of course, is 'How in group testing circumstances can you optimize testing conditions for everyone simultaneously?' In the commentary following I2, the *Standards* attempt to indicate how this might be done without ever convincing. Moreover, most of these suggestions are implementable only in a one-to-one testing situation. One attempt at relaxing typical conditions, which may even go beyond what the *Standards* had in mind, is a group test devised by the Educational Testing Service. The test is called PAYES, and ETS believes that

> it differs significantly from most standardized tests, particularly in the way supervisor and student interact. To begin with, the supervisor actually participates in the exam. No longer a combination timekeeper and proctor to prevent cheating, the supervisor reads each item to the student group — allowing time for low-verbal skill students to ask clarifying questions about individual items and to respond thoughtfully without fear of time running out ... from all indications, people like it because it's designed to help people, not label them. (*ETS Developments*, 1979)

Note how theme 6 is touched on. It is necessary to pay attention to the way tests are administered but the greater threat to optimality may lie in the tests themselves, as Coffman (1979), among others, has warned. He, like others, draws the conclusion that only if students are given tests of appropriate difficulty will the problems of low motivation, test anxiety and withdrawal from the competition be minimized. The use of tailored testing and its variants is obvious but there is more to this than meets the eye. Tailored testing theory calls for examinees to be presented with items of 50 per cent difficulty *for them*, that is, they would be expected to get one out of every two items correct, once their level is found. But when I worked in this area a few years ago I was never convinced that such a policy would be optimal for the student *psychologically*. I believe we do not know enough about how motivation, task difficulty and immediate past experience work on each other.

The distinction underlying all of the foregoing discussion is that between *maximum* performance and *typical* performance. According to Brown (1980), maximum performance is to be identified with 'do your best' and typical performance with 'present an honest picture of yourself'. The first is associated with achievement and aptitude tests, the second with personality inventories, self-respect scales, etc. I

wonder, however, if it is not typical rather than maximum performance which is wanted from tests of attainment, and particularly public
examinations. If it were maximum performance we were after, we
would not so readily deride the 'flash in the pan' performance. That
phrase may serve as a sort of statistical judgment in the long run but
the fact remains that the performance was produced. We are not even
sure it was a maximum performance, just a lot better than expected.
Conversely, consider those hackneyed phrases 'had an off day' and
'did not do himself justice'. Do these mean that the candidate failed to
turn in a typical performance or that he failed to turn in a maximum
performance? Note that both terms must be interpreted against the
opportunities offered in the paper. There is a maximum performance
beyond the ceiling. We have invented the terms 'over' and 'under'
achiever to describe these kinds of performance. Is there such a thing
as an 'overachiever'? Isn't he just an 'achiever'? It is time this
wretched terminology was scrapped.[10]

I believe that the idea of maximum performance deserves more
attention. Those interested in a fundamental treatment might look at
the work of Andrew Sutton who is trying to popularize some Russian
thinking on the subject (see, for instance, Sutton, 1979, also Sternberg, 1981). The core is Vygotsky's concept of the *zone of next
development* which is the gap between the present level of development and the potential level of development. It indicates the level of
task that a child is ready to undertake on the basis of what he can
already do, *as long as he receives the best possible help from an adult*
(my emphasis). The inappropriateness of standardized testing, and its
administrative trappings, is obvious, since the actual content and
manner of the help given will depend very much on the match
between the needs of the child and the skills and styles of the teacher.
Here, then, we have the idea that the teacher/tester and student
*collaborate* actively to produce a best performance — a sentiment
expressed also by McClelland — instead of the tester and the agencies
he serves conniving, through secrecy, witholding of information and
impersonal, unrealistic conduct, to produce typical performances, or
worse. Here, too, is the valuable idea of achievement as *becoming* as
well as being and experiencing (Harris, 1969).


## Preaching into Practice

It is easy to say that educational measurement should be child-
centred, rather more difficult to work out constructive proposals for

doing so. Recent proposals from a Yale psychologist, Sandra Scarr, deserve consideration (Scarr, 1981). They represent a considerable extension of what has hitherto been regarded as the province of educational measurement. That statement can be checked by reviewing the contents of *Educational Measurement* (Thorndike, 1971).

In Scarr's view, what is missing from discussions of what should be assessed in school is any reference to children's motivational and adjustment problems, whose expression she sees as decisive. This view derives from a developmental theory, or perhaps it is the other way round; there is no need to go into it here. Scarr maintains that we are assessing children's *functioning* in a school setting but only part of that functioning is cognitive. To capture what she is after she coins the term 'intellectual competence'. (The word is not used in the same way as McClelland but connections could be made.) Scarr calls for a 'new wave' of assessments and although she does not make that point explicitly, it is clear she believes that we should stop regarding motivational and adjustment problems as confined to children we label as 'slow learners', 'maladjusted', 'retarded' and so forth, but as inherent in all children. Is it asking too much of educational measurement to take on assessment in the round of 'normal' children? (It is certainly a long way from the impoverished view of achievement as the realization of behavioural objectives.) I do not think so, but much remains to be done in creating suitable assessment instruments (Wood, 1984b).

### The British Measurement Scene

Much of this chapter has been concerned with the American experience because that is where the ideas have come from and the arguments have been fought. Differences in outlook and practices between the US and the UK are, of course, enormous. It is hard to imagine anyone in the States coming out, as McIntyre and Brown do (1978, p. 49), with the statement that the conceptualizing of attainment is a philosophical task, although they do have the grace to add that 'there are nonetheless problems which the philosopher cannot solve on his own.' Actually rather important problems, like how to put objectives in an order of priority or knowing what to do with teachers who adapt these objectives to their pupils as they go along.

In Britain, to talk of educational measurement is to talk of examinations. If Pidgeon and Yates (1969) were to rewrite or revise their book, I wager that they would begin it with the same sentence:

'Educational measurement is not accorded a generous measure of public esteem, largely because it tends to be identified with the complex system of public examinations which, in this country, regulate educational opportunity and vocational choice.' Moreover, their estimation of public esteem for educational measurement is probably still correct.

Actually public examinations are an interesting case because they constitute a subtle cross between educational and psychological measurement philosophies and practices. The tradition is psychometric — emphasis on individual differences, fiercely rigorous administration procedures defended in the name of fairness — but, increasingly, the practice, reflecting a changing outlook, is of the kind I have been claiming is characteristic of educational measurement — concern with content overriding statistical considerations, and acceptance of techniques of assessment, notably teacher assessment, which palpably cannot meet psychometric desiderata, however hard people try to make them.

That said, I cannot agree with those critics of psychological testing who were prepared to credit examinations with a 'lack of pretence to a scientific rationale' (Daniels and Houghton, 1972) and therefore could not be regarded as psychometric in character. The pretence has been and still is there — why else do the boards have research units? — and there is continuing uncertainty about whether examinations qualify as psychological tests.[11]

In that other department of British educational measurement — the school testing scene — functions associated historically with psychometrics, or at least not with educational measurement as I have expounded it, are quite evident. When we looked at testing practices in English and Welsh local authorities (Gipps and Wood, 1981; Wood and Gipps, 1982) we heard many protestations that testing and assessment are meant to be in the interest of children — otherwise why do it? — but practice seemed to indicate otherwise, that test results were used as often for record-keeping purposes and as political ammunition — the 'external management' function of tests — and, for providing, in the words of Gordon and Terrell (1981), 'an aid to pedagogical and/or rehabilitative intervention'. I might mention too the persistent belief, symptomatic of a regression to determinism, that administering verbal and non-verbal reasoning tests along with achievement tests is a good thing to do because it tells teachers (and managers) what to expect from children (under- and over-achievement again).

I would not wish to visit on Britain litigation of the kind and magnitude seen in the US. I would be inclined to agree with Lerner (1981) that it leads to rigidity and the stifling of reform, although it is significant that the reasons she offers for rejecting legislation[12] do not apply in Britain to anything like the same extent. It may be, however, that some test cases — on security or exposure, on cheating and generally on the theme of examinee's rights — might clear the air and help to clarify and determine what educational measurement should be, how it should be conducted and for whose benefit.[13] With Britain now a pluralist society in which the arguments concerning equal opportunity heard in the US apply well enough to be taken seriously, and where some legislation and institutions are already in place, American observers must wonder how British test givers are able to escape challenge, or else how a changed social context has not led to a noticeable shift in the predominant functions associated with assessment. The Dunning Report had the wholesome title *Assessment for All* (HMSO, 1977), which would seem to constitute an appropriate reaction but, as we know, it has long been a bone of contention whether the interests of the 'unexamined' are best served by being examined in the conventional way and the prominence Dunning gives to the guidance aspect of assessment, while welcome, is not enough to convince that some 'New Deal' is to be inaugurated.

## Measurement and Instruction

Perhaps the most often expressed, and least regarded, platitude about educational measurement is that it is only of value when related to instruction. Test results, it is said, have at least as much to tell us about the teacher as the taught. It follows that teachers can learn something from test results. Allowing that the job of partitioning the variation into what is ascribable to the teacher and what is ascribable to the taught is about as difficult as you could imagine, I still find this model a refreshing counter to the prevailing view that information from test results is only about children, a view which must be responsible in part for the preoccupation with labelling and sentencing. Unfortunately it is this model which teachers resist most, with some justification, it must be said. Many teachers have evolved an elaborate defence mechanism to ward off tests and this seems to be true whether they are British (Gipps *et al.*, 1983), American (Salmon-Cox, 1981) or Irish (Kellaghan *et al.*, 1980). There is resentment at what is seen as surveillance, a conviction that tests give only 'part of the picture' and therefore can never be relied upon, overlaid with a belief, often demonstrable, that the tests and their instructional efforts do not match. Clearly, with this attitude towards tests, teachers are not going to take the rap from test results nor are they going to be prepared to learn from something which is seen as threatening. How do you persuade teachers to trust tests? I don't know, but I suspect the answer lies in coming to terms with the inevitably partial view of people's abilities which tests afford and in overcoming the rather natural inclination to blame tests because they do no more.

## Notes

1 This revised version of the article that appeared in *Educational Analysis*, Vol. 4, No. 3, draws on material published elsewhere (Wood, 1982).
2 I have in mind Meredith's (1974) charge that 'generations of educational psychologists have been reared on a diet of psychometrics whose function is to demonstrate degrees of *ineducability*, to assign educational failure unequivocally to defects in the child, in his home, in his parents, and in his heredity, and *never* to failures of teaching, failures in school organization, failures in urban conditions, failures in commercial ethics, or failures in educational legislation.'
3 Bereiter (1970). In a later paper (Bereiter, 1980), he contended that it is the uncertainty introduced by genetic variation — making determinism manifestly unworkable — which is the most important contribution of genetic ideas to education.
4 Was Hamilton (1929) the first to do so?
5 Nunnally (1975) refers darkly to a 'philosophy of education spawned by the Skinnerian movement in operant learning.' Glaser was working on teaching machines and programmed learning at the time he wrote the paper.
6 And the major distinction impossible to sustain. 'The problem of the standard is usually finessed in mastery learning studies through some sort of normative comparison' (Messick, 1981, p. 585).
7 Bloom, B.S. (1971).
8 Many of the points made by Levy (1973) with respect to testing and psychology apply with even more force to education.
9 'This is what I want to measure; how do I construct tests to do it?'
10 Wood (1983 and 1984a) makes a case for doing so.
11 It is instructive to decide if examinations fit the criteria for a psychological test suggested by a BPS Working Party (BPS, 1983). Although the Working Party themselves excluded examinations, in fact they fit the criteria rather well.
12 Educational policy *constitutionally* belongs to local educators who are informed about their communities' needs.
13 Bersoff (1981), again from an American perspective, writes that although legal interpretations of psychometric concepts can and do wreak havoc

among test givers and test takers — not to mention test constructors — legal scrutiny has made everyone more sensitive to the pervasiveness of bias, has engendered more professional accountability and has accelerated the search for improved and alternative assessment techniques.

## References

AMERICAN PSYCHOLOGICAL ASSOCIATION (1974) *Standards for Educational and Psychological Tests*, Washington, APA.

AYRES, L.P. (1918) 'History and present status of educational measurement', in WHIPPLE G. (Ed.) *The Measurement of Educational Products: The 17th Year-book of the National Society for the Study for Education*, Part II, Bloomington, Ill, Public School.

BEREITER, C. (1970) 'Genetics and educability', in HELLMUTH, J. (Ed.) *The Disadvantaged Child*, Vol. 3, New York, Brunner-Mazel.

BEREITER, C. (1980) 'The relevance of genetic ideas to education', in VAN DER KAMP et al. (Eds) *Psychometrics for Educational Debates*, London John Wiley and Sons Ltd.

BERSOFF, D.N. (1981) 'Testing and the law', *American Psychologist*, 36, pp. 1047–56.

BLOOM, B.S. (1971) 'Individual differences in school achievement: A vanishing point?' *Phi Delta Kappa Monograph*, Bloomington, Ind.

BLOOM, B.S. et al., (1956) *Taxonomy of Educational Objectives*, Vol. 1, New York, Longmans Green.

BRITISH PSYCHOLOGICAL SOCIETY (1983) *Bulletin*, 36, p. 192.

BROWN, F.A. (1980) *Guidelines for Test Use: A Commentary on the Standards for Educational and Psychological Tests*, Washington, NCME.

BROWN, J. (Ed.) (1976) *Recall and Recognition*, London, John Wiley and Son.

CARVER, R.C. (1974) 'Two dimensions of tests: Psychometric and edumetric', *American Psychologist*, 29, pp. 512–18.

COFFMAN, W.E. (1979) 'Classical test development solutions', *Iowa Testing Programs Occasional Papers*, 23.

DANIELS, J. and HOUGHTON, V. (1972) 'Jensen, Eysenck and the eclipse of the Galton paradigm', in RICHARDSON, K. and SPEARS, D. (Eds) *Race, Culture and Intelligence*, Harmondsworth, Penguin.

DAVIDSON, K. (1974) 'Objective text', *The Use of English*, 26, pp. 12–18.

DONALDSON, M. (1978) *Children's Minds*, London, Fontana/Collins.

EDUCATIONAL TESTING SERVICE (1979) *ETS Developments*, 26, 1.

GAGNÉ, R. (1970) 'Instructional variables and learning outcomes', in WITTROCK, M.C. and WILEY, D.E. (Eds) *The Evaluation of Instruction*, New York, Holt, Rinehart and Winston.

GIPPS, C.V. and WOOD, R. (1981) 'The testing of reading in LEAs: The Bullock Report seven years on', *Educational Studies*, 7, pp. 133–43.

GIPPS, C.V. et al. (1983) *Testing Children*, London, Heinemann Educational.

GLASER, R. (1963) 'Instructional technology and the measurement of learning outcomes: Some questions', *American Psychologist*, 18, pp. 519–21.

GOLDSTEIN, H. (1979) 'Consequences of using the Rasch model for educational assessment', *British Educational Research Journal*, 5, pp. 211–20.

GORDON, E.W. and TERRELL, M.D. (1981) 'The changed social context of testing', *American Psychologist*, 36, pp. 1167–71.

GREEN, B. (1981) 'A primer of testing', *American Psychologist*, 36, pp. 1001–11.

GUY, W. and CHAMBERS, P. (1973) 'Public examinations and pupils' rights', *Cambridge Journal of Education*, 3, pp. 83–9.

GUY, W. and CHAMBERS, P. (1974) 'Public examinations and pupils' rights revisited', *Cambridge Journal of Education*, 4, pp. 47–50.

HAMILTON, E.R. (1929) *The Art of Interrogation*, London, Kegan Paul.

HARRIS, C. (1969) 'Comments', in *Towards a Theory of Achievement Measurement*, proceedings of the Invitational Conference on Testing Problems, Princeton, N.J., Educational Testing Service.

HAWKES, H.E., LINDQUIST, E.F. and MANN, C.R. (1936) *The Construction and Use of Achievement Examinations*, Boston, Houghton Mifflin.

HER MAJESTY'S STATIONERY OFFICE (1977) *Assessment for All. Report of the Committee to Review Assessment in the Third and Fourth Years of Secondary School in Scotland* (the Dunning Report), Edinburgh, HMSO.

JENSEN, A.R. (1969) 'How much can we boost IQ and scholastic achievement?', *Harvard Educational Review*, 39, pp. 1–123.

KELLAGHAN, T., MADAUS, G.F. and AIRASIAN, P.W. (1980) *The Effects of Standardized Testing*, Dublin, Educational Research Centre, St. Patrick's College and Chestnut Hill, Mass., School of Education, Boston College.

LERNER, B. (1981) 'The minimum competency testing movement, social, scientific and legal implications', *American Psychologist*, 36, pp. 1057–66.

LEVINE, M. (1976) 'The academic achievement test: Its historical context and social functions', *American Psychologist*, 31, pp. 228–37.

LEVY, P. (1973) 'On the relation between test theory and psychology', in KLINE P. (Ed.) *New Approaches in Psychological Measurement*, London, John Wiley and Son.

MCCLELLAND, D.C. (1973) 'Testing for competence rather than for "intelligence"', *American Psychologist*, 28, pp. 1–14.

MCINTYRE, D. and BROWN, S. (1978) 'The conceptualization of attainment', *British Educational Research Journal*, 4, 2, pp. 41–50.

MEREDITH, P. (1974) 'A century of regression', *Forum*, 16, pp. 36–39.

MESSICK, S. (1981), 'Constructs and their vicissitudes in educational and psychological measurement', *Psychological Bulletin*, 89, pp. 575–88.

MONROE, W.S. (1923) *An Introduction to the Theory of Educational Measurements*, Boston, Houghton Mifflin.

NUNNALLY, J.C. (1975) 'Psychometric theory — 25 years ago and now', *Educational Researcher*, 4, pp. 7–21.

PIDGEON, D.A. and YATES, A. (1969) *An Introduction to Educational Measurement*, London, Routledge and Kegan Paul.

RESNICK, D.P. (1981) 'Testing in America: A supportive environment', *Phi Delta Kappan*, 62, pp. 625–8.

RYLE, G. (1949) *The Concept of Mind*, London, Hutchinson's University Library.

SALMON-COX, L. (1981) 'Teachers and standardized achievement tests: What's really happening', *Phi Delta Kappan*, 62, pp. 631–4.

SCARR, S. (1981) 'Testing *for* children: Assessment and the many determinants of intellectual competence', *American Psychologist*, 36, pp. 1159–66.

SCHMIDT, F.L. and HUNTER, J.E. (1981) 'Employment testing: Old theories and new research findings', *American Psychologist*, 36, pp. 1128–37.

SHAYER, M., KÜCHEMANN, D.E. and WYLAM, H. (1975) *Concepts in Secondary Mathematics and Science*, SSRC Project Report, London, Chelsea College.

STERNBERG, R.J. (1981) 'Cognitive-behavioural approaches to the training of intelligence in the retarded', *Journal of Special Education*, 15, pp. 165–83.

SUTTON, A. (1979) 'Measures and models in developmental psychology', in WOOD, R. (Ed.) *Rehabilitating Psychometrics: A Report on a Seminar Sponsored by the SSRC*, London, Social Science Research Council.

THORNDIKE, R.L. (Ed.) (1971) *Educational Measurement*, Washington, American Council on Education (2nd edn).

THORNDIKE, R.L. (1982) *Applied Psychometrics*, Boston, Mass., Houghton Mifflin Co.

WOOD, R. (1976) 'A critical note on Harvey's "Some thoughts on norm-referenced and criteria-referenced measures"', *Research in Education*, 14, pp. 69–72.

WOOD, R. (1982) 'Aptitude and achievement', *Caribbean Journal of Education*, 9, pp. 79–123.

WOOD, R. (1983) 'Quantifying underachievement', *Bulletin of the British Psychological Society*, 36, p. 415.

WOOD, R. (1984a) 'Doubts about "underachievement" particularly as operationalized by Yule, Lansdown and Urbanowicz', *British Journal of Clinical Psychology* (in press).

WOOD, R. (1984b) 'Assessment has too many meanings and the one we want isn't clear enough yet', *Educational Measurement: Issues and Practices* (in press).

WOOD, R. and GIPPS, C.V. (1982) 'An enquiry into the use of test results for accountability purposes', in MCCORMICK R. *et al.*, (Eds) *Calling Education to Account*, London, Heinemann Educational.

# Contributors

Mr. H.D. Black, Schools' Assessment Research and Support Unit, Scottish Council for Research in Education, 15 St. John Street, Edinburgh, EH8 8JR, Scotland.

Dr. P.M. Broadfoot, School of Education, University of Bristol, Helen Wodehouse Building, 35 Berkeley Squate, Bristol, BS8 1JA, ENGLAND.

Dr. C.V. Gipps, Screening and Special Educational Provision in Schools Project, 18 Woburn Square, London, WCIH ONS, ENGLAND.

Professor H. Goldstein, Department of Mathematics, Statistics and Computing, University of London Institute of Education, 20 Bedford Way, London, WCIH OAL, ENGLAND.

Dr. J. Gray, Division and Institute of Education, University of Sheffield, Arts Tower Floor 9, Sheffield, S10 2TN, ENGLAND.

Mr. A.E. Lapointe, Executive Director, National Assessment of Educational Progress, Box 2923, Princeton, New Jersey 08541, USA.

Mr. H.G. Macintosh, Southern Regional Examinations Board, Avondale House, 33 Carlton Crescent, Southampton, S09 4YL, ENGLAND.

Professor L.D. McLean, Educational Evaluation Centre, Ontario Institute for Studies in Education, 252 Bloor St. West, Toronto, Ontario, Canada, M5S 1V6.

Professor D.L. Nuttall, School of Education, Open University, Walton Hall, Milton Keynes, MK7 6AA, ENGLAND.

Dr. S. Ranson, Institute of Local Government Studies, University of Birmingham, P.O. Box 363, Birmingham, B15 2TT, ENGLAND.

Mr. G. Withers, Australian Council for Educational Research, P.O. Box 210, Hawthorn, Victoria 3122, Australia.

Dr. R. Wood, School of Education, Flinders University, Bedford Park, South Australia 5042, Australia.

# Author Index

# Subject Index

7845